ON BEING HERE

Treaties and Aboriginal

What, other than numbers and power, justifies the Canadian state's assertion of sovereignty and jurisdiction over its vast territory? Why should Canada's original inhabitants have to ask for rights to what was their land when non-Aboriginal people first arrived?

These questions – which lie at the heart of every court judgment on Indigenous rights, every demand that treaty obligations be fulfilled, and every land-claims negotiation – have occupied anthropologist Michael Asch for nearly thirty years. In *On Being Here to Stay*, Asch re-examines the history of Canada, focusing on fundamental issues concerning Aboriginal rights and the relationship between First Nations and Settlers.

Taking its title from the statement by Chief Justice Lamer in *Delgamuukw v. British Columbia* ("Let us face it, we are here to stay"), this book addresses the grounds upon which Settlers can claim their right to stay, beyond their power to insist on it. Asch provides evidence – long articulated by First Nations – that, in treaties negotiated immediately after Confederation, the shared understanding was one of an open-ended relationship that permitted Settlers to inhabit the land, on a shared basis, in return for fulfilling certain obligations. Considering a range of possibilities and alternative views, Asch proposes a way forward built on respecting the "spirit and intent" of these treaties, through which, he argues, First Nations and Settlers can establish an ethical way for both communities to be here to stay.

MICHAEL ASCH is a professor emeritus in the Department of Anthropology at the University of Alberta and a professor (limited term) in the Department of Anthropology and adjunct professor in the Department of Political Science at the University of Victoria.

MICHAEL ASCH

On Being Here to Stay

Treaties and Aboriginal Rights
in Canada

UNIVERSITY OF TORONTO PRESS
Toronto Buffalo London

ISBN 978-1-4426-4028-3 (cloth)
ISBN 978-1-4426-1002-6 (paper)

Printed on acid-free, 100% post-consumer recycled paper
with vegetable-based inks

Library and Archives Canada Cataloguing in Publication

Asch, Michael, author
On being here to stay: treaties and Aboriginal rights
in Canada / Michael Asch.

Includes bibliographical references and index.
ISBN 978-1-4426-4028-3 (bound). – ISBN 978-1-4426-1002-6 (pbk).

1. Native peoples – Legal status, laws, etc. – Canada.   2. Native peoples –
Canada – Government relations.   3. Native peoples – Land tenure – Canada.
4. Native peoples – Canada – Claims.   I. Title.

E92.A74 2014   323.1197'071   C2013-907135-0

This book has been published with the help of a grant from the Canadian
Federation for the Humanities and Social Sciences, through the Awards to
Scholarly Publications Program, using funds provided by the Social Sciences
and Humanities Research Council of Canada.

University of Toronto Press acknowledges the financial assistance to its
publishing program of the Canada Council for the Arts and the Ontario
Arts Council.

Canada Council   Conseil des Arts
for the Arts   du Canada

ONTARIO ARTS COUNCIL
CONSEIL DES ARTS DE L'ONTARIO
50 YEARS OF ONTARIO GOVERNMENT SUPPORT OF THE ARTS
50 ANS DE SOUTIEN DU GOUVERNEMENT DE L'ONTARIO AUX ARTS

University of Toronto Press acknowledges the financial support of the
Government of Canada through the Canada Book Fund for its publishing
activities.

Contents

Preface

I started out to write a book that would need little further research. It was to be a book that put in one place a position on the political relationship between Indigenous peoples and the Canadian state that I had been developing for thirty years and more. But that is not the book I have written.

The first four chapters did go as planned. They are largely a rendering of key features of my argument on the theme just mentioned. But beginning with the fifth chapter, I embarked on an adventure that led me to include information of which I was already knowledgeable but never thought would be relevant, as well as information that was entirely new, at least to me. That is the manuscript I presented to the University of Toronto Press. Here is what happened.

The position I have long held rests on the principle, as confirmed in the 1960 United Nations Declaration on the Granting of Independence to Colonial Countries and Peoples (or simply the Declaration on De-Colonization), to which Canada is a signatory, that, at least with respect to colonized peoples, it is wrong legally as well as morally to move onto lands belonging to others without first obtaining their permission. The centrepiece of my approach to reconciling this principle with the fact that Canada is on lands that belong to Indigenous peoples was to determine what permission from them might entail; and to that end I chose to look in particular at what Indigenous peoples today explain are the terms of treaties made with the Crown in the past that permitted settlement on their lands. I had no intention to delve into whether there had been agreement on these terms in the past. Rather, I reasoned that, whether or not such agreement had existed when the treaties were negotiated, the terms of these treaties, as Indigenous peoples present them today, serve as a proxy (by which I also mean an approximation) for what would be their position on the terms of an arrangement with the state were Canada now seeking to act in compliance with the UN Declaration.

My reason for avoiding the issue was not that I disbelieved the description of these terms provided by Indigenous authorities on the matter (by which I mean in particular elders but also other leaders and knowledge bearers). I fully expected that what they described would conform well with evidence of what transpired derived from other sources. Instead, my concern was that the representatives of the Crown acted fraudulently in the sense that they did not mean what they said – a view that is abundantly confirmed by the manner in which the government of Canada has acted when it comes to implementing the terms, even those that appear in the government's version of them.

However, in re-reading recent Supreme Court of Canada judgments on treaties, I returned to a set of principles that I had previously not taken seriously enough. To use this illustration, there is this passage in *R v. Badger*: 'First, a treaty represents an exchange of solemn promises between the Crown and the various Indian nations. Second, the honour of the Crown is always at stake; the Crown must be assumed to intend to fulfil its promises. No appearance of "sharp dealing" will be sanctioned' (*Badger* 1996: Preface). In short, I now read this to mean that, in the Court's view, what the Crown represented at the negotiations had to be considered as truthful regardless of original intent. I decided to adopt that perspective.

With that in mind, I looked more closely at the degree of correspondence between what Indigenous authorities today render as the treaty terms and what the treaty commissioners actually said. And as luck would have it, the record of the treaty I had chosen to use as my exemplar of the terms of treaties as represented by Indigenous peoples, Treaty 4, contained an abundance of information from contemporaneous accounts (and in particular a shorthand transcript) on what was said by all parties when it was negotiated. Reading the words of the lead commissioner, Alexander Morris, led me to contemplate the possibility that he actually meant what he said: a possibility that, as you will see, is reflected in my conclusions to chapter 5. This led me to recalibrate my interpretation of the written version of Treaty 4 and other similar treaties (including the cede and surrender clause).

It then became important to me to see if there was evidence to support my sense that, at least in this treaty, the Crown's representative acted in good faith, and that headed me in a direction I had never anticipated this book would go: research into positions on the proper approach to relations with Indigenous peoples taken by the British (and Canadians) in the period leading up to and after Treaty 4 was negotiated in 1874. And that led me to information I otherwise would never have found. To take one example, in 1840 the then influential Aborigines' Protection Society (APS) advocated model legislation for interaction with Indigenous peoples based on 'the indefeasible rights of every people, (not under allegiance to any other power,) to the natural rights of man, comprehending,

1 Their rights as an independent nation. That no country or people has a right by force or fraud to assume the sovereignty over any other nation
2 That such sovereignty can only be justly obtained *by fair treaty, and with their consent.*' (Aborigines' Protection Society 1840: 14; emphasis added)

From this and information from other sources, I concluded that there is every possibility that, were he of a similar view, not only did Morris mean what he said, a position for which there is further support (at least as I read the text) in Robert J. Talbot's recent biography of the man (Talbot 2009), but there was every likelihood that in so doing he was advancing a position shared by many others (a position further confirmed in the position taken by then Canadian Governor General Lord Dufferin, who was Morris's superior when the latter was acting in his capacity as lieutenant governor of Manitoba). In other words, at least in some treaties, there is good reason to conclude that the representation of the agreement Indigenous authorities offer is by and large an accurate depiction of what was, at the time, a shared understanding.

I approach this conclusion cautiously. It is hardly definitive, for much of the information on which it is based is new to me and so I have as yet had no opportunity to further explore the direction in which it may be leading. That is, the 'yes, but' that I imagine in the heads of many readers is also in my head. There are other facets to this story, and its darker aspects must never be overlooked. Indeed, overall I have not changed my view of the original intent of the Crown in most treaties. But my research has led me to conclude that there is at least a case to be made for the proposition that there were those who acted in good faith in the past, and thus the possibility that, while to act honourably now is to depart from how we have acted in the past, it is also to keep faith with it.

The book headed me in another unanticipated direction worth mentioning. As originally conceived, I was going to leave the words of Indigenous authorities uninterpreted, and, beyond paraphrasing, for the most part that is what I have done. However, there is at least one place in which I decidedly do not. It pertains to my discussion of what constitutes the treaty relationship. Among the phrases Indigenous authorities often use to describe it is a 'nation-to-nation' relationship. One might take this and others (such as the use of the term 'brother' to describe the relationship between nations) as loose metaphors. But I decided that this was not good enough. If we are to have a treaty relationship, and if it is to be founded on terms we share with Indigenous peoples, then it is incumbent on those of us I describe as Settlers (I will explain my choice of words in chapter 1) to understand to what we are agreeing; and that means confronting at least this fundamental problem: to the Western-trained mind, terms like 'nation-to-nation' and 'brothers' do not, at first blush, appear to make sense in this context.

A relationship between equals, which is what both terms suggest, requires (at least as modernity describes it) that each party is a state with sovereignty and jurisdiction over a territory. Yet Indigenous authorities inform us that we did not acquire sovereignty and jurisdiction over any territory. Therefore, we cannot be equals, for a party that does not have sovereignty and jurisdiction in a territory cannot have the same standing as one that does.

The question, then, is whether there is a way to make sense of this; and to that end, I suggest that what is most important is to work with Indigenous peoples on the matter. However, I also offer a suggestion on a way to begin that brings into conversation the ideas of, among others, Thomas Hobbes, the Mohawk Chief Kiotseaeton, Claude Lévi-Strauss, and Harold Johnson regarding the principles on which society is organized. While that portion of the book is the product of much work and many iterations, I offer my interpretation gingerly. It is simply my best effort at explanation: words offered to stimulate dialogue rather than establish authority.

In this book, I rely on contributions of many people who have communicated their understandings regarding the aspects of the topics covered, and for the integrity with which these have been offered I am thankful. I am grateful in particular to those among my colleagues who took the time to consider and comment on drafts of various chapters, among whom are: Seth Asch, John Lutz, Warren Magnusson, Brian

Noble, D.A. Sonneborn, Heidi Stark, and Jim Tully. I would like to ac-
knowledge too a number of people with whom I have had many pro-
ductive conversations on the various topics addressed, a group that
includes Taiaiake Alfred, Jessica Asch, John Borrows, Aimée Craft,
Alison Du Bois, Avigail Eisenberg, Tony Fisher, Rachel Flowers, Joyce
Green, Rob Hancock, Al Hanna, Johnny Mack, Joëlle Alice Michaud-
Ouellet, Marc Pinkoski, Peter Stephenson, Neil Vallance, Rob Walker,
Jeremy Webber, Allyshia West, and Kelsey Wrightson. I thank Rob
Hancock as well for his invaluable assistance in assembling this volume. I also wish to express my appreciation for the comments of the
three anonymous readers of the manuscript, all of whom helped me
reflect on the clarity of what I had written and, where I could, improve
on it. Also deserving of thanks are Virgil Duff and Douglas Hildebrand
at the University of Toronto Press for their support throughout, my ed-
iter, Curtis Fahey, and my indexer, Judy Dunlop.

Researching the book was made easier through the funding assistance provided by SSHRC – through the standard research grants program as well as through two Major Collaborative Research Initiatives,
the Indigenous Peoples and Governance Project and the Intellectual
Property Issues in Cultural Heritage – and, at the University of Victoria,
by the Office of the Vice-President (Research), the Dean of Law, and the
Dean of Social Science. I am thankful equally to logistical assistance and
the home provided me by the Department of Anthropology at the
University of Victoria.

The book could not have been written were it not for the efforts of my
wife, Margaret Asch, and Carl Urion, who both sought to help me by
offering their insights on the adequacy of my argument and my rendering. I will be forever grateful for the caring way in which they reviewed
what I wrote, and the supportive manner in which they conveyed their
comments on it to me. While I am the author and thus take ultimate
responsibility for what it contains, the book in fact is the fruit of our
joint efforts.

This book is dedicated to Mrs Jessie Hardisty (1885–1985)[1] of Wrigley
(Pehdzeh Ki), Northwest Territories, whose kindness and wisdom have
nurtured Margaret and me since we, then in our mid-twenties, first
arrived in that community in August 1969.

ON BEING HERE TO STAY

Treaties and Aboriginal Rights in Canada

Chapter One

Overview

Ultimately, it is through negotiated settlements, with good faith and give and take on all sides, reinforced by the judgments of this Court, that we will achieve what I stated in *Van der Peet, supra*, at para. 31, to be a basic purpose of s. 35(1) – 'the reconciliation of the pre-existence of aboriginal societies with the sovereignty of the Crown.' Let us face it, we are all here to stay.
(Chief Justice Antonio Lamer, *Delgamuukw* 1997, para. 186)

Introduction

Chief Justice Lamer speaks a truism: 'we are all here to stay.' Those of us whose ancestors were here prior to European settlement are here by dint of that fact. But that does not go far enough. What about those of us who came after? What, beyond the fact that we have the numbers and the power to insist on it, authorizes our being here to stay?

It is admittedly not an issue that confronts most of us in our daily lives. Still, the topic perennially bedevils us. It lurks in the background when Indigenous peoples protest developments on what they describe as 'their lands'; when courts make judgments on their rights; when we are challenged to fulfil our treaty obligations; and in every 'land-claims' negotiation. Why do they have 'land claims'? Were they not here, already living on the land, when Settlers came? If so, how did they lose 'their land,' and by what authority do we claim the right to determine what is to be negotiated? Each of these matters, and a myriad others, from residential schools to governance, traces itself back to the answer to that question: 'What, beyond the fact that we have the numbers and the power to insist on it, authorizes our being here to stay?'

The question is one that manifestly requires an answer, for among those who came after, like myself, are people who believe firmly that it is not right to move onto lands that belong to others without their permission. Yet there are many places in Canada where we did just that. What is our justification for asserting that we are here to stay in those places? There are also places where we did follow our principles by gaining permission to be here to stay through agreements we negotiated with those who were already here. However, as I will show, it is also clear that these agreements did not give us the authority to live as though these lands now belong to us. What, then, is the basis for asserting that we are here to stay in those places?

Most of us can go about our lives as though questions such as these do not require addressing. We take for granted the idea that we are all here to stay because we are Canadians and Canada has sovereignty and jurisdiction over these territories. But that just begs the question: If this is so, then how did Canada gain the authority to govern lands that were already being governed by others, and if not, what then is the basis for our right to be here to stay? In short, while these questions may seem abstruse, they lie at the heart of the matter, for, if we are to move beyond the mere assertion that we are here to stay because we have the power to do so, we must reconcile that fact with our sense that it is wrong to simply move onto lands that belong to others.

Addressing the origin of Canada's assertion of sovereignty and jurisdiction has occupied me for nearly thirty years. My first reflections appeared in *Home and Native Land* (Asch 1984), where I sought to understand the meaning of 'Aboriginal rights' in section 35 of the then recently adopted Canadian Constitution Act of 1982. At that time, I took the view that the adoption of this term reflected Canada's acknowledgment that Indigenous peoples had the right to self-determination held by colonized peoples in places where the 1960 United Nations Declaration on De-Colonization applied. It recognized that Indigenous peoples here held the same right to free themselves from colonial domination, notwithstanding that (primarily) European states had claimed sovereignty and jurisdiction over these territories, as did others in those parts of the world where the colonized represented a majority of the population. That determination led me to consider the status of those such as myself whose only claim to be here to stay rests on our belonging to the kind of state that elsewhere in the world Canadians might well condemn as illegitimate, as is attested to by our support for the 1960 UN Declaration and our resolve to end South African apartheid.

This book presents the development of my thinking on this matter. It begins, in chapter 2, with a brief review of the history of political relations between Indigenous peoples and Canada from 1973 to the present. I start there because it is commonly accepted that the contemporary relationship originates in a judgment in which the Supreme Court of Canada recognized that, at the time of European settlement, Indigenous peoples had rights based on the fact that there were already here, living in societies. It is with this judgment, I suggest, that the question of whether these rights survived European settlement, and if so what they are, came to the foreground. The first was answered affirmatively with the inclusion of Aboriginal rights in the 1982 constitution, and as to the second, while the full scope of these rights has yet to be determined, it has become clear that, if the courts and the government have their way, Aboriginal rights will never be interpreted as including many political rights, and certainly not the right to self-determination of colonized peoples. I conclude by indicating that Chief Justice Lamer summarized this proposition when he asserted that to be 'here to stay' requires reconciling 'the pre-existence of aboriginal societies with the sovereignty of the Crown,' rather than the other way around.

In chapter 3, I take up the proposition that the very idea of assuming that Aboriginal rights might include political rights is absurd. It focuses in particular on the arguments presented in *First Nations? Second Thoughts* (2008) by political scientist Tom Flanagan, who is likely the most prominent proponent of this view in the academy. I respond to his invitation to those whose views are akin to my own 'to reply in kind' (Flanagan 2008: 10) by entering into a dialogue with those portions of his text in which he lays out arguments in Western political and legal thought that favour the view that the legitimacy of Canada's sovereignty and jurisdiction arises independently of the fact that Indigenous peoples were already living here when we first arrived. The result, I hope, is to show that arguments in Western political and legal thought favouring the view I support are more compelling.

With that in mind, I turn in chapter 4 to a detailed discussion of the implications of taking that view. It is based on the understanding that, as I first outlined in *Home and Native Land*, the United Nations Declaration on De-Colonization applies to Indigenous peoples who find themselves within Canada. My conclusion is that, while the argument is irrefutable in principle, the implications are so extreme that the principle could be applied only with the consent of those who now constitute the majority of the population in this country. This, I argue, has led to the introduction of caveats intended to exclude Canada and countries in circumstances like our own from the declaration's purview; or, as in the position advanced by Alan Cairns: the fact that 'European migrants' now constitute the majority in itself is sufficient to conclude that 'the end of the Canadian version of empire over Aboriginal peoples ... could not mean independence for the colonized or the departure of the colonizers' (Cairns 2000: 26). But that, I argue, is merely to rely on our power to justify our legitimacy. To square legitimacy with principle, I suggest, requires that we Settlers do not have to choose between our right to be here to stay and our recognition that Indigenous peoples have the same right to self-determination as do others who have been subjected to colonialism. I conclude by introducing the issue of treaties, which I suggest offer one such alternative in that they encourage Settlers to see the legitimacy of their settlement on these lands as linked to the fact that they gained permission to settle on them from people who had the authority to grant such permission.

The rest of the book advances this possibility. Chapter 5 addresses the nature of that permission as exemplified in Treaty 4. I chose that treaty for a number of reasons, not the least of which is that Commissioner Morris, who negotiated it on behalf of the Crown, provided a detailed shorthand transcript of the proceedings in his 1880 book, *Treaties with the Indians of Canada*.[1] Relying on the Supreme Court of Canada's directive to presume that both parties were negotiating in good faith, I conclude that, first, the agreement we reached was one in which we were permitted to settle on lands that we were to share with Indigenous peoples, and in return we would promise to treat them 'with kindness'; and second, that notwithstanding our conventional view that they surrendered sovereignty and jurisdiction to us, the treaties did not effect such a transaction. Instead, they established a nation-to-nation relationship between Canada and Indigenous peoples which parallels that between Canada and New Zealand: that is, 'brothers to each other,' and 'children of the Queen.'

Chapter 6 investigates the possibility of implementing a 'nation-to-nation' relationship based on principles in contemporary Western political thought. I suggest that the path forward would be easier to conceptualize were the relationship parallel to that between two states (within the Commonwealth). But it is not. Canada is one state and this kind of relationship never exists in such a situation. That requires that each party has sovereignty and jurisdiction in its own territory, and we do not have such standing since we did not acquire it by treaty.

Therefore, following our traditions, our only option was to become incorporated into the polities of those who do. Yet that is not what happened either. I end the chapter by suggesting that to implement these treaties we need first to conceptualize how to form a relationship that falls outside the range of possibilities offered to us in contemporary political thought.

Chapter 7 takes up this point. I begin by indicating how our partners have described the nation-to-nation relationship, and conclude that to understand it requires that we move away from the strain of political thought based on the understanding that the determination of sovereignty over a territory is the surest building block on which to establish political relations between nations. I use Thomas Hobbes's *Leviathan* to provide an iteration of the thesis on which this understanding is grounded. I then rely on the understanding of the treaty relationship offered by Mohawk Chief Kiotseaeton at a 1645 treaty and particularly on his depiction of what I am calling the 'linking principle,' as well as Claude Lévi-Strauss's discussion of this principle in *The Elementary Structures of Kinship* (Lévi-Strauss 1969), to revisit key elements of the argument Hobbes develops, and in that way to open up the possibility of imagining the nation-to-nation relationship within the contours of Western political thought.

Chapter 8 discusses two aspects of implementing treaties on this basis: the role that linking plays in organizing relations; and what keeping the promises we made entails. With regard to the former, I discuss how our partners in Treaties 4 and 6 formed communities at the time those treaties were negotiated; and with the latter, I argue that the spirit and intent of the treaties as we represented them was to ensure that, as is suggested in the 'famine clause' in Treaty 6, our presence would be beneficial, not harmful. Then, after reviewing the state's disregard for the implementation of these promises, I take the position that it is still possible to rely on the guarantees that Indigenous peoples gave us in the treaties, but first we must keep the promises that we made.

I conclude, in chapter 9, by seeking a way to ensure that our government lives up to this commitment. I suggest that the fact that these are contractual obligations ought to be sufficient, but that this is not the case. I then propose that a more secure method would be to gain sufficient public support for this approach so that governments understand the stakes involved. To that end, I advance the idea that the place to begin is to retell the story of Canada in such a way that the treaties by which the Crown secured the legitimate right of those it represented to settle on these lands are understood as its founding moment. This approach would bring contemporary practice in line with the under-standing expressed by the Earl of Dufferin, Canada's third post-Confederation governor general, in 1876 that we 'acknowledge that the original title to the land existed in the Indian Tribes' so that 'before we touch an acre we make a treaty with the chiefs representing the bands ... but not until then do we consider that we are entitled to deal with a single acre' (Dufferin 1882: 209). It is an admonition that continues to serve as a guide both on lands where treaties have been negotiated and at those places where, over 150 years after Confederation, the Crown has yet to do so.

A Note on Terminology

In the above discussion, I have referred to two communities. One of these I have consistently labelled 'Indigenous.' The label identifies that group that the Constitution Act of 1982 terms the 'aboriginal peoples of Canada' and stipulates as including 'the Indian, Inuit and Métis peoples of Canada' (s. 35[2]). Another term, First Nations, is now commonly used instead of 'Indians.' The *Oxford Dictionary* defines 'Indigenous' as 'relating to, or intended for the native inhabitants ...' Thus, it imposes a collective identity on a wide range of communities with diverse histories, solely on the grounds that these peoples were (already) here at a certain point in time (Fran Hunt-Jinnouchi, qtd. in Moneo 2011: 98). Nonetheless, I will use that term because I find that the specification of a collectivity is of central relevance to the argument I make in this book. That is, 'Indigenous' refers to those whom I have described above as 'already here to stay.'[2]

Usually the group I have referred to as 'those who came later' is glossed by the prefix 'non,' as in 'non-Indigenous,' 'non-Aboriginal, and 'non-Native.' However, I do not take this approach because the prefix 'non' describes people like myself solely on the basis of a quality we do not have. My group's stake in resolving the relationship with Indigenous peoples does not derive from my non-belonging in an-other group. In fact, the group to which I do belong is identifiably dif-ferent from 'Indigenous peoples' but also here to stay. Some scholars, such as historian J.R. Miller, have used the term 'Newcomers' to desig-nate this group. I have chosen 'Settlers,' for two reasons. First, 'settling on the land' well describes the purpose of those in this group who ar-rived here; and second, the term 'Settler' follows the distinction made in the recent post-colonial literature between 'settler colonies,' where members of this group became the majority, and colonies of 'occupation' or 'exploitation,' where colonists constituted a minority (Imperial Archive n.d.).[3]

In this book, I will also follow an understanding memorialized as early as the Royal Proclamation of 1763. That document, even when it claims sovereignty over the land and those who live on it, recognizes that, in treaty negotiations involving the securing of permission to settle on Indigenous territory, 'the Crown' represents the interests of Settlers alone and Indigenous parties are represented by leaders of their own choosing.[4]

Chapter Two

Aboriginal Rights and
the Canadian Constitution

Section 35(1): The existing aboriginal and treaty rights of the aboriginal peoples of Canada are hereby recognized and affirmed.

Section 35(2): In this Act, 'aboriginal Peoples of Canada' includes the Indian, Inuit and Métis peoples of Canada.

(Constitution Act, 1982)

Aboriginal Rights as Political Rights

In my 1984 book *Home and Native Land*, I suggested that at that time there was as yet no consensus as to the meaning of the term 'aboriginal rights,' and that this matter was to be addressed in a series of conferences to be held between first ministers and leaders of key Indigenous organizations. However, I also concluded, based on the result of the first of these conferences, that the issue of 'whether or not the definition of aboriginal rights included "special" political rights such as the right to self-determination for aboriginal peoples' would become the focus of political and judicial deliberation (Asch 1984: 7).

Thirty years later, I can say that, while it still remains to be defined in full, the Canadian state has directed the parties to a definition of the general scope of this term. In fine, as I suggested in 'From *Calder* to *Van der Peet*' (Asch 1999), this has encompassed an acknowledgment that Indigenous peoples have rights that flow from ways of life that were established in the period prior to the Crown's assertion of sovereignty. These rights may extend to, among other things, economic practices, protection of spiritual practices, and landholding. At the same time,

Canada has made it clear that it will not accept that 'aboriginal rights' include robust political rights, much less any that might call into question the final legislative authority of the Crown. In that regard, the prevailing view precludes the possibility that Indigenous peoples here have the same right to self-determination that elsewhere we have acknowledged to be accorded to colonized peoples. And that has created an impasse that this book seeks to address.

This practice of defining the scope of Aboriginal rights in a manner acceptable to the Crown is well described in the passage in the *Delgamuukw* decision where then Chief Justice Lamer states: 'Let us face it, we are all here to stay.' As he says: 'Ultimately, it is through negotiated settlements, with good faith and give and take on all sides, reinforced by the judgments of this Court, that we will achieve what I stated in *Van der Peet, supra*, at para. 31, to be a basic purpose of s. 35(1) – "the reconciliation of the pre-existence of aboriginal societies with the sovereignty of the Crown"' (*Delgamuukw* 1997: para. 186).

That is, there can be no doubt that negotiated settlements based on good faith on all sides represent an appropriate way in which to come to agreement on the meaning of Aboriginal rights, and that, as Lamer suggests earlier in that same paragraph, 'the Crown is under a moral, if not a legal, duty to enter into and conduct those negotiations in good faith.' However, expressing the terms of the agreement as 'the reconciliation of the pre-existence of aboriginal societies with the sovereignty of the Crown' prejudices the outcome, for in this formulation the fundamental matter, 'the sovereignty of the Crown,' which I take to mean having 'supreme dominion, authority, or rule,'[1] is not to be questioned. As a result, what at first blush reads as an open-ended process becomes one based on this singular pre-condition: the agreement on the part of Indigenous peoples that the scope of their political rights, and in particular their right to self-determination, is circumscribed by the fact that, at the end of the day, whatever rights they may have are subordinate to the legislative authority of the Canadian state. Yet this logically ought not to be the case, if for no other reason than that the political rights of Indigenous peoples already existed at the time that Crown sovereignty was asserted and, therefore, it is the question of how the Crown gained sovereignty that requires reconciliation with the pre-existence of Indigenous societies and not the other way around. Thus, to be open-ended, the negotiations logically ought to concern 'the reconciliation of the sovereignty of the Crown with the pre-existence of aboriginal societies' or at the very least 'the reconciliation of the sovereignty of the Crown *and* the pre-existence of aboriginal societies.' And, to put it succinctly, working through the implications of the first of these formulations is the objective to which this book is directed.

However, there is a long way to go, and, notwithstanding my critique, there is much even in the Crown's formulation that requires further consideration. In 1969 the government of Canada asserted in its 'White Paper' on Indian policy, which expressed the conventional wisdom of the time, that 'the policies proposed recognize the simple reality that the separate legal status of Indians and the policies which have flowed from it have kept the Indian people apart from and behind other Canadians' (qtd. in Asch 1984: 8). And yet, only a little more than a decade later, Indigenous rights were included in section 35(1) of the Canadian constitution. This chapter, then, will recapitulate in brief the history of an evolving process by which Canada moves from a position where Aboriginal and treaty rights are relics of a misguided past to be discarded to one where they occupy a central place in our constitution – a place that then Prime Minister Pierre Trudeau described at the first constitutional conference in 1983 in this way: 'Canada's constitutional process cannot be held to be fulfilled if the peoples, whose ancestors have been here the longest, find that their particular rights are not adequately reflected or protected in the Constitution' (qtd. in ibid.: 10).

We begin with the court judgments in a case entitled *Calder v. Attorney General of British Columbia*.

Setting the Context: *Calder v. Attorney-General of British Columbia*

What is often referred to as the 'Calder Case' was brought in 1967 by Nisga'a leader Frank Calder. It sought a declaratory judgment that the Nisga'a held 'the aboriginal title, otherwise known as the Indian title ... to their ancient tribal territory,' and that this title, which had 'never been lawfully extinguished,' encompassed an interest to benefit from activities on their ancestral lands (including pursuit of subsistence activities). That is, as the lawyers for the Nisga'a put it, their interest might well be described as one 'which is a burden on the title of the Crown; an interest which is usufructuary[2] in nature; a tribal interest inalienable except to the Crown and extinguishable only by legislative enactment of the Parliament of Canada' (*Calder* 1973: 352). While the analogy is not perfect, the judgment they sought was akin to asserting that the 'title' the Nisga'a held, like the legal title to one's home, remains valid even when sovereignty is transferred from one power to another. Or, to put it another way, the Nisga'a asserted that, as Indigenous peoples, they had rights that derived from the fact that they were already here to stay when Europeans arrived and that, notwithstanding a presumed change in sovereignty, unless they had been lawfully extinguished their rights continued to exist.

The case was tried in April 1969, and in October of that year Justice J. Gould handed down his judgment. In it, he found that Nisga'a title had been voided. His argument rested on his observation that 'all of the proclamations, ordinances and proclaimed statutes affecting land in British Columbia emanating from the Crown Imperial showed a unity of intention to exercise and the legislative exercising of absolute sovereignty over all lands in the colony, a sovereignty which was inconsistent with any conflicting interest, including one as to aboriginal or Indian title' (*Calder* 1969: summary). As a result, he was persuaded that 'any rights the Indian bands had in the lands in question were totally extinguished' (ibid.). However, Justice Gould elided the question as to whether the Nisga'a (or by implication other Indigenous peoples) in principle ever held rights based on the pre-existence of their societies that might require recognition by the Crown, for he concluded that, given that these rights had been lawfully extinguished, 'it is not necessary to explore what "aboriginal title, otherwise known as the Indian title" may mean, or in earlier times may have meant, in a different context' (ibid.: 1969).

The matter was taken up by the Appeals Court of British Columbia. In a unanimous judgment rendered in 1970, justices H.W. Davey, C.W. Tysoe, and H.A. Maclean agreed with Justice Gould's finding that any rights the Nisga'a may have once held had been extinguished by general legislation. Further, Chief Justice Davey explicitly took up the question whether the Nisga'a had rights that required recognition by the Crown.[3] His answer was 'no.' In reaching that conclusion, he relied on the notion that the Nisga'a were a 'primitive people' who had no rights reconcilable with English law. Here is how he put it: 'In spite of the commendation of Mr. Duff, a well-known anthropologist, of the native culture of the Indians on the mainland of British Columbia, they were undoubtedly at the time of settlement a very primitive people with few of the institutions of civilized society, and none at all of our notions of private property.' Therefore, he went on: 'I see no evidence to justify a conclusion that the aboriginal rights claimed by the successors of these primitive people are of a kind that it should be assumed the Crown recognized them when it acquired the mainland of British Columbia by occupation' (*Calder* 1970: 483).

Thus, taken together, the lower courts concluded that there was no need to reconcile 'the pre-existence of aboriginal societies with the sovereignty of the Crown' for at least one of two reasons: 1) these societies did not hold the kind of rights that required recognition by the Crown when it asserted sovereignty; and 2) to the extent that they did hold such rights, they were of the kind that could be extinguished by the passage of general legislation, such as legislation regulating hunting, that was inconsistent with their exercise. As I will discuss in the next chapter, speaking broadly, Chief Justice Davey's depiction of the 'primitive nature' of Indigenous societies mirrors one of the central arguments deployed by Flanagan and others who support the view that the Crown ought not to recognize that Indigenous peoples have Aboriginal rights, particularly those, like self-determination, that are associated with political rights.

In 1973 the Supreme Court of Canada rendered its decision. It consisted of three separate judgments; one penned by Mr Justice Wilfred Judson, with justices Ronald Martland and Roland Ritchie concurring; another (which was a dissent) written by Mr Justice Emmett Hall, with Justice Wishart Spence and Justice (soon to be Chief Justice) Bora Laskin concurring; and a third by Mr Justice Louis-Philippe Pigeon, which did not deal with the substance of the matter. The decision first took up the issue of whether the Nisga'a had rights based on the pre-existence of their societies that were recognized by the Crown. On this point, the six justices who rendered substantive judgments all agreed: the Nisga'a did have such rights. As Justice Judson put it, quoting the work of anthropologist Wilson Duff:

> It is not correct to say that the Indians did not 'own' the land but only roamed over the face of it and 'used' it. The patterns of ownership and utilization which they imposed upon the lands and waters were different from those recognized by our system of law, but were nonetheless clearly defined and mutually respected. Even if they didn't subdivide and cultivate the land, they did recognize ownership of plots used for village sites, fishing places, berry and root patches, and similar purposes ... Except for barren and inaccessible areas which are not utilized even today, every part of the Province was formerly within the owned and recognized territory of one or other of the Indian tribes. (*Calder* 1973: 318f)

In so saying, the judgment of Justice Hall made clear, the Canadian courts were acting consistently with the 'wealth of jurisprudence affirming common law recognition of aboriginal rights to possession and enjoyment of lands of aboriginees precisely analogous to the Nishga [Nisga'a] situation' (*Calder* 1973: 315). It is a position consonant with that taken by those for whom the view that Indigenous peoples had rights based on the pre-existence of their societies is beyond doubt. Furthermore, in coming to this position, Justice Hall articulated a rationale that remains current when he said in a rebuke to Chief Justice Davey: 'The assessment and interpretation of historical documents and enactments tendered in evidence must be approached in the light of present-day research and knowledge, disregarding ancient concepts formulated when understanding of the customs and cultures of our original people was rudimentary and incomplete and when they were thought to be wholly without cohesion, laws, or culture, in effect a sub-human species' (ibid.: 346).

The judgments differed, however, on the question of whether, as the lower courts had said, the general legislation passed by the colony of British Columbia had the legal effect of voiding Indigenous title. Justices Judson, Martland, and Ritchie said that it did, but justices Hall, Spence, and Laskin took the contrary view. As the summary of Hall's judgment makes clear, from their perspective

> once aboriginal title is established, it is presumed to continue until the contrary is proven. When the Nishga people came under British sovereignty they were entitled to assert, as a legal right, their Indian title. It being a legal right, it could not thereafter be extinguished except by surrender to the Crown or by competent legislative authority, and then only by specific legislation. There was no surrender by the Nishgas and neither the Colony of British Columbia nor the Province, after Confederation, enacted legislation specifically purporting to extinguish the Indian title nor did the Parliament of Canada. (*Calder* 1973: 316)

In short, absent legislation that specifically extinguished these rights, they are presumed to remain in force. As Hall stated, 'it would, accordingly, appear to be beyond question that the onus of proving that the Sovereign intended to extinguish the Indian title lies on the respondent [the Province of British Columbia] and that intention must be "clear and plain." There is no such proof in the case at bar; no legislation to that effect' (*Calder* 1973: 404). Thus: 'The essence of the action is that such rights as the Nishgas possessed in 1858 continue to this date. Accordingly, the declaratory judgment asked for implies that the *status quo* continues and this means that if the right is to be extinguished

it must be done by specific legislation in accordance with the law'
(ibid.: 353). Furthermore, the Nisga'a's possession of such rights has
consequences for the Crown. As Hall commented: 'The exact nature
and extent of the Indian right or title does not need to be precisely
stated in this litigation ... The precise nature and value of that right or
title would, of course, be most relevant in any litigation that might follow extinguishment in the future because in such an event, according
to common law, the expropriation of private rights by the government
under the prerogative necessitates the payment of compensation'
(ibid.: 352).

Justice Pigeon ruled against the Nisga'a's position based on technical
grounds, and as a result the Supreme Court upheld the position of the
lower courts 4 to 3. However, the dissenting judgment of Justice Hall
was sufficiently persuasive that, although under no legal requirement
to do so, in August 1973, the government of Canada chose to acknowledge that Indigenous interests exist and that their extinguishment requires compensation. As a policy statement put it:

> The present statement is concerned with claims and proposals for the settle-
> ment of long-standing grievances. These claims come from groups of Indian
> people who have not entered into Treaty relationship with the Crown. They
> find their basis in what is variously described as 'Indian Title,' 'Aboriginal
> Title,' 'Original Title,' 'Native Title,' or 'Usufructurary Rights.' In essence,
> these claims relate to the loss of traditional use and occupancy of lands in
> certain parts of Canada where Indian title was never extinguished by treaty
> or superseded by law ... It is basic to the position of Government that these
> claims must be settled and that the most promising avenue to settlement is
> through negotiation. It is envisaged that by this means agreements will be
> enshrined in legislation, enacted by Parliament, so that they will have the
> finality and binding force of law ... The Government is now ready to negoti-
> ate with authorized representatives of these native peoples on the basis that
> where their traditional interest in the lands concerned can be established, an
> agreed form of compensation or benefit will be provided to native peoples
> in return for their interest. (Qtd. in Asch 1984: 65)

In short, Hall's judgment set the foundation for Canada's recognition
that rights deriving from the pre-existence of Indigenous societies have
to be reconciled with the sovereignty of the Crown. With the government's acceptance of his argument, Canada took its first step along the
path we are exploring in this book.

From James Bay to the Mackenzie Valley

At that time, Canada seemed convinced that reconciliation would focus on the payment of compensation for the loss of a way of life, for, as the 1973 policy statement also intimated, 'claims are not only for money and land, but involve the loss of a way of life. Any settlement, therefore, must contribute positively to a lasting solution of cultural, social and economic problems' (qtd. in Asch 1984: 66). However, two events disabused the government of that view, and in so doing set the course for what has followed.[4] These events were: a plan to construct hydroelectric dams in the James Bay region, and a proposal to run a pipeline through the Mackenzie River valley. In each case, governments learned that the projects were opposed by the Indigenous peoples of the region (the James Bay Cree in the former, the Dene, Métis, and Inuvialuit in the latter) on a number of grounds, of which among the most significant was that the developments would virtually destroy a still-viable subsistence economy based on hunting, fishing, and trapping.

As a result of their concerns, the James Bay Cree sought an injunction against the construction of the dams, arguing that they would have a negative impact on their way of life and provoke 'irreversible and irremediable damages' to their subsistence economy (Harvey Feit, cited in Hancock 2007: 79). Persuaded by the evidence, on 13 November 1973, Mr Justice Albert Malouf granted the injunction. As he said:

a) The Cree Indians and Inuit populations occupying the territory and the lands adjacent thereto have been hunting, trapping and fishing therein since time immemorial.
b) They have been exercising these rights in a very large part of the territory and the lands adjacent thereto including their trap lines, the lakes, the rivers, and the streams.
c) These pursuits are still of great importance to them and constitute a way of life for a very great number of them.
d) Their diet is dependent, at least in part, on the animals which they hunt and trap, and on the fish which they catch.
e) The sale of fur-bearing animals represents a source of revenue for them; and the animals which they trap and hunt and the fish which they catch represent, if measured in dollars, an additional form of revenue.
f) The hides of certain animals are used as clothing.

g) They have a unique concept of the land, make use of all its fruits and
   produce including all animal life therein and any interference therewith
   compromises their very existence as a people.
h) They wish to continue their way of life.[5]

Although the injunction was immediately suspended and then overturned on appeal (*La Société de développement de la Baie James et al. v.
Kanatewat et al.* 1975), the governments of Canada and Quebec moved to
resolve the matter by negotiations. This led to the 1975 James Bay and
Northern Quebec Agreement (JBNQA) in which it was stipulated that,
in exchange for agreeing to extinguish rights based on the pre-existence
of their societies, the Cree and the other Indigenous communities (including the Inuit of the region) would receive both cash compensation
and specified rights, including some that provided significant protection for and enhancement of their traditional economy and society in
lands not flooded. Of these, perhaps the most sweeping was a guaranteed level of harvesting protected from unilateral intervention by the
state (except in the case of species at risk), income support, and provisions promoting sensitivity to Indigenous culture in education and the
administration of justice. Nonetheless, at the end of the day, sovereignty
and jurisdiction rested with the state, for the agreement asserts:

2.1 In consideration of the rights and benefits herein set forth in favour of
the James Bay Crees and the Inuit of Quebec, the James Bay Crees and the
Inuit of Quebec hereby cede, release, surrender and convey all their Native
claims, rights, titles and interests, whatever they may be, in and to land in
the territory and in Quebec, and Quebec and Canada accept such surrender. (JBNQA 1998: 5)

This agreement, with minor modifications, became the precedent upon
which all subsequent successful settlements of what are called 'comprehensive claims' (respecting Aboriginal rights) in northern Canada are
based.

The Dene, Métis, and Inuvialuit who lived along the proposed corri-
dor for the Mackenzie valley pipeline brought up the same concerns at
the inquiry struck to consider the project. Initiated by the government
of Canada in 1974, this inquiry, conducted by Mr Justice Thomas Berger,
was to investigate the potential social, economic, and environmental
impact of the proposed pipeline. As in the Malouf case, the Indigenous
peoples affected were successful in persuading the commissioner that

construction of the pipeline would have a deleterious effect on their still-viable subsistence economy and that efforts ought to be made to strengthen that economy prior to pipeline development. As Commissioner Berger put it to Minister of Indian Affairs and Northern Development Warren Allmand in April 1977: 'Although there has always been a native economy in the North, based on the bush and the barrens, we have for a decade or more followed policies by which it could only be weakened and depreciated. We have assumed that the native economy is moribund and that native people should therefore be induced to enter industrial wage employment. But I have found that income in kind from hunting, fishing and trapping is a far more important element in the northern economy than we had thought' (Berger 1977: xix). Thus: 'The real economic problems in the North will be solved only when we accept the view the native people themselves have expressed so often to the Inquiry: that is, the strengthening of the native economy. We must look at forms of economic development that really do accord with native values and preferences' (ibid.: xxi).

However, in contrast to the Cree and Inuit in Quebec, the Dene (joined for much of the time by the Métis and Inuvialuit) also asserted that, whether described as 'Aboriginal rights,' 'Aboriginal title,' or some other term, their political right to determine their own destiny with Canada had to be recognized. As Berger explained: 'Native people desire a settlement of native claims before a pipeline is built. They do not want a settlement – in the tradition of the treaties – that will extinguish their rights to the land. They want a settlement that will entrench their rights to the land and that will lay the foundations of native self-determination under the Constitution of Canada' (Berger 1977: xxiif). Or, as the Dene put it in their 1975 Dene Declaration, passed by the Dene National Assembly:

The Dene find themselves as part of a country. That country is Canada. But the Government of Canada is not the Government of the Dene. The Government of the Northwest Territories is not the Government of the Dene. These governments were not the choice of the Dene, they were imposed upon the Dene.

What we the Dene are struggling for is the recognition of the Dene nation by the governments and peoples of the world.

What we seek then is independence and self-determination within the country of Canada. This is what we mean when we call for a just land settlement for the Dene nation. (Qtd. in Asch 1984: 128f)

In effect, this meant, as the Dene explained in 1977 in their proposed Agreement in Principle between the Dene Nation and Her Majesty the Queen in Right of Canada, the powers associated with Crown sovereignty must be reconfigured so as to provide Dene the opportunity to exercise final legislative authority in their traditional territories: 'There will therefore be *within* Confederation, a Dene Government with jurisdiction over a geographical area and over subject matters now within the jurisdiction of either the Government of Canada or the Government of the Northwest Territories' (qtd. in Berger 1977: 180; emphasis in original).

The government of Canada rejected this position categorically and in the strongest of terms, as is indicated by the following 1977 press release:

> In the Northwest Territories, the initial position put forward by the Indian Brotherhood and the Inuit Tapirisat ranges well beyond the policy the Federal Government is prepared to follow. As has been indicated, the Government has no wish to see the cohesion of ethnic communities undermined and quite the reverse. In the North, as in the South, the government supports cultural diversity as a necessary characteristic of Canada. However, political structure is something quite different. Legislative authority and governmental jurisdiction are not allocated in Canada on grounds that differentiate between the people on the basis of race. Authority is assigned to legislatures that are representative of all the people within any area on a basis of complete equality ...
>
> Accordingly, unless Indian and Inuit claimants are seeking the establishment of reserves under the Indian Act, as in the South, the government does not favour the creation in the North of new political divisions, with boundaries and governmental structures based essentially on distinctions of race and involving a direct relationship of the Federal government. (Qtd. in Asch 1984: 68f)

Instead, Canada offered the Dene, Métis, and Inuvialuit a settlement that reflected the terms of the James Bay Agreement. The Inuvialuit accepted the offer and negotiated the Inuvialuit Final Agreement (1984), which was ratified by Parliament in 1984. The Dene refused. As a result, no agreement with them was reached, notwithstanding a decade or more of negotiations. Subsequently, in 1992, 1994, and 2003 respectively, the Dene and Métis in the Gwich'in, Sahtu, and Tlicho regions reached final settlements (Gwich'in First Nation 1992; Sahtu Dene and Métis 1993; Tlicho 2003) that mirrored the Inuvialuit Final Agreement but also included (either separately or in the same document) rights of local self-government that in some cases supersede those of the Northwest Territories. However, two regions, the Dehcho and those in Treaty 8, have still not come to agreement, largely because they find that these provisions are inadequate. In the words of the 'Dehcho Process Report' issued by the Dehcho First Nations in June 2011, a final agreement acceptable to them must 'recognize a Dehcho public government "*based on Dene laws and customs, and other laws agreed to by the parties,*" which will be the *primary government for all residents of the Dehcho territory*. Canada and the GNWT will continue to play a role in governing the Dehcho, but the Dehcho Government will be the primary government for the Dehcho' (Dehcho First Nation 2011: 1–2; emphasis in original).

As can be seen, the position taken by the government of Canada in the 1970s generated a precedent that largely remains in place today. As a result, to reach a successful conclusion, an Indigenous party must agree to exchange whatever rights derive from their pre-existence as societies for financial compensation and state recognition of specified rights, on the understanding that governments in Canada (except, as will be discussed below, where they choose to relinquish it) has final legislative authority with respect to the exercise of these rights.

The Constitution and Its Aftermath

After a period of intense discussion and debate (e.g., McWhinney 1979, 1982; Banting and Simeon 1983), the British Parliament, on the recommendation of Canada, passed the Constitution Act of 1982 by means of which all remaining colonial ties with the British Crown were severed. One of its provisions, section 35(1), entrenched 'existing aboriginal and treaty rights' in the constitution. Substantively, this meant that these rights, whatever they might be, could be extinguished only by constitutional amendment rather than merely by acts of Parliament – and thus, through a formula (section 38[1]) requiring the agreement of the Senate, the House of Commons, and the legislative assemblies of at least two-thirds of the provinces that have at least 50 per cent of the population of Canada as a whole, but not, it should be noted, the consent of the holders of those rights named in the constitution. Given that the constitution named, but did not provide a definition of, 'existing aboriginal rights,' the question became: Of what do these rights consist?

To address that question, governments in Canada and representatives of the 'aboriginal peoples of Canada'[6] agreed to hold four national meetings over five years to negotiate a common definition of the words

contained in section 35(1). It became apparent at the first of these, held
in 1983, that the central point of disagreement concerned the extent to
which Indigenous rights included political rights in general and the
right to self-determination in particular. Georges Erasmus, president of
the Dene Nation, put the position of Indigenous peoples as follows: 'We
are talking about the title that our people had prior to contact with the
European people and obviously ... the rights we also had at the first
contact was full sovereignty' (qtd. in Asch 1984: 29). James Gosnell,
Assembly of First Nations regional chief in British Columbia, then explained that this sovereignty had not been extinguished in the period
after European settlement:

> It has always been our belief, Mr. Chairman, that when God created this
> whole world he gave pieces of land to all races of people throughout
> this world, the Chinese people, Germans and you name them, including
> Indians. So at one time our land was this whole continent right from the
> tip of South America to the North Pole ...
>
> It has always been our belief that God gave us the land ... and we say
> that no one can take our title away except He who gave it to us to begin
> with. (Qtd. in ibid.: 29)

To this, Prime Minister Trudeau responded:

> Going back to the Creator doesn't really help very much. So he gave you
> title, but you know, did He draw on the land where your mountains
> stopped and somebody else's began ...? God never said that the frontier of
> France runs along the Rhine or somewhere west of Alsace-Lorraine where
> the German-speaking people of France live ... I don't know any part of the
> world where history isn't constantly rewritten by migrations and immi-
> grants and fights between countries changing frontiers and I don't think
> you can expect North America or the whole of the Western Hemisphere to
> settle things differently than they have ben settled everywhere else, hope-
> fully peacefully here. (Qtd. in ibid.: 31)

In other words, the prime minister took the view that, even if Indigenous peoples had a right to self-determination at one time, the fact
that they found themselves within Canada was sufficient to have these
rights extinguished. Thus, notwithstanding the entrenchment of these
rights in the constitution, governments in Canada remained faithful to
the position that they alone had the final legislative authority with
respect to the exercise of Indigenous rights.

Undeterred, Bill Wilson of British Columbia made an analogy be-tween what Indigenous peoples believed to be their right and the right to self-determination of those under foreign occupation: 'When the German forces occupied France, did the French people believe they didn't own the country? I sincerely doubt that there was one French person in France during the war that ever had the belief that France belonged to Germany, which is why, of course, they struggled with our assistance to liberate their country and once again take it back for them-selves' (qtd. in Asch 1984: 29). Thus, he concluded that, notwithstand-ing Trudeau's 'history lesson': 'What we say is we have title and that is why we are talking to you about aboriginal rights, but we are not talk-ing English Common Law definitions ... international law definitions that have been interpreted and re-interpreted and sometimes extin-guished by conquest and ceding treaties and other agreements like that. We are talking about the feeling that is inside ... all of us as Métis, Indian and Inuit people that this country belongs to us' (qtd. in ibid.: 30).

In effect, then, as I am suggesting, this position is consonant with that taken by the United Nations respecting the right to self-determination of colonized peoples. Four years and three constitutional conferences later, no progress had been made on this matter. Given the power differential, it was the viewpoint of the state that took precedence, as it does today.

Current Federal Negotiations Policy and Its Development

Canada first advanced its current view of the scope of Aboriginal politi-cal rights in a 1995 document entitled *The Government of Canada's Approach to Implementation of the Inherent Right and the Negotiation of Aboriginal Self-Government* (INAC 1995). It is based largely on terms on which governments and national Indigenous organizations had appeared to be in agreement during constitutional negotiations that led to the Charlottetown Accord some three years earlier.[7] The Accord itself failed in a national referendum among Canadians, and thus was never enacted. While there is no hard data on the matter, the available evidence indi-cates that it may well have succeeded in Inuit communities, but it was rejected at the very least by those First Nations communities for which results could be implied (Scholtz 2008: 1). It thus imposes a policy that, it would seem, failed to garner support within Indigenous communities.

Consonant with the majority in *Calder*, this policy takes as its point of departure the principle, that, whatever their content, Indigenous peoples' political rights derive from the fact that they constituted self-governing communities prior to the arrival of Europeans, and are recognized on that basis in the constitution. That is, using the language of the day, the policy accepts 'the inherent right of self-government as an existing right within Section 35 of the *Constitution Act, 1982*' (INAC 1995: 1). It also takes the view, advanced in Hall's judgment in *Calder*, that these rights may continue to exist notwithstanding Canada's assertion of sovereignty, for it states that political and other rights 'may be enforceable through the courts' (ibid.). However, it also notes that negotiations are 'clearly preferable' on the grounds that litigation is 'lengthy, costly, and would tend to foster conflict' (ibid.). That is, it advocates that the parties begin by agreeing that Canada has sovereignty and jurisdiction, which would signal acceptance of the proposition that any political rights that derive from the pre-existence of Indigenous societies will come into effect only by agreement with the Crown.

Furthermore, the *Approach* specifies the terms on which the government is prepared to conduct negotiations. The first of these is that 'the inherent right to self-government does not include a right to sovereignty in the international law sense' (INAC 1995: 2). Thus, it sets as a precondition the principle that Indigenous political rights exist only to the extent that they can be reconciled *with* Crown sovereignty. It also specifies that 'self-government agreements, including treaties, will, therefore, have to provide that the *Canadian Charter of Rights and Freedoms* applies to Aboriginal governments and institutions in relation to all matters within their respective jurisdictions and authorities' (ibid.: 2f). It then anticipates that the scope of the political rights included in these agreements will likely be limited 'to matters that are internal to the group, integral to its distinct Aboriginal culture, and essential to its operation as a government or institution' (ibid.: 3), specifying those pertaining to matters such as group membership, education, health, social services, and adoption.[8] Additionally, it explicitly excludes matters from negotiations that it describes as those 'where there are no compelling reasons for Aboriginal governments or institutions to exercise law-making authority' for they 'cannot be characterized as either integral to Aboriginal cultures, or internal to Aboriginal groups' (ibid.: 4). Among the subjects identified in this respect are 'powers related to Canadian sovereignty' and 'other national interest powers,' including any related to the Criminal Code.

Finally, the policy identifies a third category of governing authority:

There are a number of other areas that may go beyond matters that are integral to Aboriginal culture or that are strictly internal to an Aboriginal group. To the extent that the federal government has jurisdiction in these areas, it is prepared to negotiate some measure of Aboriginal jurisdiction or authority. In these areas, laws and regulations tend to have impacts that go beyond individual communities. Therefore, *primary law-making authority would remain with the federal or provincial governments, as the case may be, and their laws would prevail in the event of a conflict with Aboriginal laws.* (INAC 1995: 4; emphasis added)

Among the areas covered in this category are: environmental protection, assessment and pollution prevention, fisheries co-management, administration of justice, and emergency preparedness.[9] The fact that 'marriage' (or at least the solemnization of marriage, which is a provincial responsibility) is in the first category but 'divorce,' which is a federal responsibility, falls into the third is perhaps an indication that the underlying rationale for the latter group of subjects was a desire to protect the national government's powers.[10]

Yet, as it happens, the distinction the policy draws between the first and third categories has little practical effect since in many cases Indigenous governments do not have final legislative authority even with respect to powers associated with the first. For example, the provision for Health Services in the 2007 Tsawwassen Agreement reads: '89. Tsawwassen Government may make laws in respect of health services, including public health, provided by a Tsawwassen Institution on Tsawwassen Lands (Tsawwassen First Nation 2007: 16). However, these powers are restricted by the following: '92. Federal or Provincial Law prevails to the extent of a Conflict with a Tsawwassen Law made under clause 89' (ibid.). Similarly, lawmaking authority may be restricted even in areas where final legislative authority rests with the Indigenous government. Thus, with respect to education, where the Tsawwassen Agreement stipulates that laws made by the Indigenous government must prevail, the clause enabling that government to exercise its right 'to make laws in respect of kindergarten to grade 12' ensures that the results conform to standards set by the province of British Columbia in that it requires that the local authorities 'establish curriculum, examination, and other standards that permit students to transfer between school systems at a similar level of achievement and permit students to enter the provincial post-secondary education systems' (ibid.: 14f). In sum, while it was presented as an opportunity to negotiate, the policy introduced in 1995 dictated the conditions for government participation in the process to such a degree that it amounted to a final offer, made on a take-it-or-leave-it basis.

In its 1996 report, the Royal Commission on Aboriginal Peoples[11] responded to this policy. It argued that Indigenous peoples in Canada had a right to self-determination that arises 'from their status as distinct or sovereign peoples' (RCAP 1996: II, 12), by dint of which they were 'entitled to negotiate freely the terms of their relationship with Canada and to establish governmental structures that they consider appropriate for their needs' (ibid.: II, 81). However, the commission agreed with Canada's position that this right, 'except in the case of grave oppression or disintegration of the Canadian state,' did not 'give rise to a right of succession' (ibid.). As with the 1995 policy, the commission distinguished between two classes of authorities associated with self-government: core and periphery. The former, as in the 1995 policy, the commissioners defined as including 'all matters that (1) are vital to the life and welfare of a particular Aboriginal people, its culture and identity; (2) do not have a major impact on adjacent jurisdictions; and (3) are not otherwise the object of transcendent federal or provincial concern' (ibid.: II, 73).[12]

The 'inherent right of self-government within Canada,' the commission concluded, 'stems from the original status of Aboriginal peoples as independent and sovereign nations in the territories they occupied, as this status was recognized and given effect in the numerous treaties, alliances and other relations maintained with the incoming French and British Crowns.' As a consequence, in contrast to the 1995 policy, the commission asserted that the right of self-government, at least within the sphere of core powers, is already recognized and affirmed in the constitution, and thus 'an Aboriginal group has the right to exercise authority and legislate at its own initiative, without the need to conclude self-government treaties or agreements with the Crown' (RCAP 1996: II, 73). Hence, when it came to such matters, Indigenous law would take priority over federal law, except where 'the need for federal action can be shown to be compelling and substantial and the legislation is consistent with the Crown's basic trust responsibilities to Aboriginal peoples' (ibid.: II, 103). The commission then recommended that all governments in Canada recognize that 'in the core areas of jurisdiction, as a matter of principle, Aboriginal peoples have the capacity to implement their inherent right to self-government ... without the need for agreements' (ibid.: II, 141).

The government of Canada's response to the royal commission report is contained in its 1997 'Gathering Strength: Canada's Aboriginal Action Plan,' which was 'designed to renew the relationship with the

Aboriginal Peoples of Canada' (Ministry of Indian Affairs and Northern Development 1998: 1). There, Canada expresses its 'regret for the historic injustices experienced by Aboriginal people' (ibid.: 5), apologizing especially 'to those individuals who experienced the tragedy of sexual and physical abuse at residential schools' (ibid.: 3). However, the promise of 'renewal' did not extend to the report's recommendations concerning the recognition of Aboriginal rights, either with respect to self-determination within Canada or to the holding of final legislative authority on any matter. Instead, the government reiterated its 1995 policy that, while Canada recognized 'the inherent right of self-government as an existing Aboriginal right within section 35 of the Constitution Act, 1982,' it intended to limit that recognition to places where 'self-government arrangements' were then being negotiated, mentioning eighty such places in particular (ibid.: 8). This point was repeated in a 2000 'Progress Report' on 'Gathering Strength,' which proclaimed that, as a result of the government's policy, 'more than 80 *self-government negotiations*, representing more than half of all the First Nations and Inuit communities across Canada, are underway' (Ministry of Indian Affairs and Northern Development 2000: 9; emphasis in original); and in a 2003 statement entitled 'Resolving Aboriginal Claims' (Ministry of Indian Affairs and Northern Development 2003), a reiteration of the 1995 policy that was also intended to 'share the Government of Canada's domestic experiences ... with other nations' (ibid.: 1).

The result has been that negotiations are successful in concluding settlements only when the Indigenous party agrees that the terms of self-government as described in the 1995 policy represent in full the expression of the political rights associated with the pre-existence of their societies – as stipulated in the Tsawwassen Final Agreement (Tsawwassen First Nation 2007: 22):

FULL AND FINAL SETTLEMENT

11. This Agreement constitutes the full and final settlement in respect of the aboriginal rights, including aboriginal title, in Canada of Tsawwassen First Nation.

SECTION 35 RIGHTS OF TSAWWASSEN FIRST NATION

12. This Agreement exhaustively sets out the Section 35 Rights of Tsawwassen First Nation, their attributes, the geographic extent of those rights, and the

limitations to those rights to which the Parties have agreed, and those rights
are:
    a. the aboriginal rights, including aboriginal title, modified as a result of
this Agreement, in Canada, of Tsawwassen First Nation in and to Tsawwassen
Lands and other lands and resources in Canada;
    b. the jurisdictions, authorities and rights of Tsawwassen Government;
    and
    c. the other Section 35 Rights of Tsawwassen First Nation.

In short, the negotiations process is one in which Indigenous peoples
confirm that they are reconciling their political rights with Crown sovereignty. Or to put it another way, in return for recognition of a limited
set of rights, Indigenous peoples affirm that Canada has sovereignty
and jurisdiction, and thus that settlers are legitimately here to stay. That
is the consequence of choosing the path that the 1995 policy describes
as 'clearly preferable as the most practical and effective way to implement the inherent right to self-government' (INAC 1995: 2). But negotiations are not the only path, for, as the 1995 policy confirms, 'the
Government acknowledges that the inherent right of self-government
may be enforceable through the courts' (ibid.).What, then, is the outcome when what the policy aptly describes as the lengthy, costly, and
conflictual path of litigation is taken?

Aboriginal Rights and Litigation

Notwithstanding Chief Justice Lamer's admonition that the courts
would seek to ensure that negotiations between Canada and Indigenous
peoples would be undertaken in 'good faith,' the results are about the
same: Aboriginal rights are subordinated to the legislative authority of
Canada. This was made clear in *Sparrow*, the Supreme Court of Canada's
first substantive judgment on the meaning of Aboriginal rights. That
judgment determined that, while governments could no longer extinguish Aboriginal rights through legislation, 'federal legislative powers
continue, including the right to legislate with respect to Indians'
(*Sparrow* 1990: 4). In practice, the Court declared, this meant that with
constitutionalization 'the government is required to bear the burden of
justifying any legislation that has some negative effect on any aboriginal right protected under s. 35(1)' (ibid.: 5) To that end, it proposed a
test to legitimize such legislation, which, in the case at hand, directed
attention to the Aboriginal right of the Musqueam to fish for food.

The test imposed these criteria:

1: 'Whether the legislation in question has the effect of interfering with
   an existing aboriginal right.'
2. 'If a *prima facie* interference is found, the analysis moves to the issue
   of justification. This is the test that addresses the question of what
   constitutes legitimate regulation of a constitutional aboriginal right.'
3. 'If a valid legislative objective is found, the analysis proceeds to
   the second part of the justification issue. Here, we refer back to the
   guiding interpretive principle (that) the honour of the Crown is at
   stake in dealings with aboriginal peoples. The special trust relationship and the responsibility of the government vis-à-vis aboriginals
   must be the first consideration in determining whether the legislation
   or action in question can be justified.' (*Sparrow* 1900: 5–6)

If these criteria can be met, then the law is valid. Thus, in *Sparrow*,
government is required to regulate the fishery in such a way that, unless conservation requires banning fishing completely, the Musqueam
right to benefit from the fishery must be ensured before the interests of
non-Musqueam fishers are to be considered.

In addition, the judgment added this observation that directs attention to the existence of Aboriginal political rights: 'It is worth recalling
that while British policy towards the native population was based on
respect for their right to occupy their traditional lands, a proposition to
which the Royal Proclamation of 1763 bears witness, there was from the
outset never any doubt that sovereignty and legislative power, and indeed the underlying title, to such lands vested in the Crown' (*Sparrow*
1990: 30). In other words, in the very first judgment on section 35(1),
Supreme Court of Canada took the view that with our settlement the
sovereignty and jurisdiction of the political societies of those who were
here already was nullified.[13]

In a second judgment, *R. v. Van der Peet*, rendered six years later, the
majority of the Court reinforced this idea. Delivered by then Chief
Justice Antonio Lamer, the judgment asserted that the 'aboriginal rights'
guaranteed in section 35 are to be distinguished from rights that are
'general and universal' and 'in the liberal enlightenment view' are thus
'held by all people in society because each person is entitled to dignity
and respect' (*Van der Peet* 1996: para. 18). Aboriginal rights, Lamer concluded, 'are rights held only by aboriginal members of Canadian society' (ibid.: para. 19) and 'arise from the fact that aboriginal people are

aboriginal' (ibid.: para. 31; emphasis in original), by which he means that the rights derive from 'the fact that aboriginals lived in distinctive societies, with their own practices, traditions and cultures.'[14] Furthermore, Lamer suggested that 'aboriginal rights' are themselves not 'general and universal' among the 'aboriginal peoples of Canada.' That is, 'a court cannot look at those aspects of the aboriginal society that are true of every human society (e.g., eating to survive) or at those aspects of the aboriginal society that are only incidental or occasional to that society' (ibid.: preamble). Rather, 'to be an aboriginal right an activity must be an element of a practice, custom or tradition integral to the distinctive culture of the aboriginal group claiming the right' (ibid.) In other words, this judgment excludes the right of self-determination and of self-government from the definition of Aboriginal rights on two grounds: these are rights of the kind that are 'held by all people in society' and, like eating to survive, 'are true of every human society.' The point was put this way in *Pamajewon*, a case in which an Aboriginal right to self-government was adjudicated: 'Assuming without deciding that s. 35(1) includes self-government claims, the applicable legal standard is nonetheless that laid out in *Van der Peet, supra*. Assuming s. 35(1) encompasses claims to aboriginal self-government, such claims must be considered in light of the purposes underlying that provision and must, therefore, be considered against the test derived from consideration of those purposes' (*Pamajewon* 1996: para. 24).

Counter to Justice Hall's admonition to eschew 'ancient concepts,' the majority in *Van der Peet* also concluded that it could define the Aboriginal rights of an Indigenous people based on the presumption that communities can be rated as to their level of civilization. Thus, in the case at hand, the majority determined that Mrs Dorothy Van der Peet, a member of the Sto:lo Nation, did not have an existing Aboriginal right to sell her fish commercially because 'the Sto:lo were at a band level of social organization' and therefore lacked 'specialization in the gathering and trade of fish' requisite to demonstrate that the exchange of fish was a central part of their culture prior to European settlement' (*Van der Peet* 1996: para. 90). Or, to put it another way, contrary to the fact that trade is important for all peoples, the Court determined that the Sto:lo did not have such a right based on the presumption that they were so primitive at the time of contact that trade in fish could have become central to their culture only after it had been introduced to them by people (i.e., Europeans) who belonged to a more advanced culture.

It is true that the Court's position on Aboriginal political rights has been leavened in more recent judgments. For example, in her dissent in

Van der Peet, then Justice Beverley McLachlin had suggested that section 35 of the constitution 'recognizes not only prior aboriginal occupation, but also a prior legal regime giving rise to aboriginal rights which persist, absent extinguishment' (*Van der Peet* 1996: para. 230). It is a point she reiterates in her judgment as chief justice in *Mitchell*, a 2001 case in which the Court unanimously determined that constitutional recognition of Aboriginal rights did not exempt Grand Chief Michael Mitchell (also known as Kanentakeron), a Mohawk of Akwesasne, from paying duties on goods imported into his traditional territories. She argued that 'English law, which ultimately came to govern aboriginal rights, accepted that the aboriginal peoples possessed pre-existing laws and interests, and recognized their continuance in the absence of extinguishment, by cession, conquest or legislation' (*Mitchell* 2001: para. 9).

In another judgment in the same case, Justice Ian Binnie introduced the possibility, derived from the *Report of the Royal Commission on Aboriginal Peoples*, that 'First Nations were not wholly subordinated to non-Aboriginal sovereignty, but over time became merger partners,' thereby introducing to the concept of Crown sovereignty 'the idea of a "merged" or "shared" sovereignty' (*Mitchell* 2001: para. 129). Thus, he argues that, when Canada patriated its constitution and 'all aspects of our sovereignty became firmly located within our borders,' 'Crown sovereignty' incorporated 'at least the idea that aboriginal and non-aboriginal Canadians *together* form a sovereign entity with a measure of common purpose and united effort. It is this new entity, as inheritor of the historical attributes of sovereignty, with which existing aboriginal and treaty rights must be reconciled' (ibid.) Nonetheless, the Court concluded that, while 'the enactment of s. 35(1) of the *Constitution Act, 1982* accorded constitutional status to existing aboriginal and treaty rights ... the government retained the jurisdiction to limit aboriginal rights for justifiable reasons in the pursuit of substantial and compelling public objectives' (ibid.: summary).

This view is repeated in a more recent judgment, *Haida Nation*. There, Chief Justice McLachlin asserts that governments retain final legislative authority, for, even when 'the right and its potential infringement is of high significance to the Aboriginal peoples, and the risk of non-compensable damage is high' (*Haida Nation* 2004: para. 44), ultimately 'a commitment to the process [of consulation and perhaps negotiation prior to enacting legislation that could infringe on an Aboriginal right] does not require a duty to agree. But it does require good faith efforts to understand each other's concerns and move to address them' (ibid.: para. 49).

Conclusion

In short, notwithstanding Lamer's assurance that reconciliation will rely on 'good faith and give and take on all sides, reinforced by the judgments of this Court,' the courts to date have adhered to the same position as that of the government of Canada: Aboriginal rights, whatever their content, are subordinate to the sovereignty of Canada. And, to reiterate, this formulation begs the most fundamental question: If Indigenous peoples had legitimate sovereignty when Europeans first arrived, how did the Crown legitimately acquire it? It is the question that then Chief Justice Lamer avoided when, in *Van der Peet* and later in *Delgamuukw*, he asserted that a basic purpose of constitutionalizing Aboriginal rights was 'the reconciliation of the pre-existence of aboriginal societies *with the sovereignty of the Crown*' rather than the other way around.

However, there now appears to be the glimmer of a possibility that the Court has become concerned with this elision. For example, in the unanimous 2004 judgment in *Taku River*, Chief Justice McLachlin modified Lamer's formulation, writing: 'The purpose of s. 35(1) of the *Constitution Act, 1982* is to facilitate the ultimate reconciliation of prior Aboriginal occupation with *de facto* Crown sovereignty' (*Taku River* 2004: para. 42; emphasis in original). That is, she both replaced 'pre-existence of aboriginal societies' with 'prior Aboriginal occupation' and modified 'the sovereignty of the Crown' with the phrase 'de facto' – which, as defined in the *Oxford English Dictionary*, means 'in reality, in actual existence, force or possession as a matter of fact.' That this is her intent is underscored by her stress in *Haida* on 'the need to reconcile prior Aboriginal occupation of the land with *the reality* of Crown sovereignty' (*Haida Nation* 2004: 26; emphasis added). In other words, the phrase 'de facto' correctly emphasizes that Crown sovereignty is a fact; however, it does not speak to the *legitimacy* of that fact in law, and, as *Duhaime's Law Dictionary* suggests, it is often used in situations in which 'something which, while not necessarily lawful, exists in fact.'[15] Thus, the possibility arises that the Court is suggesting that, while Crown sovereignty exists, the legitimacy of its acquisition (or its 'de jure'[16] status) remains in doubt. That this is a possibility is reinforced by the repeated use of the phrase 'assumed sovereignty' or 'assertion of sovereignty' throughout *Haida Nation*, as for example, in the following passage: 'This process of reconciliation flows from the Crown's duty of honourable dealing toward Aboriginal peoples, which arises in turn from the Crown's assertion of sovereignty over an Aboriginal people and *de facto* control of land and resources that were formerly in the control of that people' (*Haida Nation* 2004: para. 32).

Evidence that this language might be interpreted as implying that, at least in principle, Indigenous peoples retain a robust set of political rights is found in paragraph 25, which reads: 'Put simply, Canada's Aboriginal peoples were here when Europeans came, and were never conquered. Many bands reconciled their claims with the sovereignty of the Crown through negotiated treaties. Others, notably in British Columbia, have yet to do so. The potential rights embedded in these claims are protected by s. 35 of the *Constitution Act, 1982*' (*Haida Nation* 2004: para. 25).

There is, then, the possibility that the Supreme Court might be alluding to a conclusion that, at least in places where their rights have not been reconciled to Crown sovereignty through treaties, Indigenous peoples in Canada retain the same right to self-determination enjoyed by other peoples whose lands have been colonized or are under foreign occupation; and if so, that is what may be implied by the change from 'pre-existence of aboriginal societies' to 'prior Aboriginal occupation.'

But likely I go too far. What I do believe is that the language of the Court in *Haida Nation* and *Taku* invites us to think that, when it comes to reconciliation with Indigenous peoples, the presumption that 'might makes right' is not good enough. Rather, it suggests that we begin by asking ourselves what the shape of a relationship with Indigenous peoples would be were we to replace the de facto 'assertion of Crown sovereignty' with an approach that asks how that would look were we to base reconciliation on the de jure principle that, in our way of understanding, it is simply wrong to move onto lands we know belong to others without permission.

However, let me begin by examining the proposition that the path we have taken since *Calder* is misguided; that somehow it is not in keeping with our principles to acknowledge that Indigenous peoples have rights merely because they were here when Settlers first arrived. To that end, I will next discuss and evaluate the arguments raised by University of Calgary political scientist Tom Flanagan.

Chapter Three

Aboriginal Rights and Temporal Priority

... Temporal priority is one of the great ordering principles of human society, memorialized in proverbs such as 'first come, first served.' We follow rules of priority in such daily-life situations as standing in line to pay a cashier or waiting for a speaker to finish rather than interrupting. When I go trout fishing on a stream and I find another fisherman already working a pool, I don't cast into the same pool, I walk away to find one that is unoccupied (by fishermen, not by trout!).

(Flanagan 2008: 20)

Introduction

Let me begin by introducing the proposition that the path the Supreme Court encourages us to take is misguided; that somehow it is wrong for us to recognize that Indigenous peoples have legal rights because they were here before us. While this proposition is not as popular as it once was, it is one with deep roots, and continues to have its adherents. Of these, there has been no greater a champion of it in the academy than political scientist Tom Flanagan, who in *First Nations? Second Thoughts* lays out what I count to be five arguments to persuade us that we ought not to continue on the road we have been taking, notwithstanding its support by the Supreme Court (2008: 231–2). In fine, they are all based on this idea: there are compelling reasons for us to ignore the principle of 'temporal priority,' which holds, in the case at hand, that people who were here before European settlement have rights which those who came later must recognize.

In this chapter, I will address these arguments in some detail, for it is my view that, were any found to be beyond dispute, as Flanagan infers, then I would have to rethink the basic premise upon which I am beginning; that, whatever the solution we arrive at, we need to start by recognizing that, as then Supreme Court Justice Judson put it, 'when the settlers came the Indians were there, organized in societies and occupying the land as their forefathers had done for centuries.'

But let me begin at a point of agreement. Tom Flanagan and I concur: temporal priority is a central tenet in our culture, one that we use to order relationships in matters that range from scientific explanations (cause and effect) to practices in serving groups of people (those who come later are served later). In fact, I am also convinced that we agree that it is a central tenet of English law, in that when someone settles in territory under our jurisdiction that person is subject to our laws. Nor do I believe that we would disagree with the understanding that, normally, when we seek sovereignty somewhere else, English law demands that we acquire it from those who hold it (Halsbury's Laws of England 5th ed.: Vol. 13, s. 4[1], ss. 801), so that, even when land is taken by force of arms, the private rights of the conquered remain in place until expressly changed by the conqueror (ibid.: ss. 867).

The question, then, is not in the rule but in the exception, for I also agree with Flanagan that 'we do not follow temporal priority blindly and inflexibly' (Flanagan 2008: 20). The issue is whether the situation here is such an exception, one that would be widely accepted had the judgment of society as a whole and the Supreme Court in particular not been clouded in the past thirty years, as Flanagan asserts, by 'aboriginal orthodoxy' and 'historical revisionism' (ibid.: ch. 1).

Thus, in this chapter I ask whether Flanagan's arguments make it clear that the principle of temporal priority does not apply in Canada. To that end, I will describe these arguments as fairly as I can, and then reply to each. I begin with the one that asserts temporal priority does not apply because, as Flanagan argues (principally in chapter 4, 'The Fiction of Aboriginal Sovereignty'), it has long been held in international law that the principle of temporal priority applies to sovereignty only if at the time of European arrival Indigenous peoples were living in that form of political community we call 'the state.' Since that is not the case with respect to Indigenous peoples at the time of European settlement, the principle of temporal priority does not hold in this case.

1. Indigenous Sovereignty and Convention

At its heart, Flanagan's argument is that the international community has for centuries identified circumstances in which the principle of

temporal priority does and does not apply. In that regard, a distinction
is drawn between Indigenous peoples and others. One approach, which
I will discuss more fully with respect to Flanagan's fifth argument, divides humanity between those who cultivate the soil and those who do
not. In support of this position, Flanagan cites eighteenth-century Swiss
political philosopher Emer de Vattel, who, as Flanagan describes it,
held the view that people who 'did not practice agriculture ... had only
an "uncertain occupancy" of the land that did not amount to sovereign
possession' (Flanagan 2008: 55).

The division of humanity that pertains explicitly to the matter of
Indigenous sovereignty distinguishes between the state and other
forms of political community, with the former being the only form to
which sovereignty may be attributed. Hence, as Indigenous peoples
did not live in states, it would be misplaced to attribute sovereignty to
their communities. Among the prominent proponents of this view, as
Flanagan points out, was the sixteenth-century Spanish theologian and
political theorist Francisco de Vitoria, who argued that 'the aboriginal
inhabitants of the Americas did not possess sovereignty because they
were not organized into territorial states with stable governments and
thus were not actors under the law of nations' (Flanagan 2008: 54).
Flanagan makes that point in these words: 'Sovereignty in the strict
sense exists only in the organized states characteristic of civilized societies' (ibid.: 58f). Thus, temporal priority does not apply because 'aboriginal peoples in Canada had not arrived at the state level of political
organization prior to contact with Europeans' (ibid.: 6).

While Flanagan offers 'evidence,' which I will take up below, to
support aspects of this claim, in this iteration the argument rests on
convention. That is, his justification for the categorical nature of his
conclusion that 'sovereignty is an attribute of statehood' is founded on
the premise that the proposition that it applies only to states is a tenet
of such long standing as to be beyond dispute. Therefore, as there were
no states here when settlers arrived on these lands, the principle of temporal priority did not apply. To apply it now is to revise history, for it
seeks to overturn an understanding that is so well established as to be
considered a settled conclusion, and to replace it with a fiction invented
recently by a powerful lobby intent on advancing its agenda.

RESPONSE

Let me offer this counter. In the first place, convention, even when of
long standing, is hardly sufficient in and of itself to uphold a principle.

No precedent, no matter how long it has been held, is beyond challenge. A norm or a convention must stand up to scrutiny, and if it is found wanting, like, for example, the principles that justified slavery or declared the world flat, then it ought to be overturned no matter the length of time that it has been held to be true or just. Thus, acceptance or rejection of the application of temporal priority in Canada ought to stand on its merits: Is the fact that one party is not a state, does not practise agriculture, or is not (in the eyes of the other) 'civilized' a reasonable basis to deny the application of that principle? This is a matter to which I will return below. However, my point here is the following: whether there has been at least a partial revision of our views with respect to the application of temporal priority, and whether the change may have been influenced by 'aboriginal orthodoxy,' is of no significance. Merely because the principle was not applied in earlier times is not a justification in and of itself for not applying it today.

Second, it is simply inaccurate to declare that the convention is based on an internationally recognized norm, when in fact Indigenous peoples were not parties to establishing it. In this I am following the view expressed nearly two hundred years ago by United States Senator Frederick Frelinghuysen on the occasion of the removal of the Cherokee:

> In light of natural law, can a reason for a distinction exist from the mode of enjoying that which is my own? If I use the land for hunting, may another take it because he needs it for agriculture? I am aware that some writers have, by a system of artificial reasoning, endeavored to justify, or rather excuse, the encroachments made upon Indian territory, and to denominate these abstractions the law of nations, and, in this ready way, the question is dispatched. Sir, as we read the sources of this law, we find its authority to depend upon either the conventions or common consent of nations. And when, permit me to inquire, were the Indian tribes ever consulted on the establishment of such a law? Whoever represented them or their interests in any congress of nations, to confer upon the public rules of intercourse and the proper foundation of dominion and property? (Frelinghuysen 1977 [1830]: 6)

My third point is that, as the above quote makes clear, Flanagan is incorrect to represent the position he rejects as 'revisionist.' The fact is that, while the convention he espouses has been dominant in Western political and legal thought since the Enlightenment, it has met with robust counter-arguments from at least the mid-eighteenth century. Of these, the principal one is based on the concept often referred to as 'equality of standing,' which asserts that the international standard for applying the principle of temporal priority is the presence of an organized society, not the specific form that it takes. One exponent of this point of view was Montesquieu, who argued in 1748 that 'all nations have a right of nations, and even the Iroquois, who eat their prisoners, have one. They send and receive embassies; they know rights of war and peace'[1] (Montesquieu 1989 [1748]: 8). And that: 'In addition to the right of nations, which concerns all societies, there is a *political right* for each one. A society could not continue to exist without a government.'

In the late eighteenth century, Johann Herder made a similar argument when he defended the right of Indigenous peoples in North America to oppose our taking of their lands: 'Even when the natives are reasonably well treated by the European, they feel cheated, and can scarcely conceal their hatred. "You have no business here, for this land is ours," is a thought they cannot suppress. Hence the "treachery" of all the so-called savages ... To us this seems horrible; and so it is, no doubt. Yet it was the European who first induced them to this monstrous deed. Why did they come to their country? Why did they enter it as despots, arbitrarily practicing violence and extortion?' (Barnard 1965: 286f).

In other words, not only is the fact that a position has been long held not sufficient rationale for it to prevail today, the position Flanagan opposes cannot be dismissed as 'revisionist' for it also has a long history in Western thought. Flanagan may advocate returning to the prior precedent; that is his right. But there is nothing in this argument to persuade me to abandon the position that the principle of temporal priority does indeed apply in Canada.

2. Temporal Priority and Prescription

A second argument Flanagan advances is that temporal priority is irrelevant, for, over time and whatever the justice of our acquisition of Indigenous land, it is a well-accepted principle in international law (known as 'prescription') that, so long as it is recognized by others, the exercise of the Crown's sovereignty over Indigenous peoples and their territories has, in and of itself, legitimatized that sovereignty. As he says: 'Maybe it was wrong for John Cabot, Jacques Cartier, and all the other explorers to claim sovereignty for Britain and France. Nonetheless, Canada, the United States, and all the other states of the Americas exist and their sovereignty is recognized throughout the world. In a free country like Canada, aboriginal leaders can talk all they want about their own inherent sovereignty, but the expression is only a rhetorical turn of phrase. It may produce domestic political results by playing on guilt or compassion, but it has no effect in international (or domestic) law' (Flanagan 2008: 61).

In support of this assertion, Flanagan cites the definition of 'prescription' that appears in *The Acquisition of Territory in International Law*, published in 1963 by the renowned scholar of international law Sir Robert (R.Y.) Jennings. The excerpt that appears in Flanagan's text reads: 'Prescription ... is a portmanteau concept that comprehends both a possession of which the origin is unclear or disputed, and an adverse possession which is in origin demonstrably unlawful. For prescription, therefore, the possession must be long-continued, undisturbed, and it must be unambiguously attributable to a claim to act as a sovereign' (qtd. in Flanagan 2008: 61). Thus, Flanagan concludes with the following categorical assertion: 'State practice, interpretive works, and decisions of international tribunals unanimously agree that long-continued possession and effective control, combined with declarations of sovereignty, eventually confer title by prescription' (ibid.).

In other words, there can be no doubt that to assert in this day and age that Indigenous peoples retain their sovereignty is to violate a long-settled principle of international law. In short, it would appear that, based on prescription, an appeal to temporal priority is irrelevant in that in law any right to political self-determination that Indigenous peoples may have, based on their presence here prior to European settlement, has been nullified through the passage of time.

RESPONSE

Prescription identifies a set of conditions that, in international law, legitimatize the taking of land that originally belonged to others. My response is that, while this may be lawful, it is transparently unjust to presume that a people lose their right to self-determination solely because someone else has been able to suppress their ability to exercise that right for a sufficient length of time. Rather than accede to what is unjust, then, as would be the case with respect to other such laws, I would seek to change it.

But this response is premised on the assumption that Flanagan's definition of 'prescription' reflects its meaning in full. It does not. The sentence in the Jennings quote that immediately follows what Flanagan chooses to reproduce reads as follows: *"It depends as much on the quies-cence of the former sovereignty as on the consolidation of the new"* (Jennings 1963: 23; emphasis added). That is, in addition to the criteria Flanagan sets out, for prescription to apply requires 'the quiescence' in its appli-cation by those whose authority to govern has been adversely effected by it. That this is well understood is confirmed in the following passage from Joshua Castellino and Steve Allen's *Title to Territory in International Law*: 'The possession must be peaceful and uninterrupted,' a require-ment that 'manifests itself in two respects, the display of authority by the prescribing state *and the necessary acquiescence of the other state'* (Castellino and Allen 2003: 53; emphasis added).

Other works seek to spell out the meaning of 'non-acquiescence' more explicitly, as in this textbook in international law: 'Effective con-trol by the acquiring state probably needs to be accompanied by acqui-escence on the part of the losing state; *protests, or other acts or statements which demonstrate a lack of acquiescence, can probably prevent acquisition of title by prescription'* (Malanczuk 1997: 150; emphasis added). Indeed, that is the way 'prescription' is defined in the authoritative text on English law. 'Prescription,' states Halsbury, 'denotes the acquisition of title to territory by means of de facto exercise of state authority in the mistaken belief that it is part of the territory of the state which is pre-scribing for it. The exercise of authority must be undisturbed and *not protested against by the state against which it is exercised'* (Halsbury's Laws of England 5th ed.: Vol. 61, s. 7, ss. 118; emphasis added).

So, the question becomes, did and do Indigenous peoples 'protest' or 'by other acts or statements' demonstrate that they have not acqui-esced? The answer, as the evidence clearly shows, is 'yes.' Here are two examples. The first is contained in a letter written in 1727 by Panaouamskeyen, the spokesperson for the Abenaki, disputing that his people are subjects of the Crown:

> Much less, I repeat, did I, become his subject, or give him my land, or ac-knowledge his King as my King ... He again said to me – But do you not recognize the King of England as King over all his states? To which I an-swered – Yes, I recognize him King of all his lands; but I rejoined, do not hence infer that I acknowledge thy King as my King, and King of my lands. Here lies my distinction – my Indian distinction. God hath willed that I have no King, and that I be master of my lands in common. He again asked me – Do you not admit that I am at least master of the lands I have purchased? I answered him thereupon, that I admit nothing, and that I knew not what he had reference to. (Panaoumskeyen 1991[1727])

The second example was penned two and a half centuries later by the Chilcotin (now spelled Tsilhqot'in) Nation:

> The Chilcotin Nation affirms, asserts, and strives to exercise full control over our traditional territories and over the government within our lands.
>
> Our jurisdiction to govern our territory and our people is conferred upon us by the Creator, to govern and maintain and protect the traditional territory in accordance with natural law for the benefit of all living things existing on our land, for this generation and for those yet unborn.
>
> We have been the victims of colonization by Britain, Canada and the province of British Columbia. We insist upon our right to decolonize and drive those governments from our land. (General Assembly of the Chilcotin Nation 1983)

In short, it is far from clear that the situation in Canada fits the definition of 'prescription' as cited in legal authorities. Indeed, my initial response may well be settled law, for, as the Supreme Court of Canada stated in the Quebec Reference case:

> Our law has long recognized that through a combination of acquiescence and prescription, an illegal act may at some later point be accorded some form of legal status. In the law of property, for example, it is well known that a squatter on land may ultimately become the owner if the true owner sleeps on his or her right to repossess the land. In this way, a change in the factual circumstances may subsequently be reflected in a change in legal status. It is, however, quite another matter to suggest that a subsequent condonation of an initially illegal act retroactively creates a legal right to engage in the act in the first place. The broader contention is not supported by the international principle of effectivity or otherwise and must be rejected. (*Reference re Secession of Quebec* 1998: para. 146)

That is, at least in the view of the Supreme Court, the legal doctrine of 'prescription' is to be applied when an owner 'sleeps on his or her right,' not to convey legitimacy on an act that was illegal in the first place. If the principle of temporal priority applies, then 'prescription' does not negate the rights that flow from it.

3. Aboriginal Rights and the Peopling of America

In fine, Flanagan suggests that we would not come to the view that Indigenous peoples have temporal priority were we to attend to these facts respecting the peopling of North America: 1) all of us migrated from other parts of the world, and in particular, while some Indigenous peoples arrived long ago, the most recent wave of Indigenous immigration migrated only a few centuries before the arrival of the first Europeans; 2) Indigenous peoples 'did not follow a rule of temporal priority themselves,' for 'only the first migrants, whoever they were and whenever they came, found a truly empty continent. Later arrivals had to push their way in just as the European colonists did' (Flanagan 2008: 2); and 3) Indigenous migrants did not occupy lands in a manner that conforms to the conditions under which the principle of temporal priority applies.

From the first observation, Flanagan concludes that, given that we are all equally immigrants to this continent, it is unreasonable to accord Indigenous peoples rights based on the fact that they arrived here before Europeans, particularly since the first European migrants arrived so soon after the most recent wave of Indigenous migration was completed. From the second, he suggests that it is unreasonable to accord Indigenous peoples rights based on temporal priority with respect to European settlement when later waves of Indigenous peoples did not apply that principle with respect to those already living here. Doing so, he argues, 'is a kind of racism,' for 'it contends that the only legitimate inhabitants of the Americas have been Indians and Inuit. According to this view, they had the right to drive each other from different territories as much as they liked, even to the point of destroying whole peoples and taking over their land, but Europeans had no similar right to push their way in' (Flanagan 2008: 25). The third argument contends that the principle of temporal priority applies only to the extent that migration resulted in a circumstance in which specific communities of Indigenous peoples controlled specific territories and used land in specific ways. Thus, for example, given the manner in which the land was used, the principle of temporal priority does not pertain to ownership of land. That is, as Flanagan puts it, 'aboriginal peoples cannot justifiably claim "property rights ... by virtue of their occupation upon certain lands from time immemorial." There may be specific cases where a native community has dwelled continuously upon the same territory for thousands of years (if such cases exist in Canada, they lie on the coast of British Columbia), but, in general, Native peoples in Canada, like hunter-collectors around the world, moved a great deal' (ibid.: 19).

RESPONSE

I do not find any of these arguments persuasive. With regard to the first, it does not matter (using facts relied upon in Western scholarship on the peopling of the New World) that Europeans arrived soon after some communities of Indigenous peoples. What matters is that the migration of Europeans came *after* the last migration of Indigenous peoples. That is, as commonly understood, temporal priority is a relative measure, and this case is analogous to the fact that the temporal priority of the person immediately ahead of you in line is not altered by the length of time between his/her arrival and yours. Ahead of you is ahead of you. All that counts is that you arrived after. In this regard, to designate that a right derives from 'time immemorial' does not require that the community possessing that right has been in a certain place 'from the beginning of time' For this phrase means only 'ancient beyond memory or record; extremely old' (*OED*). And that certainly is accurate with respect to our memory with respect to the presence of Indigenous peoples on these lands before we arrived. 'Time immemorial' can also refer to an arbitrary date. For example, 'time immemorial' may be the time before legal memory was fixed by the Statute of Westminster as 3 September 1189, the day that King Richard I (Richard the Lionheart) ascended the throne.[2] In *Van der Peet*, the Supreme Court of Canada determined that the date akin to 'time immemorial' with respect to Aboriginal rights is 'prior to contact,' whereas in *Delgamuukw* it held that the date relevant to 'Aboriginal title' is the one on which the Crown asserted sovereignty in a particular region, and therefore differs from one part of the country to another (see *Delgamuukw* 1997: para. 144).

I have two difficulties with the second argument. First, as Flanagan admits, there is no direct evidence derived from Western science to substantiate the assertion that later waves of Indigenous immigrants did not adhere to the principle of temporal priority with respect to those who were already here. As he says: 'Theories of conquest and displacement based purely on archaeological evidence are conjectural' (Flanagan 2008: 17). Accordingly, he derives his conclusion by extrapolation from what he claims to be evidence that 'from the sixteenth century onward, as soon as European explorers could report their observations ... aboriginal peoples contested with each other for the control of territory and ... conquest, absorption, displacement, and even extermination were routine phenomena' (ibid.). Yet elsewhere he suggests that in the same period such struggle was not always the norm even among those most frequently represented as enemies in the popular literature. As he says: 'A party of Cree might ride for days in Blackfoot territory without encountering any Blackfoot. If they met, they might fight, or they might establish friendly relations and the Blackfoot might allow the Cree to hunt without opposition' (ibid.: 115). In short, Flanagan's assertion that later waves of Indigenous peoples did not respect the principle of temporal priority is not substantiated by the evidence that he himself provides.

But for the sake of argument, let us presume that his evidence on this point is compelling. Does it follow, then, that it would be 'racist' to insist that European migrants adhere to the principle? I think not. Temporal priority, Flanagan and I agree, is a crucial principle in Western thought. Neither of us claims that it also holds among Indigenous peoples (although it may well). Therefore, there can be no expectation that they would act in the same way as we would. To adhere to temporal priority is to remain true to standards we set for ourselves regardless of what others may do, and that means in this case that, as immigrants to lands over which others have sovereignty, we are required to subordinate our laws to theirs, and by extension, it is incumbent upon us to ensure that we adopt their legal regime in all other respects.

Flanagan's third contention is that to apply the principle of temporal priority to any 'right' requires that Indigenous peoples prove that this right existed prior to European settlement. Thus, the principle of temporal priority cannot apply with respect to land ownership because Indigenous peoples did not settle in one place long enough to establish possession, nor did they use the land in ways we consider to be characteristic of land ownership ('in general, native peoples in Canada, like hunter-collectors around the world, moved a great deal'). Of course, at one level this is an argument by convention, and thus objections, such as the one advanced by Senator Frelinghuysen, are relevant. To those, I would add two. First, Flanagan's approach places a burden on Indigenous peoples that we do not apply to ourselves. In our society, my ownership of a parcel of land is not determined by how long and for what purposes I have used it. It is determined by the recognition that it belongs to me. Thus, so long as I have title, I retain the ownership of a parcel of land even if I never set foot on it or use it only for hunting (and whether or not I permit others to do so as well). By corollary, it is only reasonable to assume that the same holds (albeit likely with a very different kind of 'recognition regime') among Indigenous peoples; and, if so, one may conclude that there was a lawful regime in place prior to European settlement. In other words, Flanagan's argument assumes, incorrectly, that Indigenous peoples did not live in rule-governed political communities.

And that leads to my second, more general, objection: Flanagan's argument asserts that the principle of temporal priority does not apply except when Indigenous peoples prove (to our satisfaction? beyond reasonable doubt?) that it does. But this reverses the burden of proof. In our way of thinking, the principle of temporal priority is presumed to apply except when it can be demonstrated that it does not. Hence, to prove that it does not apply with respect to land ownership (or to any other matter) requires that we demonstrate (to their satisfaction? beyond reasonable doubt?) that Indigenous peoples did not live in societies that were regulated by rules that attended in some manner to these matters. Similarly, it follows that the application of the principle of temporal priority depends on the fact that, collectively, Indigenous peoples arrived before settlers ('when the settlers came the Indians were there, organized in societies and occupying the land as their forefathers had done for centuries') rather than on the ability of specific Indigenous communities to demonstrate that they were in control of specific territories.

4. Choosing between Aboriginal Rights and Democracy

In this argument, Flanagan takes the view that to apply the principle of temporal priority to one group in society violates a value fundamental to democratic society – that each citizen is to be treated as equal regardless of ancestry. He puts it this way, in the process referring to Indigenous peoples as 'Siberian-Canadians': 'The attribution of privileges to Siberian-Canadians on the basis of ancestry is anomalous in a liberal democracy because it contradicts a fundamental aspect of the rule of law – treating people for what they do rather than for who they are. Indians did not do anything to achieve their status except to be born, and no one else can do anything to join them in that status because no action can affect one's ancestry' (Flanagan 2008: 22). Hence, making 'race the constitutive factor of the political order' would establish 'aboriginal nations as privileged political communities with membership defined by race and passed on through descent. It would redefine Canada as an association of racial communities rather than a polity whose members are individual human beings' (ibid.: 194). And, he suggests, to act in this manner not only contradicts the values on which our polity is built but also sets us on a path that we know from history threatens democracy itself. As he says: 'Through painful trial and error, the Western world has developed a form of polity – liberal democracy – which, though patently imperfect, confers upon ordinary people a degree of freedom, respect, and security of expectations unmatched in any other political system. Do we really want to jeopardize this accomplishment by embarking upon the troubled waters of racial and ethnic politics?' (ibid.: 196f).

Here Flanagan evokes for me, and no doubt for many others, the image of a society where the democratic value of equality of citizenship provides vulnerable individuals and communities with protection against discriminatory laws, such as those in the United States during the era of 'Jim Crow' permitting segregation based on race. But that is not his point. Rather, he heads in the opposite direction, for he avows that applying the principle of temporal priority to Indigenous peoples (i.e., 'Siberian-Canadians') creates problems because it gives them an (undeserved) advantage over their fellow citizens. That is, it 'creates a sense of entitlement among those inside the magic circle while fostering resentment among those who are excluded, thus poisoning the political atmosphere' (Flanagan 2008: 22). At the same time, Flanagan leavens his argument by suggesting that the number of 'Siberian-Canadians' is sufficiently small that granting such 'entitlements' would not in and of itself be fatal to the viability of the Canadian state. However, he suggests, a privileged class of citizens, no matter how small, would constitute a threat to stability by acting as a 'continuous irritant' to the political community' and, moreover, would encourage further irritations of this kind: 'Its very existence would be a standing invitation to other racial or ethnic communities to demand similar corporate status' (ibid.: 194).

RESPONSE

Flanagan's argument rests on the premise that treating citizens as 'individual human beings' is an inviolable democratic value. That is, there is simply no place in a democracy for recognition of 'ancestry,' 'race,' or 'ethnicity.' Each of us is a citizen, and nothing more. As with his argument on convention, Flanagan presents this view as though it was the only possibility that reason would permit. But the matter is hardly beyond reasoned debate. States, with some limited exceptions, always contain communities that differ with respect to 'ancestry,' 'race,' or 'ethnicity'; and it is clear from experience that very often this fact in itself can be an 'irritant,' one that, at times, may even threaten the stability of the state. Ignoring these differences, however, may well exacerbate tensions, as when, for example, a state insists that all ethno-national communities, regardless of the language each speaks, interact with it in the language spoken by the majority community.

How to manage the irritants that may result from tempering the strict adherence to the value of 'citizenship equality' has long been a consideration relevant to statecraft. Flanagan has taken one position, but it is hardly the only one. Indeed, I think it fair to say that his position does not *appear* to overlap significantly with the direction Canada has taken with regard to the recognition of the linguistic and educational rights of francophones and the governance rights of the primarily French-speaking population in Quebec.[3] I say *appear* because nowhere in his book does Flanagan either indicate that he disagrees with the approach taken in Canada or, by reasoned argument, explain how his rejection of rights respecting 'Siberian-Canadians' does not equally apply to 'francophones.'

Furthermore, as with his argument on convention, Flanagan pays no attention to the arguments of those with whom he disagrees, limiting his engagement on this matter, as far as I can see, to the use of the word 'troubling' to characterize the position developed by James Tully, one of Canada's leading political philosophers (who Flanagan seems to suggest is a member of the 'aboriginal orthodoxy'), in his book *Strange Multiplicities*. It is a position to which I will refer in chapter 6. However, here I wish to focus on what I consider a more striking omission. Canada is renowned for the breadth and depth of scholarship on multiculturalism, and Will Kymlicka is arguably this country's leading political theorist on the subject. Kymlicka, I think it is fair to say, has devoted much of his vast scholarship to addressing the matter from many perspectives, one of which is explicitly the issue of whether it is consistent with democratic values to apply the principle temporal priority with regard to the political and other rights of Indigenous peoples in Canada. While Kymlicka's argument is laid out in many places, one significant venue is *Multicultural Citizenship*. Although this work was published five years before the first edition of *First Nations? Second Thoughts*, and directly challenges the nub of his argument, Flanagan does not mention it.

In *Multicultural Citizenship*, Kymlicka concludes that there is no conflict between ethno-cultural rights and democratic citizenship under certain conditions. These conditions are: 1) that the different ethno-cultural communities belong to what he calls 'societal cultures' or societies that provide 'members with meaningful ways of life across the full range of human activities' (Kymlicka 1995: 76); and 2) that these societies were already in existence 'at the time of their incorporation' into the state (ibid.: 79). In Canada, Indigenous peoples meet both tests. Indigenous communities, Kymlicka claims, were fully independent political actors prior to 'incorporation' and thus (to use the language being deployed here) the principle of temporal priority applied with respect to their political rights at that time (i.e., they have an inherent right to self-determination). Therefore, he argues explicitly that, in Canada, when incorporation has been voluntary, agreements (treaties) between Indigenous peoples and the state are voided 'morally if not legally' 'if the Canadian government reneges on these promises' (ibid.: 117); and, speaking more broadly, 'if incorporation was involuntary (e.g. colonization), then the national minority might have a claim to self-determination under international law' (ibid.) Given this circumstance, recognition of the minority's rights based on their ancestry is the position that adheres most consistently with democratic (or liberal) values: 'So long as liberals believe in separate states with restricted citizenship, the burden of proof (with respect to denying rights based on ancestry) lies as much with opponents of group-differentiated rights as with their defenders' (ibid.: 126).

In short, one might conclude from Flanagan's argument that to base rights on temporal priority so violates democratic values that it can only be categorically rejected by all reasonable people. However, as I hope this discussion indicates, his argument is hardly sufficient to support his opinion on this matter, much less provide the basis upon which to dismiss all other points of view.

5. Civilization and Temporal Priority

Flanagan's fifth argument is based on the premise that, as our way of living is objectively better at providing for our material well-being than is theirs, we have a right to impose it so long those on the receiving end obtain the requisite benefits. That is, Flanagan argues that the principle of temporal priority does not apply whenever the benefits of civilization are offered to the uncivilized, for the imposition improves their lives while benefiting humanity as a whole. He puts his case this way:

> Let me put this line of argument in the simplest terms. Initially, all people, whether hunters or farmers, have an equal right to support themselves from the bounty of the earth. But the hunting mode of life takes up a lot of land, while agriculture, being more productive, causes population to grow and leads to civilization. As their numbers increase, civilized peoples have a right to cultivate the additional land necessary for their support. If the hunters deny them that opportunity by keeping their hunting grounds as a game preserve, they impede the equal access of the farmers to the bounty

of the earth. It is wrong for the hunters to insist on maintaining their way of life; rather they should adopt agriculture and civilization, which would actually make them better off while allowing more people to live. *The farmers are justified in taking land from the hunters and defending it as long as they make the arts of civilization available to the hunters.* (Flanagan 2008: 42f; emphasis added)

As with the argument on convention, this argument has a long history in Western thought, with Flanagan tracing it to the Papal Bull of 1493 in which Pope Alexander VI asserted that the purpose of European settlement in the New World was to 'spread ... Christian rule' and 'bring to the worship of our Redeemer and the profession of the Catholic faith their residents and inhabitants.'[4] As Flanagan points out, it is also associated with the work of Adam Smith and Jean-Jacques Rousseau, both of whom portrayed 'civil society as resulting not from a single decisive moment in time – the initial social contract – but from a long and gradual process of development' (Flanagan 2008: 29). The Marquis de Condorcet used the following words in *Outlines of an Historical View of the Progress of the Human Mind* (published in French as *Esquisse d'un Tableau Historique des Progrès de l'Esprit Humain* in 1793/4, and in English in 1795) to express this idea:

In one place will be found a numerous people, who, to arrive at civilization, appear only to wait till we shall furnish them with the means; and, who, treated as brothers by Europeans, would instantly become their friends and disciples. In another will be seen nations crouching under the yoke of sacred despots or stupid conquerors, and who, for so many ages, have looked for some friendly hand to deliver them: while a third will exhibit either tribes nearly savage, excluded from the benefits of superior civilization by the severity of their climate, which deters those who might otherwise be disposed to communicate these benefits from making the attempt; or else conquering hordes, knowing no law but force, no trade but robbery. The advances of these two last classes will be more slow, and accompanied with more frequent storms; it may even happen that, reduced in numbers in proportion as they see themselves repelled by civilized nations, they will in the end wholly disappear, or their scanty remains become blended with their neighbours. (Condorcet 1795: 324–5)

However, unlike the argument on convention, here Flanagan relies on reason rather than precedent to make his case. His position begins

with the thesis (which proponents would call an evidence-based observation) that humanity as a whole progresses through time from lower
to higher stages of development in a process that some call 'Universal
History' and others 'Cultural Evolution.' Commonly portrayed as the
movement from 'primitive' to 'civilized' or, as Flanagan terms it, from
'uncivilized' to 'civilized,' it is understood to occur in 'stages' and is
thus sometimes referred to as 'the stadial theory of history.' These stages, while once described by such value-laden terms as 'savagery' (a
term no longer in current use, although Flanagan uses it on at least one
occasion – see below), 'Barbarism' (again not currently used), and
'Civilization' – all found in the schema of nineteenth-century anthropologist Lewis Henry Morgan – contemporary proponents now em-
ploy more neutral words based on either how people make a living
(foraging, nomadic pasturalism, horticulture, agriculture, and modern
commerce) and/or forms of political organization (bands, tribes, chief-
doms, primitive states, and 'modern' state systems).

A key aspect of this argument is the assertion (again presumed by
adherents to be an evidence-based observation) that, while humanity as
a whole has progressed through these stages, not all segments of humanity have yet done so. As a result, today there are portions of humanity ('cultures') living at each stage of development so that, while some
have attained the highest level (which Flanagan labels 'civilization'),
others exist at lower levels and some at the first (which Flanagan labels
'uncivilized' or 'savage'). In that calculus, at the time of their arrival,
European Settlers represented humanity at its highest level of development and, for the most part, Indigenous peoples in North America
represented its lowest.

However, Flanagan does not suggest that such differences make
Indigenous peoples less worthy of being human than are the Settlers,
for he argues that, regardless of level of development, all of us equally
live in societies that have 'norms of reciprocity and justice, and ways
of making collective decisions' as well as 'standards of goodness and
beauty.' Therefore it would be erroneous to conclude that Indigenous
peoples are 'necessarily any less intelligent, wise, kind, courageous,
or trustworthy than their counterparts in a civilized society; indeed
they may possess more of all these virtues' (Flanagan 2008: 34). At the
same time, he cautions, we must not ignore the fundamental truth
that 'human history and prehistory record an evolutionary process
of increasing technical mastery over nature and increasing size and
complexity of social organization' (ibid.: 33) and that therefore 'in

addition to this horizontal tableau of variability within wide limits, there is also a vertical dimension of development through time' (ibid.), a development that is nonetheless uneven and that has resulted in some societies being more advanced than others.

On this foundation, Flanagan builds his argument on temporal priority. The first step is to draw from the finding that societies differ with respect to their size and complexity the conclusion that these reflect a hierarchy, with those that are bigger and more complex ranked higher than those that are smaller and more simple. As he says, 'if one culture is simple and another complex, is not the latter also superior to the former in some sense? Increasing complexity is a hallmark of progress in scholarship and science, as well as of technical advances in engineering, commerce, and athletics. Why not culture generally?' (Flanagan 2008: 31). Based on this finding, Flanagan takes the step of suggesting that superior forms will expand territorially. Thus he suggests that, given time, the Iroquoian peoples, who 'practiced food production in the form of horticulture,' thereby making them the 'most advanced' Indigenous community in Canada, 'might well have produced an agricultural civilization and an imperial state' on their own (ibid.: 36). However, this possibility was thwarted when representatives of 'civilization,' a 'collective advance' fully five thousand years ahead of any society in the Americas (ibid.: 46) that had 'gradually emerged and spread around the world' (ibid.: 34), arrived in the New World. Thus: 'The entry of Europeans into North America, as into Australia, was the last act of a great drama – the spread of agriculture around the world. Meanwhile another play was being enacted as organized states extended their sway over stateless societies. The two processes fit together naturally when agricultural peoples organized as states come into contact with small-scale, stateless, hunter-gatherer societies' (ibid.: 39).

As Flanagan argues, what ensued was a contest 'between civilization and savagery' (Flanagan 2008: 42) that pitted 'Indian cultures and all the civilizations of the Old World taken together.' It was one that Indigenous peoples were bound to lose because, 'for reasons having nothing to do with race, the European colonists had enormous advantages over the aboriginal inhabitants of Canada' (ibid.: 46). In other words, the inevitable result of the spread of the more advanced form of development ('civilization') to North America was the demise of the less advanced one (small-scale, stateless, hunter-gatherer societies), as, with the success of the former, 'agriculture, settlement, and resource extraction started to make the aboriginal way of life impossible' (ibid.: 45).

However, according to Flanagan, this finding does not in itself justify his argument on temporal priority. To get there, he makes two further claims. The first, which follows the principles of utilitarianism,[5] is
that the relevant measure of success is the relative ability of a society to
provide for the material well-being of its members. And using this calculus, civilization is clearly the superior form, for, as he asks rhetori-
cally: 'Though one might dislike many aspects of civilization, would it
be morally defensible to call for a radical decline in population, neces-
sitating early death and reproductive failure for billions of people now
living?' (Flanagan 2008: 35). Therefore, to return to a portion of an earlier quote: 'It is wrong for the hunters to insist on maintaining their
way of life; rather they should adopt agriculture and civilization, which
would actually make them better off while allowing more people to
live.' Hence, the European settlement of North America is justified on
moral grounds.

    With that in mind, Flanagan lays out the final step in the argument
that the principle of temporal priority does not extend to North
America. It rests on the proposition that the principle should not be
applied when 'the civilized' offer 'the uncivilized' the opportunity to
learn and benefit from the ways of civilization. That is: 'The farmers are
justified in taking land from the hunters and defending it as long as
they make the arts of civilization available to the hunters.' This did not
happen everywhere, for 'in some instances, colonial states exterminated or enslaved aboriginal inhabitants without any attempt to civilize
them' (Flanagan 2008: 45). However, this was not the case in Canada.
Rather, we offered the uncivilized the opportunity to learn the ways of
civilization and invited them to become fully equal members of the
body politic. To this end, 'the Canadian government, with or without
treaties, set aside land reserves for Indians, offered agricultural instruction and assistance, provided both basic and industrial education,
and facilitated the work of Christian missionaries' (ibid.: 42). Furthermore, 'generally speaking,' the reserved areas of land were 'large
enough that the surviving groups of Indians (admittedly much reduced
by disease and frontier warfare) could, and often did, support themselves by adopting the agricultural technology of the day' (ibid.). In
Flanagan's eyes, this process has been successful: 'The aboriginal population of Canada ... is now larger than it was before the arrival of the
Europeans. Indians and Inuit have adopted the civilized mode of life.
They work, buy and sell, and invest in the economy. They acquire
literacy and education ... They vote and in other ways participate in

politically decision-making ... In the largest context, the policy of civilization has succeeded' (ibid.: 45). And I presume he is suggesting that this ought to satisfy us that we have treated Indigenous peoples properly.

In sum, as I read it, Flanagan's argument is that the superiority of our way of life, our offer to share it, and the benefits that have accrued to Indigenous peoples through our presence here justifies the position that the principle of temporal priority does not apply when it comes to taking their lands.

RESPONSE

While he does not rely on convention, Flanagan's argument has such an eerie similarity to a position that was once widely held in the West that it invites mention. This position, which came to dominance in the latter part of the nineteenth century, justified colonialism as a 'civilizing mission' put into place on the understanding that 'a temporary period of political dependence or tutelage was necessary in order for "uncivilized" societies to advance to the point where they were capable of sustaining liberal institutions and self-government' (*Stanford Encyclopedia of Philosophy*, entry on 'colonialism,' p. 1).[6] It found expression in such international agreements as the Berlin Act of 1885 respecting the colonization of Africa, in which Clause VI reads:

> All the Powers exercising sovereign rights or influence in the aforesaid territories bind themselves to watch over the preservation of the native tribes, and to care for the improvement of the conditions of their moral and material well-being ...
>
> They shall, without distinction of creed or nation, protect and favour all religious, scientific, or charitable institutions and undertakings created and organized for the above ends, or which aim at instructing the natives and bringing home to them the blessings of civilization. (Qtd. in Phipps 2002: 25)

It also found its way into Article 22 of the 1924 Covenant of the League of Nations, which states:

> To those colonies and territories ... which are inhabited by peoples not yet able to stand by themselves under the strenuous conditions of the modern world, there should be applied the principle that the well-being and development of such peoples form a sacred trust of civilisation and that

securities for the performance of this trust should be embodied in this Covenant.

The best method of giving practical effect to this principle is that the tutelage of such peoples should be entrusted to advanced nations who by reason of their resources, their experience or their geographical position can best undertake this responsibility, and who are willing to accept it, and that this tutelage should be exercised by them as Mandatories on behalf of the League.

The character of the mandate must differ according to the stage of the development of the people, the geographical situation of the territory, its economic conditions and other similar circumstances. (Avalon Project 2008: 5)

It thus looks as though Flanagan is reiterating this position, but with one exception: whereas in this version the putative goal of tutelage is to prepare the presumptively less advanced to become fully self-determining, in Flanagan's it is to enable them to disappear as a distinct community by assimilating into ours.

Taking that view in 1900 or even perhaps 1950 is one thing. But today it is another. With the passing of the era of European colonization, the world community has come to understand that the notion of the West's 'civilizing mission' is a presumption born of arrogance that constituted nothing more than a self-serving rationalization designed to justify European powers' subjugation of peoples with a legitimate right to self-determination. This perspective is expressed succinctly in the United Nations Declaration on De-Colonization: 'Inadequacy of political, economic, social or educational preparedness should never serve as a pretext for delaying independence' (United Nations 1960a: 67). That is, to put it in the language Flanagan adopts, whether or not one can rate societies on a scale of development based on universal history, no society rates so low on that putative scale that it is not fully capable of determining its destiny for itself. Therefore, there is no need for 'tutelage.' Furthermore, one might argue that, given the success Flanagan attributes to the 'civilizing mission' in Canada, it seems clear that, under our guidance, Indigenous peoples have attained the preparedness requisite for independence.

As that is the current view, I am tempted to stop there; it strikes me that it is up to Flanagan to explain why he seems to rely on a discredited convention that is a holdover from the colonial era, or that, if he agrees with the UN Declaration's position that colonized peoples have the right to self-determination, it is incumbent on him to explain why the Declaration's clause expressly excluding exceptions based on level of preparedness does not apply to Indigenous peoples in Canada. But I will continue, for, like Flanagan, I believe that an argument based on reason ought not to be rejected through guilt by association, whether that association is to 'aboriginal orthodoxy' or to 'imperial powers,' or through the use of such pejorative labels as 'repugnant' or 'self-serving' and 'racist' or 'revisionist.' I will thus discuss the reasoning in this argument on its own terms. That is, I will explore the merits of Flanagan's assertion that reason compels the conclusion that, because civilized people have a way of life that is objectively superior, they 'are justified in taking land from the hunters and defending it as long as they make the arts of civilization available to the hunters.'

While the nub of my response will focus on the word 'taking,' let me begin by raising concerns with some of the steps leading to that conclusion. The first is with the assertion that humanity participates in a universal history in that as a whole we pass through the same stages of development. As Flanagan points out in some detail in his book, this argument has long been challenged by those who hold a view called 'cultural relativism,' which the Oxford English Dictionary defines as 'the theory that there are no objective standards by which to evaluate a culture and that a culture be understood in terms of its own values and customs.' This matter is by no means settled, and Flanagan's argument does not resolve it. However, to rely on this disagreement would mean that I avoid addressing Flanagan's position on its own terms.

Therefore, for the sake of argument, I will accept the proposition that societies can be compared on objective standards and that in so doing some may be determined to be 'more advanced' than others. At the same time, I do not agree that it follows that there must be a universal history in the sense that all of humanity is on a single path that passes through the same stages of development. That is, even if history is the story of a movement from simplicity to complexity, it does not follow that the development of complexity takes one form.

My reasoning is that if, like Flanagan, I assume that humanity is uniform in its abilities (we are all intelligent, wise, kind, courageous, and trustworthy in equal measure), then it is reasonable to suppose that we all have an equal ability to accumulate knowledge and transmit what we have accumulated to future generations. Thus, over time, all societies acquire knowledge and in that regard must become more complex, even if, as has been argued,[7] some intend to remain the same. The

inevitable result is that, while it may be that, when measured on what
is taken to be an objective scale, Indigenous societies are 'simple' with
respect to a dimension such as technology, it does not follow that they
are 'simple' in every way. That is, because a society may be evaluated
as more advanced in some ways, it does not follow that it must be more
advanced in *every possible way*. It is a point that the renowned anthropologist Claude Lévi-Strauss put this way in his magnum opus, *The
Elementary Structures of Kinship:* 'Today we know that the archaic nature
of the material culture of the Australian aborigines has no correspondence in the field of social institutions. By contrast, their social institutions are the result of a long series of deliberate elaborations and
systematic reforms. In short, the Australian sociology of the family is,
as it were, a "planned sociology"' (Lévi-Strauss 1969: 314).

This means that, objectively speaking, each society, not just our own,
is likely to have accumulated knowledge of benefit to all of humanity.
And what this suggests to me is that, even for those who accept the notion that societies can be rated on a scale of development, the arrogant
presumption of the tutelage argument – that Indigenous peoples have
much to learn from us about how to improve their lives, but virtually
nothing to offer us about improving ours – does not hold. In fact, as I
will discuss in a later chapter, I have come to see that it will help us
greatly in understanding how our relationship with those who were
here already might be resolved were we to be open to the possibility
that Indigenous peoples have much to teach us about the building of
relationships among political communities.

However, I will concede, for the sake of argument, that 'civilization'
is objectively superior in every possible way to the manner in which
Indigenous peoples in North America lived when Europeans first arrived. If that is so, then the issue is whether that 'fact' justifies settlers
taking the land, so long as we make the benefits of civilization available to them. As I will indicate, the answer remains 'no.' Here are my
reasons.

First, it does not follow that taking land from others is justified at all
times and under all conditions. It is a point that John Stuart Mill, a
founder of utilitarianism, made early in his career when he said that
there is not much satisfaction to be found

in contemplating the world with nothing left to the spontaneous activity
of nature; with every rood of land brought into cultivation, which is

capable of growing food for human beings; every flowery waste or natural pasture ploughed up, all quadrupeds or birds which are not domesticated for man's use exterminated as his rivals for food, every hedgerow or superfluous tree rooted out, and scarcely a place left where a wild shrub or flower could grow without being eradicated as a weed in the name of improved agriculture. If the earth must lose that great portion of its pleasantness which it owes to things that the unlimited increase of wealth and population would extirpate from it, for the mere purpose of enabling it to support a larger, but not a better or a happier population, I sincerely hope, for the sake of posterity, that they will be content to be stationary, long before necessity compel them to it. (Mill 1848: II, 331)[10]

In other words, for the good of all, we must refrain from imposing civilization in some places in the world; and one of these places may well be North America. Furthermore, there is no reason for such places to be devoid of human activities, for, as Flanagan admits, Indigenous peoples made a living in places that were not 'brought into cultivation' or 'developed' in other ways.

But let me take Flanagan's argument to its limiting condition: Would Settlers be justified in taking the land were it true that the welfare of humanity as a whole depended on using all of the land everywhere in North America in ways incompatible with the activities of Indigenous peoples; and that this necessity existed from the outset of European settlement? The answer is 'no,' for there is one other condition that would need to be met: the people living on that land would have to refuse to allow the world community to use it in that manner, even though they, in common with humanity as a whole, faced a catastrophe of biblical proportions. That is, taking the land might be tenable only when, notwithstanding these dire conditions, we failed to conclude agreements that allowed us to do so.

But of course all of this is hypothetical in the extreme. We know that, whatever were the crises that stimulated migration to Canada, the needs of civilization (as Flanagan defines it) proceeded at a sufficiently slow pace that those who came later had time to enter into agreements prior to their settlement, and indeed often did exactly that. In sum, even if one concedes that Flanagan is correct in his argument at every step, he still provides no justification for ignoring the principle of temporal priority. In other words, this argument does not convince me to abandon my position.

Conclusion

In this chapter, I have addressed five arguments Flanagan raises to justify the proposition that temporal priority ought not to apply with respect to European settlement in Canada. While I hope that I have been successful in describing these fairly, I know that nothing can substitute for reading them in full, and I urge my readers to do so. Similarly, I know that my responses may be amenable to some, but certainly not to all. There are, after all, different opinions on these topics. But my goal has not been to silence viewpoints. Rather, it has been to show that Flanagan offers no compelling reason for me to abandon mine. As well, I hope I have shown that Flanagan is unfair in dismissing opinions with which he disagrees as the fruit of 'historical revisionism' foisted on the general public by an 'aboriginal orthodoxy' prepared to play fast and loose with fact and truth. They are the products of mature thought.

In sum, after reviewing Flanagan's arguments, I remain as convinced about my position as when I started. The place to begin is with the understanding that 'when the settlers came the Indians were there, organized in societies and occupying the land as their forefathers had done for centuries.' The question, then, is not whether the principle of temporal priority applies, but what are the consequences of applying it? It is to that issue I now turn.

Chapter Four

Aboriginal Rights and Self-Determination

Although non-Aboriginal Canadians would not have described their relation to indigenous peoples in Canada as imperialist, they – if sometimes only
unconsciously – had an imperial mentality. Unlike Africa and Asia, however,
where the indigenous populations vastly outnumbered the European intruders
– even in settler colonies – the waves of European migrants in Canada quickly
outdistanced the indigenous population. The end of the Canadian version of
empire over Aboriginal peoples accordingly could not mean independence for
the colonized or the departure of the colonizers.

(Cairns 2000: 26)

The Right to Self-Determination of Colonized Peoples

The view that Indigenous peoples have the right to self-determination
follows this reasoning: once we accept that they were living in political
societies when Europeans arrived, then we must conclude that they
were politically self-determining at that time. Therefore, even by the
standards of the era, Settlers could not treat their lands as unoccupied.
But what if they did? What are the consequences of setting up a political community in the territory of an existing political community without permission?

While there are many situations in which this may not lead to a right
to self-determination, there are two, as explained by Antonio Cassese,
where there is no doubt it applies. As he says: 'The right to external self-
determination, which entails the possibility of choosing (or restoring)
independence, has only been bestowed upon two classes of peoples

(those under colonial rule or foreign occupation), based upon the assumption that both classes make up entities that are inherently distinct from the colonialist Power and the occupant Power and that their "territorial integrity," all but destroyed by the colonialist or occupying Power, should be fully restored' (qtd. in the *Reference re Secession of Quebec* 1998: para. 131). Therefore, as the Supreme Court states in the passage that follows this quote: 'The right of colonial peoples to exercise their right to self-determination by breaking away from the "imperial" power is now undisputed' (ibid.: para. 132). That is, whether or not the Court would concur were it required to make a judgment on such a question pertaining to the rights of Indigenous peoples, in situations analogous to the one in Canada, the most applicable answer lies in the principle of self-determination contained in the 1960 United Nations Declaration on De-Colonization, which states that 'all peoples have the right to self-determination; by virtue of that right they freely determine their political status and freely pursue their economic, social and cultural development' (UN 1960a).

The Declaration also declares that 'any attempt aimed at the partial or total disruption of the national unity and the territorial integrity of a country is incompatible with the purposes and principles of the Charter of the United Nations' (UN 1960a). Still, Resolution 1541, the legislation implementing the Declaration, states that, to achieve 'a full measure of self-government,' the right to self-determination may include the right to 'a sovereign, independent State.'

And so the world community has agreed that the right to self-determination of a colonized people remains undiminished even though in earlier times European Settlers and their descendants asserted sovereignty over them and their territories. That is, absent voluntary consent, the right to political self-determination of colonized peoples remains, notwithstanding the subsequent assertion of sovereignty by the Crown over the same territories. In that sense, Canada is no different from other settler colonies, such as Nigeria and Southern Rhodesia (now Zimbabwe).[1]

The rationale for applying the Declaration on De-Colonization here is that Canada fits the profile in that, like other colonies, it emerged as part of the same process of European expansion.[2] That is, as Cairns puts it:

The domestic Canadian version of empire over Aboriginal peoples lacked the pomp and ceremony of the British raj, or the status-enhancing experience of a handful of officials ruling over millions in tropical Africa, Ceylon, or the Dutch East Indies. Nevertheless, we sent missionaries to Christianize, anthropologists to analyze, and Indian agents – our version of colonial district officers – to administer. Indian children were taught wounding versions of history; sacred practices and revered customs were forbidden or mocked; the use of Aboriginal languages was discouraged; customary forms of governance were bypassed; traditional healing arts were displaced; and treaties were accorded lesser significance by governments than by the descendants of the Indian leaders who signed them. In general, Aboriginal ways of life, and thus their bearers were stigmatized. (Cairns 2000: 31)

This view is shared by other leading scholars, including Will Kymlicka, who in *Politics in the Vernacular* succinctly summarizes his position in the following words: 'Indigenous peoples are ... "colonized" minorities. What I mean is that they are distinct cultural communities which were previously self-governing, but whose homeland has been included in a larger state against their will. They occupied and governed their lands before the state was even in existence' (Kymlicka 2001: 148). He then continues: 'Indigenous peoples were originally self-governing, and had the balance of power been different, they could have maintained independence. They only lost their self-government as a result of coercion and colonization. They view this, rightly I think, as a violation of their inherent right to self-government' (ibid.: 149).

And there is good evidence that Indigenous peoples themselves have long held the view that, notwithstanding the assertion of sovereignty by Europeans, they retain the right to external self-determination. For example, in 1923 one of the political leaders of the Haudenosaunee, Chief Dekaheh, presented a petition to the League of Nations that challenged the legitimacy of Canadian sovereignty on Iroquois territory. It said in part: 'We have exhausted every other recourse for gaining protection of our sovereignty by peaceful means before making this appeal to secure protection through the League of Nations. If this effort on our part shall fail we shall be compelled to resist by defensive action upon our part this British invasion of our Homeland for we are determined to live the free people that we were born' (qtd. in Corntassel 2008: 109).

A similar perspective was expressed by the Stl'atl'imx Nation of Chiefs (also known as the Lillooet Tribal Council) in its application for membership in the United Nations. There they state both that their 'title and rights to the land have not been extinguished' notwithstanding the

existence of Canada and that Canada 'does not represent the interests
of our Nation, nor, can it speak on our behalf' (Stl'atl'imx Nation of
Chiefs n.d.). They conclude by quoting a declaration published in 1911
in which they reaffirmed that they constitute 'a sovereign people.' To be
clear, I am not arguing that Indigenous peoples in Canada necessarily
seek self-determination, only that this option is included within the
definition of Aboriginal rights.

Why, then, has the Declaration on De-Colonization not applied in
Canada, even though Canada voted in favour of it? Two explanations
have been offered. The first focuses on the definition of the term 'self' in
the phrase 'self-determination'; the second involves the proposition
that the right of self-determination is self-evident only with respect to
certain kinds of colonies.

Reason 1: Indigenous Peoples Do Not Constitute a 'Self'

As I discussed in *Home and Native Land* (Asch 1984: 38n3), some political
theorists, such as Rosalyn Higgins, take the view that 'self-determination
refers to the rights of the majority within a generally accepted political
unit to the exercise of power' (qtd. in ibid.: 39). Higgins cites the example of the Naga people of India, who number over fifteen million:
'There can be no such thing as self-determination for the Nagas. The
Nagas live within the political unit of India and do not constitute a
majority therein' (ibid.) From this it follows that, since Indigenous
peoples constitute a small percentage of those living in the 'generally
accepted political unit' called 'Canada,' they do not have a right to self-
determination, notwithstanding the fact that they became a minority as
a consequence of colonialism. It is a point that Pierre Trudeau put in
this provocative way in 1969: 'Aboriginal rights, this really means saying, "we were here before you. You came and you took the land from
us and perhaps you cheated us by giving us some worthless things in
return for vast expanses of land and we want you to re-open this question. We want you to preserve our aboriginal rights and to restore
them to us." And our answer – it may not be the right one and may
not be one which is accepted but it will be up to all of you people to
make your minds up and to choose for or against it and to discuss with
the Indians – our answer is "no"' (qtd. in Cumming and Mickenberg
1972: 332).

The argument holds, then, that it is the majority that determines the
rights of Indigenous peoples regardless of how the majority came to be.

RESPONSE

To my mind, this argument is logically unsound. Regardless of our attachment to the principle, majority rule is not necessarily a just yardstick by which to measure whether or not a colonized people have a right to self-determination. A majority becomes a majority, as Higgins makes clear, only after the border of the state containing it has been drawn.[3] In this sense, state borders protect the self-determination of some of the world's minorities by making them majorities, while denying it to others; and that is what happened in Canada. Because borders were drawn in a certain way, no one doubts that Canada has a right to political self-determination equal to that of the United States, even though our population is roughly 10 per cent of theirs. However, were they drawn in another way, then we, like the Naga, would have no right to self-determination. In this case, we are justifying the inapplicability of the UN Declaration through the very act that colonized Indigenous peoples. In other words, once we accept that Indigenous peoples who find themselves within Canada constitute a colonized population, it follows that they do not lose their right to self-determination merely because a numerically larger Settler population showed up and drew borders around territories in such a way that that right could no longer apply. The fact that we now form a majority within Canada does not erase the applicability to Indigenous peoples of the right to self-determination accorded to colonized peoples in the Declaration on De-Colonization.

Reason 2: Distinguishing between Kinds of Colonies

This reasoning suggests that the Declaration extends the right to self-determination only to certain portions of those defined as 'colonized.' It is set out in these words in Principle IV of Resolution 1514: '*Prima facie* there is an obligation to transmit information in respect of a territory which is geographically separate and is distinct ethnically and / or culturally from the country administering it' (UN 1960b). In other words, there are sufficient grounds to compel colonizers to decolonize only when the colonized belong to a different ethno-cultural community *and* do not live within the colonizer's state.

This provision, according to renowned international lawyer Gordon Bennett, arose as a compromise that resolved a dispute which threatened to scuttle the Declaration. As he explains, there were some colonial powers, led by Belgium, that sought to maintain their overseas colonies by making the provisions of the Declaration so unpalatable to the world community that it would be defeated were it to come to a vote. To that end, Belgium advanced the position (which became known as 'The Belgian Thesis') that the right to self-determination of colonized peoples applies equally to all colonized peoples, for 'colonization ... is no less colonization if it is made by territorial contiguity rather than by overseas expansion' (Bennett 1978: 12). Not surprisingly, the thesis was not met with enthusiasm among many member states.

Among those most concerned with the Belgian thesis were countries that had recently become independent as part of the decolonization process (one example might be Nigeria, which had gained its independence that very year) and that contained within their borders minority ethno-cultural communities which, based on the provisions of the Declaration, might themselves claim the right to self-determination. For example, 'the Ecuadorian delegate expressed a widely shared belief when he warned that the Belgian interpretation ... was dangerous in that it would convert the whole world into a vast colonial system' (Bennett 1978: 13). Ultimately, however, 'it was the putative threat to the sovereignty of newly independent states that secured the final rejection of the Belgian thesis' (ibid.). This resulted in a compromise 'led by Latin America and supported by many anti-colonial regimes' that emphasized above all security of borders and territorial integrity. Known as 'the blue water' or the 'salt water' thesis, it was directed to ensuring that, at the most, the Declaration would apply to countries with 'overseas' colonies. Thus, for instance, it unequivocally included Belgium, while providing a rationale for the world community to avoid considering whether it applied to Nigeria.

RESPONSE

Given the wording of Principle IV, it would appear that the Declaration extends to Canada as well. I use the word 'appear' because technically it may well not. While the provision is aimed at 'overseas' colonies, the wording is 'geographically separate,' and that is not the same thing. As Bennett points out, 'it is strongly arguable that indigenous groups who are isolated from the rest of the nation by vast tracts of unoccupied land, as for example are the Eskimos of Northern Canada, must on any rational basis be regarded as "geographically separate"' (Bennett 1978: 13). It is therefore uncertain whether strict adherence to principle does not require Canada to comply with Principle IV at least with respect to some Inuit political communities.

More crucially, however, it is clear that the provision *ought not* to apply to Canada. The use of the phrase 'prima facie' indicates that the world community does not reject the Belgian thesis. Rather, it suggests that there are circumstances when it is not self-evident that decolonization must take place. This makes sense in that there may well be cases where further evidence might be required, and Nigeria may be one of these. But this does not apply to our situation. The fact is that our situation parallels that of other colonizing powers in that Canada is a product of European colonization, and Indigenous peoples do unequivocally belong to communities that are ethno-culturally distinct from the colonizing population. That is, as Cairns observes, 'the Canadian situation was simply the local version of a global phenomenon in which a handful of European powers assumed the mastery of most of the non-European world' (Cairns 2000: 24).

Were Canada not rescued by the 'geographically separate' provision, there is no doubt that it would be understood that the provisions of the Declaration extend to us as well as to Belgium, for, as Kymlicka argues, given that it applies to 'overseas colonized peoples who were forcibly included in European empires ... there is no principled reason for [the] differential treatment of internal and overseas colonized peoples' (Kymlicka 2001: 149). In short, notwithstanding Principle IV, there is no valid reason to deny that the right of colonized peoples to self-determination in this Declaration applies equally to Indigenous peoples in Canada.

The United Nations Declaration
on the Rights of Indigenous Peoples

In 2007 the United Nations passed a Declaration on the Rights of Indigenous Peoples, which has recently been adopted by Canada. Like the 1960 Declaration on De-Colonization, it contains the affirmation that, like all other peoples, 'Indigenous peoples have the right to self-determination. By virtue of that right they freely determine their political status and freely pursue their economic, social and cultural development (UN 2007a: Article 3).[4] However, unlike the implementing resolution in the 1960 Declaration, which refers to the possibility that the exercise of self-determination might legitimately lead to the creation of new states, that option is explicitly rejected in the 2007 Declaration, which states: 'Nothing in this Declaration may be interpreted as implying for any State, people, group or person any right to engage in any activity or to perform any act contrary to the Charter of the United Nations or construed as authorizing or encouraging any action which would dismember or impair, totally or in part, the territorial integrity or political unity of sovereign and independent States' (ibid.: Article 46[1]). Furthermore, the expression of the right to self-determination is limited as follows: 'Indigenous peoples, in exercising their right to self-determination, have the right to autonomy or self-government in matters relating to their internal and local affairs, as well as ways and means for financing their autonomous functions' (ibid.: Article 4).

Nonetheless, the 2007 Declaration contains provisions that are of great import to Indigenous peoples. Among these are:

> the right not to be subjected to forced assimilation (UN 2007a: Article 8.1);
> [the right to redress for] any action which has the aim or effect of disposing them from their lands (ibid.: Article 8.2[b]);
> the right to have their own representatives and to participate in decision making in matters that would affect their rights (ibid.: Article 18); and
> the right to own, use, develop, and control the lands, territories, and resources that they possess by reason of traditional ownership or other traditional occupation or use, as well as those that they have otherwise acquired. (ibid.: Article 26.2)

Perhaps most important, the Declaration also asserts that 'free, prior and informed consent' is required before a state can take actions that may have an adverse effect on Indigenous peoples. Among the articles addressing this point are:

> (UN 2007a: Article 10): Indigenous peoples shall not be forcibly removed from their lands or territories. No relocation shall take place without the free, prior and informed consent [FPIC] of the indigenous peoples concerned and after agreement on just and fair compensation and, where possible, with the option of return.

> (UN 2007a: Article 19): States shall consult and cooperate in good faith with the indigenous peoples concerned through their own representative institutions in order to obtain their free, prior and informed consent before adopting and implementing legislative or administrative measures that may affect them.

> (UN 2007a: Article 28.1): Indigenous peoples have the right to redress, by means that can include restitution or, when this is not possible, just, fair

and equitable compensation, for the lands, territories and resources which they have traditionally owned or otherwise occupied or used, and which have been confiscated, taken, occupied, used or damaged without their free, prior and informed consent.

For some, these provisions provide Indigenous peoples with a degree of protection regarding specified activities that is tantamount to a veto. As the Indigenous Environmental Network (IEN) suggests: 'At the core of the Free Prior, and Informed Consent standard is the acknowledgement that under certain circumstances, companies must accept that projects will not proceed – especially when our Native Nations / Indigenous Peoples say NO!' (IEN n.d.: 1). However, for others, the intent is not nearly that strong. Here, for example, is the position of the U.S. government: 'The United States recognizes the significance of the Declaration's provisions on free, prior and informed consent, which the United States understands to call for a process of meaningful consultation with tribal leaders, but not necessarily the agreement of those leaders, before the actions addressed in those consultations are taken' (qtd. in Tsosie 2011: 942n122). In other words, as Tara Ward suggests, 'a customary international legal principle that addresses indigenous peoples' full right to FPIC does not yet exist' (Ward 2011: 54). The concept of FPIC has yet to be authoritatively defined.

It is also unclear whether states are required to uphold any of the provisions in the Declaration, for, as two international lawyers (one of whom is James Anaya, UN special rapporteur on the rights of Indigenous peoples), state: 'The UN Declaration on the Rights of Indigenous Peoples may not be legally binding per se' (Anaya and Weissner 2007). It is a point that echoes one made by at least three states, Great Britain,[5] Colombia, and Canada (UN 2007b). Nor is it clear that the penalties would be sufficiently significant to prevent violations of the Declaration's provisions were it binding, for the document notes: 'Indigenous peoples have the right to redress, by means that can include restitution or, *when this is not possible, just, fair and equitable compensation*, for the lands, territories and resources which they have traditionally owned or otherwise occupied or used, and which have been confiscated, taken, occupied, used or damaged without their free, prior and informed consent' (UN 2007a: Article 28.1; emphasis added). Further, 'unless otherwise freely agreed upon by the peoples concerned, *compensation shall take the form* of lands, territories and resources equal in quality, size and legal status or *of monetary compensation* or other appropriate redress (ibid.: Article 28.2).

Still, although there is nothing in this Declaration to diminish
Canada's final legislative authority, implementing its provisions in good
faith would require Canada to move its position on self-government well
beyond the strictures of its 1995 policy. In that regard, I would venture
that these provisions represent the distance it is possible to go when
one presumes that it is the pre-existence of Indigenous polity that is to
be reconciled with the sovereignty of the Crown.

Power and Reason – Citizens Plus

To repeat a truism, the political world runs on power, and at the end of
the day reason serves power, not the reverse. The problem is that the
reasons advanced to justify power with respect to Indigenous peoples
are largely unconvincing. Yet we still advance them, perhaps because
we do not wish to admit to ourselves that there is no justification beyond power itself to explain why the pre-existence of Indigenous societies must be reconciled with the sovereignty of the Crown and not the
other way around.

To move past this formulation, some believe that we need to abandon
facile reasoning, lay the power card on the table, and admit that, in the
terms in which we are conceptualizing the matter, we care less about
the reasons by which we arrive at that position than the fact that we get
there. This does not mean we abandon reason, for reason has a significant role to play even when subordinated to power. Otherwise the
Supreme Court would have never concluded that temporal priority is
relevant, much less that rights might derive from its application. Chief
Justice Lamer observed: 'The doctrine of aboriginal rights exists because of one simple fact: when Europeans arrived in North America,
aboriginal peoples *were already here*' (qtd. in Flanagan 2008: 20; emphasis in original). There is reason to acknowledge that Indigenous peoples
have rights even when power enables us to avoid applying the Belgian
thesis to ourselves.

Likely the most distinguished proponent of this point of view in the
academy is the political theorist Alan Cairns. He lays out his position
with rigour and in detail in his book *Citizens Plus* (2000). As noted
above, Cairns's argument flows from the understanding that the settlement of Canada was part of a worldwide process of European colonization. For Indigenous peoples, this produced 'an unhappy record of
negative, often stigmatizing interactions with the majority society'
(Cairns 2000: 86), one that, as for other colonized peoples, altered the

trajectory of their history so that 'suddenly, they belonged to someone else's future, carried along in the Canadian case, by the majority society's momentum, driven by its own logic and sense of destiny' (ibid.: 87). As a result, today we meet neither 'as common members of a single society sharing circumstances, common memories, and mutual pride in past achievements' nor 'as strangers, confronting each other for the first time' for history divides us' (ibid.: 86). Nonetheless, he concludes, knowing full well that 'the past cannot be discarded,' for 'those who seek to shape the future have been made what they are by history,' we are now, at long last, seeking [or as Cairns puts it, 'trying') 'to escape from a past pattern of relationships viewed as counterproductive' (ibid.) Thus: 'The task is not to debate various *Aboriginal* futures as if we had a clean slate on which we could write as we wish. The beginning point for our discussion is the here and now with the brooding presence of the past intruding on every conversation' (ibid.: 80; emphasis added).

To begin with the 'here and now' means that we start with the understanding that 'in Canada, the majority is non-Aboriginal, and it cannot and will not go home, or give up power, as was the case when the independence flag was raised in colonies where white settlers were only a small minority' (Cairns 2000: 27). Unlike those places, 'the Canadian version of empire over Aboriginal peoples … could not mean independence for the colonized or the departure of the colonizers' (ibid.: 26), and that in turn means that, whatever is the substance of the relationship between us, 'Aboriginal Canadians will still be legally citizens of Canada and residents of provinces and territories from which many of the services they receive will come. They will remain entangled with the surrounding society. They will exist in the midst of the former colonizers' (ibid.: 28). In sum, Cairns is arguing that, our troubled past notwithstanding, we will need to 'meet as common members of a single society.'

Before continuing I wish to note that Cairns's conclusion is consistent with his argument in all respects but one: his use of the phrase *'former* colonizers' rather than 'colonizers' runs counter to his premise that colonizers stay only as long as they have the power to insist on it. However, elsewhere Cairns is consistent, as when he argues that the 'dilemma' Indigenous peoples face is that, 'although the Canadian state may lack legitimacy, [they] unlike Québec, cannot opt out of it' (Cairns 2000: 27). The question, then, is how to deal justly with the consequences of this political reality.

As Cairns reports, at one time we unjustly took the view that it was appropriate to absorb Indigenous peoples in the Canadian society through assimilation. As he says, 'the goal of a common Canadianism was explicitly pursued … Many of their cherished customs and rituals were banned … Residential schools were designed as agents of assimilation – to remove children from the influence of their parents, punish them for speaking Indian languages, introduce Christianity, and inculcate negative attitudes to their own cultures' (Cairns 2000: 50). However, he continues, beginning in the 1960s and particularly with the response of Indigenous peoples to the 1969 'White Paper' (Canada 1969), there was a growing recognition on our part that Indigenous peoples would remain a permanent presence in Canada. The result was that 'we now have to think about relationships between societies rather than the disappearance of the smaller into the larger' (Cairns 2000: 70). It a process that came to maturity when, with the inclusion of provisions acknowledging the collective existence of 'aboriginal people' with certain rights, the Constitution Act of 1982 'signaled their arrival as full partners … in a reconstituted Canada' (ibid.: 81). And so the task before us is to figure out how to fit Indigenous peoples as newly arrived 'full partners' into an existing political arrangement, or, to put it slightly differently, to reconcile the pre-existence of Indigenous societies with the sovereignty of the Crown. The question then becomes: What is the most appropriate way to accomplish this aim?

In that regard, to Cairns what is key is that Indigenous peoples now belong to two communities: those defined by an ancestry that Settlers do not share and those defined by a Canadian citizenship that they hold in common with us (Cairns 2000: 86). Of the two, *Citizens Plus* argues that the latter is primary, not only because 'the reality is that the citizens of Aboriginal nations are also part of the Canadian and provincial communities' (ibid.: 93), but also because Canadian citizenship is an identity we all share. Thus, he asks, unless Indigenous peoples are committed as individuals to membership in the 'Canadian community of citizens' (ibid.: 133), 'what will sustain our feelings of responsibility for each other?' (ibid.: 155). It is our common citizenship that provides the ground upon which to build our common future (ibid.: 200–3). Therefore, the right approach to implementing Aboriginal peoples' constitutional rights is one that balances a strong sense of Aboriginal citizenship, on the one hand, and some degree of recognition 'of the specificity of Aboriginal peoples' (ibid.: 90), on the other, the latter including 'where appropriate some self-governing powers.' 'The task … is to devise institutional incentives that over time will encourage the normal divided identities of federalism as well as an Aboriginal identity' (ibid.), and this means that the institutions of self-government need to be limited so that Indigenous peoples and Settlers are encouraged to 'feel that they belong, in one of the ways of their being, to the Canadian community of citizens' (ibid.: 109).

The concept that appropriately describes this result is 'Citizens Plus.' It is a term coined in the landmark 1966–7 report *A Survey of Contemporary Indians of Canada* (Hawthorn 1966–7) (also known as the Hawthorn Report, after the lead author, anthropologist Harry Hawthorn), in which Cairns participated. There it is ascribed this meaning: 'In addition to the normal rights and duties of citizenship, Indians possess certain additional rights as charter members of the Canadian community' (qtd. in Cairns 2000: 161f). As for specifics, with regard to political rights, Cairns's position is sympathetic to the limited provisions on self-government contained in the 1995 policy. In addition, as he discusses more fully in another text, he seeks ways to enhance Indigenous participation in decision making at the federal level, such as by guaranteeing representation in the Parliament of Canada (Cairns 2005: 55).

Given his perspective, Cairns is highly critical of the federal government's framing of its position on Aboriginal self-government for it fails to incorporate the crucial understanding that Indigenous peoples are also full-fledged members of the Canadian electorate. As he says, the government's position makes it appear as though the non-Indigenous institutions of government are alien to Indigenous peoples, for it leaves 'the impression that external controls and limits are to be imposed on Aboriginal governments, and that major powers are to be wielded by what, by inference, are non-Aboriginal governments. Of course, they are not. They are Canadian and provincial governments responsible to all of their residents/citizens, including Aboriginal citizens. To fail to underline this point is to reinforce the idea that the self-governing Aboriginal community is the only significant community to which its members belong' (Cairns 2000: 198).

Cairns lays out a far better case for limiting constitutional recognition of Indigenous political rights to what is contained in the 1995 policy than does that policy itself. In fact, to my mind, he offers the only reasonable rationale for concluding that the pre-existence of Indigenous societies should be reconciled with Crown sovereignty; and that, in my view, is because his position begins with the assumption that there is no need to justify Crown sovereignty on the basis of reasoned argument; the fact that we are in a position of power, even though that power was acquired illegitimately, is sufficient.

Power and Reason: A Concluding Response

Cairns is of course right: Canada is a democracy, and power rests with the majority. It is thus impossible to imagine that our Supreme Court, no matter how clearly it saw the justice of the analogy, would ever declare on its own – in the absence of pressure from the larger society – that 'the right of colonial peoples to exercise their right to self-determination by breaking away from the "imperial" power is now undisputed.' The matter is simply too consequential for the Settler majority to respect this principle solely on the word of nine individuals, even when they speak with the authority of Supreme Court judges. Thus, even though Chief Justice Marshall of the U.S. Supreme Court penned a judgment in 1832 upholding the Cherokees' right to remain in their homeland as guaranteed by treaty, President Andrew Johnson moved them to Oklahoma against their will and in so doing stated (quoted in a 2003 speech by U.S. Supreme Court Associate Justice Stephen Bryer): 'John Marshall has made his decision; now let him enforce it.[6] Similarly, in Canada, Prime Minister Trudeau could say, as noted earlier: 'It will be up to all of you people to make your minds up and to choose for or against it [self-determination] (qtd. in Asch 1984: 9). This means that Canada's position, rightly or wrongly, will be determined not by the Supreme Court but (at least in the foreseeable future) by those of us who came here later.

And that is the central problem. The self-determination argument puts Settlers in a no-win position. We may be convinced by reasoned argument that Indigenous peoples have the same right to self-determination as do other colonized peoples, and the consequence may well be a recognition on our part that we have no right to stay. Yet, as Lamer aptly summarized, we are here to stay. Therefore, even though the argument may be compelling, we are likely to reject it. To ask us to accept that Indigenous peoples have this right, then, is to virtually ensure that we will 'choose against it.' Indeed, I would suggest that one important reason for holding fast to arguments denying the application of the principle of temporal priority is to avoid facing the implications of accepting in full that it does.

What is needed is an approach that encourages us to see that the legitimacy of our settlement on these lands is not opposed to the fact that there were people here living in fully self-determining political societies when we first arrived. To that end, I now shift focus from what section 35(1) of the Constitution Act terms 'Aboriginal rights' to what it calls 'Treaty rights.'

Chapter Five

Treaty Relations

Treaties between the Crown and Aboriginal Peoples are one of the paradoxes of Canadian history. Although they have been an important feature of the country since the earliest days of contact between Natives and newcomers, relatively few Canadians understand what they are or the role they have played in the country's past. Unfortunately, even fewer non-Native Canadians appreciate that treaties are a valuable part of the foundations of the Canadian state.

(Miller 2009: 3)

Introduction

Of this, there can be no doubt: to move knowingly onto land belonging to others without their permission is theft. We may seek to be immigrants, we may seek a political arrangement to establish our right to govern over part or all of those lands, or we may seek a means to share jurisdiction. But we may not just move in. That is simply wrong. And, indeed, when looked at from this perspective, arguments that seek to deny the applicability of the principle of temporal priority to Canada amount to no more than justifications to avoid calling ourselves 'thieves.'

While there is considerable truth in describing what we have done as theft, that is not the whole story. By and large, from the outset we have recognized that Indigenous peoples were living in societies at the time of contact with Europeans, and that as a consequence we were required to gain their assent to settle on their lands. This recognition was articulated as policy forcefully in the Royal Proclamation of 1763, which states: 'And whereas it is just and reasonable, and essential to our Interest, and the Security of our Colonies, that the several Nations or Tribes of Indians with whom We are connected, and who live under our

Protection, should not be molested or disturbed in the Possession of such Parts of Our Dominions and Territories as, not having been ceded to or purchased by Us, are reserved to them or any of them, as their Hunting Grounds ...'

Furthermore, the Royal Proclamation introduced a specific set of rules to give us the assurance that all parties consented to these arrangements. Specifically, it insisted that agreements be drawn between representatives of our highest political office, the Crown, and confirmed in a public gathering of members of the Indigenous community. That is:

> We do, with the Advice of our Privy Council strictly enjoin and require, that no private Person do presume to make any purchase from the said Indians of any Lands reserved to the said Indians, within those parts of our Colonies where, We have thought proper to allow Settlement: but that, if at any Time any of the Said Indians should be inclined to dispose of the said Lands, the same shall be Purchased only for Us, in our Name, at some public Meeting or Assembly of the said Indians, to be held for that Purpose by the Governor or Commander in Chief of our Colony respectively within which they shall lie.

This regime remained in place for over a century and a half, so that even Treaty 11, negotiated in 1921, could state: 'And whereas, the said Indians have been notified and informed by His Majesty's said commissioner that it is His desire to open for settlement, immigration, trade, travel, mining, lumbering and such other purposes as to His Majesty may seem meet, a tract of country bounded and described as hereinafter set forth, and to obtain the consent thereto of His Indian subjects inhabiting the said tract, and to make a treaty ...' (Treaty 11 1957: 5–6).

Following this process, between 1763 and 1921 we negotiated literally hundreds of agreements that are referred to as 'the historical treaties.'[1] These include treaties of political alliance (peace and friendship treaties) and compacts (Miller 2009: 4f) to permit trading and other commercial activities on Indigenous territories in what are now Ontario, Quebec, Nova Scotia, New Brunswick, Prince Edward Island, and parts of Newfoundland (RCAP 1996: II, map 483). Among these are the 'territorial treaties' (Miller 2009: 5) through which we obtained consent to settle on much of the land mass of what is now Canada.[2]

What this indicates is that, notwithstanding any assumption we may have had about the sovereign status of Indigenous political communities or whether we believed that, for some reason or another, they had come 'under our Protection,' we have long accepted that the principle of temporal priority applies when it comes to our settlement on their lands. Treaties offer us a way of seeing the recognition of that principle as the basis for the legitimacy of our settlement here and not in opposition to it. 'Treaty rights,' then, in contrast to 'Aboriginal rights,' mean (to use rights discourse) those rights Indigenous peoples have that flow from agreements we made with them. The question is: What were the terms on which permission was granted? Or to put it another way: What did we promise in order to gain permission to settle on their lands; or, to put it in rights terms: What are the treaty rights we guaranteed to them in return for *the treaty right they guaranteed to us* to legitimatize our permanent settlement on these lands? That will be the subject of this chapter.

Let me first make it clear that, in proposing agreements by treaty, we were tapping into a long-standing institution in the territory we call 'North America.' As Les Healy explained to the Royal Commission on Aboriginal Peoples:

> The concept of treaty, *inaistisinni*, is not new to the Blood Tribe. *Inaistisinni* is an ancient principle of law invoked many times by the Bloods to settle conflict, make peace, establish alliances or trade relations with other nations such as the Crow, the Gros Ventre, the Sioux, and, more recently, the Americans in 1855 and the British in 1877. *Inaistisinni* is a key aspect of immemorial law, which served to forge relationships with other nations. *Inaistisinni* is a sacred covenant, a solemn agreement, that is truly the highest form of agreement, binding for the lifetime of the parties. So solemn is a treaty that it centres around one of our most sacred ceremonies and symbols, the Pipe. (RCAP 1996: II, ch. 2, s. 3.3)

That is, as is to be expected with respect to groups of communities living among one another, the practice of treaty making was entrenched long before we arrived. In fact, it is well understood that many of the protocols used in our treaties were adapted from those that were already in common use here.

The Numbered Treaties

My discussion of the terms permitting our settlement will focus largely on that subset of the eleven territorial treaties called the (post-Confederation) 'numbered treaties.' Negotiated over a fifty-year period beginning with Treaty 1 in 1871 and ending with Treaty 11 in 1921, they cover much of what is now Canada, including all of Manitoba, Saskatchewan, and Alberta as well as parts of Ontario, British Columbia, and the Northwest Territories (for a map that features these treaties, see Appendix II). Of further significance is that, at the negotiation of each of the numbered treaties, the parties agreed that the principal topic of discussion was the terms of an arrangement permitting Canadian settlement of these lands. As Treaty 4 reads:

> And whereas the said Indians have been notified and informed by Her Majesty's said Commissioners that it is the desire of Her Majesty to open up for settlement, immigration, trade and such other purposes as to Her Majesty may seem meet, a tract of country bounded and described as hereinafter mentioned, and to obtain the consent thereto of Her Indian subjects inhabiting the said tract, and to make a treaty and arrange with them, so that there may be peace and good will between them and Her Majesty and between them and Her Majesty's other subjects, and that Her Indian people may know and be assured of what allowance they are to count upon and receive from Her Majesty's bounty and benevolence ...
>
> (Treaty 4 1966: 5)

The simple question, then, is what was the shared understanding of the terms offered to 'the said Indians' to obtain their 'consent' for fulfilling 'the desire of Her Majesty to open up for settlement, immigration, trade and such other purposes as to Her Majesty may seem meet?' And that is where the difficulty lies. While each party is consistent in claiming that the terms were the same for each treaty, they are widely divergent in their view of the substance of these terms. Indeed, it would not be hyperbolic to say that the views are in diametric opposition.

That is, for each of the numbered treaties, governments in Canada (and others) insist that Indigenous peoples consented to transfer all authority to the Crown, thereby leaving Settlers free to do as they please with their lands. As proof, those who hold this view refer to a clause that appears with very similar wording in each of the written and signed treaty documents. The Treaty 4 version of this clause reads: 'The Cree and Saulteaux Tribes of Indians, and all other the [sic] Indians inhabiting the district hereinafter described and defined, do hereby cede, release, surrender and yield up to the Government of the Dominion of Canada, for Her Majesty the Queen, and Her successors forever, all their rights, titles and privileges whatsoever, to the lands included within the following limits.' It then describes those limits (Treaty 4, 1966: 6).

Those who adhere to this interpretation of the treaties take the position that, to obtain Indigenous peoples' consent, the Crown offered, among other things: a small portion of their former lands, the size of which would be determined based on the existing population at the time of negotiations, to be held as reserves; a one-time grant of a small number of implements, seed, and other goods for those who were taking up agriculture on those reserved lands; a small sum of money, fixed at that time in perpetuity, to be paid annually; and a school on each reserve. As well, the Crown promised that they would be free to hunt, fish, and trap on lands we had yet to take up, subject to our regulation. To illustrate, here is the clause respecting agricultural implements in Treaty 4:

> It is further agreed between Her Majesty and the said Indians that the following articles shall be supplied to any band thereof who are now actually cultivating the soil, or who shall hereafter settle on their reserves and commence to break up the land, that is to say: two hoes, one spade, one scythe and one axe for every family so actually cultivating, and enough seed wheat, barley, oats and potatoes to plant such land as they have broken up; also one plough and two harrows for every ten families so cultivating as aforesaid, and also to each Chief for the use of his band as aforesaid, one yoke of oxen, one bull, four cows, a chest of ordinary carpenter's tools, five hand saws, five augers, one cross-cut saw, one pit-saw, the necessary files and one grindstone, all the aforesaid articles to be given, once for all, for the encouragement of the practice of agriculture among the Indians.

Indigenous parties to all the numbered treaties share a very different interpretation. They speak with one voice in asserting that what the Crown asked for was permission to share the land, not to transfer the authority to govern it. As Treaty 6 Elder Norman Sunchild puts it: 'It was understood that the Queen had given Alexander Morris [the lead commissioner] instructions to say … go tell them that I am not asking for anything, just his land for the purpose of Her Majesty's subjects to make a livelihood upon this land. And everything else where he [the Indian people] lives, those things continue to belong to him and nobody can control that for him' (Cardinal and Hildebrandt 2000: 36). Similarly, Treaty 8 Chief George Desjarlais offered this testimony to the Royal Commission on Aboriginal Peoples: 'We are treaty people. Our nations entered into a treaty relationship with your Crown, with your sovereign. We agreed to share our lands and territories with the Crown. We did not sell or give up our rights to the land and territories. We agreed to share our custodial responsibility for the land with the Crown. We did not abdicate it to the Crown. We agreed to maintain peace and friendship among ourselves and with the Crown' (RCAP 1996: II, pt. 2, ch. 4, s. 3.1).

In return for agreeing to share their land, the Indigenous parties unanimously hold that we pledged to enter into the kind of caring relationship that one associates with close family members such as 'first cousins' (Elder Simon Kytwyhat, in Cardinal and Hildebrandt 2000: 33), and that, in this regard, the specifics we promised constituted not a final offer but tangible proof of our pledge to do whatever we could to ensure that they would benefit from our settlement by learning certain of our ways, including our farming methods. As Treaty 4 Elder Danny Musqua explains: 'We agreed to the relationship, a perpetual land-use agreement between us [First Nations] and them [the Crown] in Treaty 4, that would harvest the land for the purposes of agriculture, sow crops and we, along with that [would learn agricultural skills]; they would give us the technology to also do that ourselves (ibid.: 66).

Perhaps most crucially, the Indigenous parties all insist that our settlement would bring them no harm and thus that we undertook to assure them that they would be free to continue to live as they always had; no changes would be forced on them. As Treaty 6 Elder Alma Kytwyhat says: 'It was the [queen] who offered to be our mother and to love us in the way we want to live' (Cardinal and Hildebrandt 2000: 34). 'The Queen,' Elder Danny Musqua underlines, 'adopted [First Nations] as children' (ibid.) Relying on their study of the elders' interpretation of Treaty 4, the Federation of Saskatchewan Indian Nations explains the Indigenous interpretation of treaties in these words: 'The Elders state that the Indians were promised Crown protection and assistance to develop and prosper. The promise is described in general terms, with reference to a continuing, and comprehensive, Crown responsibility, and also in specific terms with respect to economic development assistance' (*Saskatchewan Indian* 1986: 10).

Treaty Interpretation

How might we come to an understanding of the terms of these treaties, given the extreme dissonance between the two positions? One possibility is to consider the two viewpoints equally valid, attributing the differences to the widely divergent cultural perspectives each party brought to the table. It is a view advanced by the royal commission, as when it poses this question: 'What if there was no agreement at all? One party thought it was purchasing land; the other thought it was agreeing to share its territory. This goes beyond the limits of legal analysis and into the grey area of contact between two alien societies entering treaty, signifying something very important to both of them, but perhaps something very different to each of them' (RCAP 1996: II, pt. 1, ch. 2, s. 2). Hence, the commission continues: 'We have concluded that the cross-cultural context of treaty making probably resulted in a lack of consent on many vital points in the historical treaties' (ibid.: s. 3.6). The result is the possibility that today there are two systems, equally legitimate, that exist side by side. That is, 'it is possible that Aboriginal title continues to coexist with the Crown's rights throughout the areas covered by treaties, despite the Crown's intention to include a cession of Aboriginal title' (ibid.: s. 3.9).

The commission suggests that the proper approach to resolving the differences is to reach a shared agreement as to the treaties' meaning based on the assumption that both interpretations carry equal weight. The procedure, which is outlined in a discussion of the 'Treaty Implementation and Renewal Process,' seeks to come to an agreement that balances two principles: 'reconciliation,' which 'requires the establishment of proper principles to govern the continuing treaty relationship and to complete treaties that are incomplete because of the absence of consensus'; and 'justice,' which 'requires the fulfillment of the agreed terms of the treaties as recorded in the treaty text and *supplemented* by oral evidence' (RCAP 1996: II, pt. 1, ch. 2, s. 3.10; emphasis added). Furthermore, the report anticipates that there may well continue to be disagreement respecting some of the terms, including what is likely the most fundamental issue: whether the Indigenous parties consented to extinguish or to share the land. In this case, the commission argues that, just or unjust, the position dominant today must be retained even though it violates basic principles of contract law: 'If the Indian treaties were contracts, conventional legal analysis might indicate that many of them are void because of the absence of *consensus ad idem*. The law of contracts then suggests that the parties would return to their original positions, as if the contract had not been made. The problem is apparent. 'After 100 years of relying on a treaty that has been assumed to be about extinguishment, the parties cannot turn back the clock and begin again' (ibid.: s. 2). But to accept this approach is to return to the proposition that we can do no better than to rely on our power to impose our will to justify our settlement on Indigenous lands.

I have a more fundamental objection. As an anthropologist I am unwilling to assume on this evidence alone that cultural difference, no matter its extent, provides an adequate explanation for the differences between the parties on a matter fundamental to both. Rather, it is my view that, despite cultural differences, there is every chance that these parties could have achieved a degree of shared understanding at the time of negotiations to conclude an agreement based on mutual consent. In other words, one cannot rule out the possibility that the position advanced by one of the parties today more closely conforms to what actually transpired at the time of treaty making than does the other.

In a sense, Tom Flanagan takes the same view. In *First Nations? Second Thoughts*, he asserts that one perspective, based on the written treaty, is more accurate than the other. His argument refers to 'the obvious meaning of the written text,' that is, the meaning of what is rendered in written form is self-explanatory (Flanagan 2008: 151). He also seems to assume, perhaps because these documents contain the signatures of all parties (albeit with our partners' signatures generally represented with the letter 'x'), that the text of a treaty also reliably reflects what took place. In contrast, he takes the view that the interpretation advanced by contemporary leaders, generally in an oral form, is inherently unreliable; 'oral traditions often contradict facts that can be established by overwhelming documentary evidence' (ibid.: 161), and can be internally inconsistent in that they 'often contradict each other' (ibid.: 162). Furthermore, he considers that the meaning of what is said is not always evident, for 'aboriginal oral traditions often contradict Western concepts of rationality and knowledge' (ibid.: 160). Thus, from his point of view, the version of the agreement in which the Indigenous parties agree to extinguish their sovereignty and jurisdiction in return for what is specified explicitly in the treaty document takes precedence over the version in which they agree to share the land and we agree to treat them as one would treat close family members.

Of course there is a third possibility: that the 'sharing' interpretation more closely reflects what transpired than does the written version. And that, in fact, is what I believe to be true. But is this just a matter of opinion? Can I substantiate it in a way that might persuade those who now hold the other view? Fortunately, Flanagan makes it clear that his conclusion is not based on dogma, for he continues: 'None of this means that oral traditions are always unreliable. In any particular instance, an oral tradition may have much to teach us. However, it does mean that we must be cautious' (Flanagan 2008: 164). Ultimately, 'it means comparing sources against each other to establish the most likely account of what happened – in what in civil litigation might be called "the balance of probabilities"' (ibid.). And he concludes: 'The use of aboriginal oral traditions in treaty litigation [and I would conclude elsewhere] will be constructive as long as these procedures are observed and as long as oral traditions are treated as one of many kinds of historical evidence' (ibid.: 165). As anthropologist Alexander von Gernet, whom Flanagan cites in support of his argument, says: 'When independent evidence is available to permit validation, some oral traditions about events centuries old turn out to be surprisingly accurate' (qtd. in ibid.: 163). In other words, Flanagan might not dismiss the view I am advancing were I able to provide sufficient evidence from other sources to confirm it; and I will presume this will also satisfy those who otherwise might conclude that the differences between the two interpretations of treaty making reflect the differing cultural lenses through which the negotiations were conducted.

Choosing Treaty 4

As it happens, there are many treaties for which such independent evidence exists. Among these are two that I expect people who hold views consonant with Flanagan's will consider reliable: Treaties 4 and 6. There, the chief commissioner for the Crown, Alexander Morris, instructed his secretary (M.G. Dickieson in Treaty 4 and A.G. Jackes in Treaty 6) to include a 'Narrative of the Proceedings,' a transcription in English of what was said by all parties to the negotiations. In 1880 Morris published these transcripts along with much other contextual information in his book *The Treaties of Canada*, with the expectation that 'such a record will prove valuable as it enables any misunderstanding on the part of the Indians as to what was said at the conference to be corrected, and … moreover will enable the council better to appreciate the character of the difficulties that have to be encountered in negotiating with the Indians' (Morris 1880: 83). While I will refer to Treaty 6 later in this book, here I will focus on Treaty 4.

In the case of Treaty 4, I rely on information from Morris's book, and in particular the thirty-eight-page 'Narrative,' which he declares to be 'accurate shorthand reports of the proceedings at Qu'Appelle and Fort Ellice, which were made at the time by Mr. Dickieson who was present at the treaty as secretary to the Commissioners.' I also draw on a report by Commissioner David Laird, an article by F.L. Hunt, a reporter who attended the negotiations, and the order-in-council that set up the commission. I propose to compare this evidence with the terms of the treaty as represented in the text of Treaty 4, on the one hand, and, on the other, with the understanding of the treaty as described by contemporary Indigenous elders and leaders in four documents: a 'Proclamation and Convention of Treaty 4 First Nations,' adopted by the Treaty 4 Chiefs Council in 1999; a 'Statement of Elders' recorded in the early 1980s and deposited at the Provincial Archives of Alberta (Treaty 4 Elders 1983); a summary of 'Elders Interpretation of Treaty 4,' which was originally produced for the Federation of Saskatchewan Indian Nations and appears on its website; and statements by elders that originated in a series of Treaty Elders Forums that were initiated jointly by the Federation of Saskatchewan Indian Nations, Canada, and the province of Saskatchewan (as observer) and reproduced in a book by Harold Cardinal and Walter Hildebrandt entitled *Treaty Elders of Saskatchewan: Our Dream Is That Our Peoples Will One Day Be Clearly Recognized as Nations*. What I hope to show is that the independent evidence confirms that, on the balance of probabilities (if not more conclusively), the interpretation provided by the contemporary elders and leaders of the Indigenous parties to the negotiations more accurately reflects the *shared understanding of both parties* as it is reflected in the record of what transpired than does the representation contained in the written text.

Treaty Interpretation – the Supreme Court of Canada

For a long time, I was convinced that treaties did not offer a way forward. This is because one possible explanation for the differing interpretations is that the Crown was not negotiating the terms in good faith: its representatives intended the outcome to be the written version of the treaty regardless of what they said during negotiations. It was a view I heard first when, during a year-long stay with my wife, Margaret, in Wrigley, Northwest Territories, conducting fieldwork, I interviewed the chief who negotiated Treaty 11 in 1921 and the nephew of one of the elders who advised him; these interviews will be discussed in the next chapter. At that time, (then) Chief Edward Hardisty, who was translating for me, said of the dissonance between the interpretations: 'The Commissioner must be a good liar because he told the Indians a good lie. He told a lie to the King too.' From this observation and many others along the same lines, I concluded that there could be no way to sort out whether the treaties might have been merely a polite way of imposing our power, amounting to nothing more than theft of the land by fountain pen.[3] I now know that I have every reason to believe that, at least in the case of Commissioner Morris, he meant what he said, but that is a topic I will discuss in a later chapter.

Here I want to begin with the assumption that the Crown was negotiating in good faith. In this respect, my approach follows the one adopted by the Supreme Court of Canada in recent years in cases relating to 'Treaty Rights.' The Court's approach is laid out in general terms in *R. v. Badger*: 'Certain principles apply in interpreting a treaty. First, a treaty represents an exchange of solemn promises between the Crown and the various Indian nations. Second, the honour of the Crown is always at stake; the Crown must be assumed to intend to fulfil its promises. No appearance of "sharp dealing" will be sanctioned. Third, any ambiguities or doubtful expressions must be resolved in favour of the Indians and any limitations restricting the rights of Indians under treaties must be narrowly construed. Finally, the onus of establishing strict proof of extinguishment of a treaty or aboriginal right lies upon the Crown' (*Badger* 1996: Preface).

Chief Justice McLachlin elaborated on these principles in later judgments. As she explains, first, the goal of an interpretation is to find the 'common intention' of the parties, and in that pursuit to 'choose from among the various possible interpretations of [that] intention the one which best reconciles the interests of both parties at the time the treaty was signed.' Second, rather than interpreting a text in a technical way, it must be understood 'in the sense they would have naturally held for the parties,' a principle that, as I take it, is intended to be consistent with the instruction in *Badger* that words 'must not be interpreted in their strict technical sense nor subjected to rigid modern rules of construction. Rather, they must be interpreted in the sense that they would naturally have been understood by the Indians at the time of the signing' (*Badger* 1996: para. 52). Third, an interpretation must remain 'sensitive to the unique cultural and linguistic differences between the parties.' And finally, although the point is not explicitly stated, to arrive at a common intention of the terms of a treaty that reconciles the interests of both parties, a valid treaty must be the product of a meeting of the minds[4] to a sufficient degree that the parties have a shared understanding of the agreement reached.[5] Otherwise it would not be possible to conclude that, as the Court says in *Badger*, 'treaties are analogous to contracts, albeit of a very solemn and special public nature. They create enforceable obligations based on the mutual consent of the parties' (ibid.: para. 76). That is: 1) a treaty is an agreement that records how parties reconciled their interests; 2) regardless of the form the language in the written version takes, the concepts to which they refer are to be interpreted in their everyday ('natural') sense; 3) interpretations must be particularly sensitive to cultural difference; and 4) however this process transpired, the result was the creation of 'enforceable obligations based on the mutual consent of the parties.'

Furthermore, what is most crucial from my perspective is the chief justice's declaration that 'the integrity and honour of the Crown is presumed,' which I take to be another way of saying that 'no appearance of "sharp dealing" will be sanctioned.' To my mind, this means that it must be assumed that the Crown always acts in good faith, and thus that its representations are honest and truthful. Hence, notwithstanding Chief Hardisty's observation to the contrary, the Supreme Court's approach compels me to accept that the treaty commissioners did not lie.

The Supreme Court also addresses the matter of reconciling oral and written interpretations. Normally, as James (Sa'ke'j) Youngblood Henderson points out, text is given precedence, which means that the oral is interpreted against what is written. As he says: 'The common rule for interpreting written documents is textualism, which is an attempt to adhere to the plain meaning of the written word. Thus, the typical first step in formal judicial reasoning is to examine the text and determine its categorization' (Henderson 2007: 100). Henderson suggests that 'the Supreme Court of Canada has rejected adherence to the plain meaning of the words in the text of a treaty' as the basis for making such judgments (ibid.).

A second possibility would be to reverse the process and privilege the oral over the written. The Supreme Court does take a step in this direction in that one of its principal objections to 'textualism'[6] is that a text cannot be relied upon to reflect the terms of the agreement in full. As it says in *Badger*, 'the treaties, as written documents, recorded an agreement that had already been reached orally and they did not always record the full extent of the oral agreement' (*Badger* 1996: para. 52); and again in *Marshall*: 'Where a treaty was concluded verbally and afterwards written up by representatives of the Crown, it would be unconscionable for the Crown to ignore the oral terms while relying on the written terms' (*Marshall* 1999: para. 78).

Given that the Crown's understandings were not transmitted orally, it follows that the Supreme Court is recognizing the possibility that, at some times and in some respects, the Indigenous parties will have a better record of what took place than does the Crown. And that is what I expect to be the case with respect to Treaty 4. Indeed, I hope that the method I adopt here will enable Settlers to gain confidence in the accuracy of what is conveyed to us orally even when corroboration by independent evidence is unavailable. Yet, despite all of this, the Supreme Court still privileges the text. As the chief justice argues,[7] 'courts cannot alter the terms of the treaty by exceeding what "is possible on the language" [of the text] or realistic' (*Marshall* 1999: para. 78), and that 'the words of the treaty clause at issue should be examined to determine their facial meaning, in so far as this can be ascertained, noting any patent ambiguities and misunderstandings that may have arisen from linguistic and cultural differences' (ibid.: para. 82).

On this point, there is good reason to demur. A provision arrived at by mutual consent cannot be ignored merely because the text does not record it; nor should it be moulded by the shape of what is written down when in fact the oral record is demonstrably the more accurate one. In short, to be fair, an interpretation must consider the possibility that the actual terms of a treaty may well exceed (or even differ from) what is in the written text. Thus, the determination of what is 'realistic' can emerge only as we become more aware of the evidence regardless of its source. Accordingly, I will follow this method rather than the one adopted by the Supreme Court.

Treaty 4 Background

I begin with the understanding that Treaty 4 was negotiated principally at Fort Qu'Appelle from 8 to 15 September 1874 between

> Her Most Gracious Majesty the Queen of Great Britain and Ireland, by Her Commissioners, the Honourable Alexander Morris, Lieutenant Governor of the Province of Manitoba and the North-West Territories; the Honourable David Laird, Minister of the Interior, and William Joseph Christie, Esquire, of Brockville, Ontario, of the one part; and the Cree, Saulteaux and other Indians, inhabitants of the territory within the limits hereinafter defined and described by their Chiefs and Headmen, chosen and named as hereinafter mentioned, of the other part. (Treaty 4 1966: 5)

The commissioners were accompanied by a detachment of one hundred soldiers (Laird 1874: 1) and an interpreter, Charles Pratt, who replaced the original selection, William Daniel (Laird 1874: 2). The Cree and Saulteaux, whose encampment near Qu'Appelle consisted of around one hundred and twenty tents (or about two thousand individuals) (Laird 1874: 1), were led by thirteen chiefs. They were supported by spokespersons, who, under their instructions, were entrusted with communicating directly with the commissioners (Hunt 1876: 179). Others present at the negotiations included parties of Métis and of Sioux as well as F.L. Hunt, who, in addition to being a reporter, was also brother-in-law of Pasqua, one of the chiefs[8] (Ray, Miller, and Tough 2002), and John Fisher, a Métis leader who described himself as president of the province of Qu'Appelle (Laird 1874: 3).[9]

Negotiations began at 4 p.m. on 8 September with a formal procession led by the commissioners riding in a carriage and ending with many in the Indigenous communities[10] singing their way into a large tent (which Laird calls a Marquee tent). The parties met formally every day except Sunday (although a brief meeting was held between the commissioners and Métis representatives that day (Laird 1874: 6). The agreement was finalized in the afternoon of the 15th. The next day the Crown fulfilled its first promise, which was to give individual members of the Indigenous parties a certain sum of money (the commissioners also met with a deputation of Sioux to discuss possible locations for reserves). The same agreement was negotiated at Fort Ellice on 21 September. Then, in August and September 1875, a party of commissioners, led by Christie, negotiated 'adhesions' to the treaty with communities of Stoney and Assiniboine[11] as well other communities of Cree and Saulteaux.

While the policy for negotiating Treaty 4 was rooted in the Royal Proclamation of 1763 and confirmed in the 'Order of Her Majesty Admitting Rupert's Land and the North-Western Territory into the Union' (which included the area to be negotiated),[12] the timing of the negotiations was determined by Canada's desire to open up these lands for settlement and in other ways extend its presence on them; the lands concerned encompassed the vast territory which Canada had recently acquired from the Hudson's Bay Company, for £300,000. The precipitating event was opposition of Indigenous peoples to attempts by Settlers to construct a telegraph line, and by the Hudson's Bay Company (HBC) to undertake land surveys, without their permission. As Morris reports, one chief told his people: 'We have done wrong to allow that wire to be placed there, before the Government obtained our leave to do so' (Morris 1880: 10); another, the Gambler, principal spokesperson for the Saulteaux, said during the negotiations: 'The Queen's messengers never came here, and now I see the soldiers and the settlers and the policemen' (ibid.: 101).

That the solution was to negotiate Treaty 4 is confirmed by Commissioner Morris, who stated: 'The government of Canada had, anticipating the probabilities of such a state of affairs, wisely resolved, that contemporaneously with the formal establishment of their rule, there should be formed alliances with the Indians' (Morris 1880: 101). Further confirmation is provided by this passage from the order-in-council setting up the commission for Treaty No. 4:

> That looking ... to the fact that the Mounted Police Force is now moving into the Territory in question with a view of taking up their winter quarters at Fort Pelly, and considering the operations of the Boundary Commission which are continually moving westward into the Indian Country, and also the steps which are being taken in connection with the proposed Telegraph Line from Fort Garry westward, all which proceedings are calculated to further unsettle and excite the Indian mind, already in a disturbed condition; [the minister] recommends that three Commissioners be appointed by His Excellency the Governor General for the purpose of making Treaties during the current year with such of the Indians Bands as they may find it expedient to deal with. (Treaty 4 1966: 3)

In short, it is clear that both parties agreed that the principal reason for negotiating a treaty at this time was to overcome the objections raised by Indigenous peoples to proceeding with settlement on their lands without one; and furthermore, as Morris points out, the Indigenous parties 'could place 5000 mounted warriors in the field' (Talbot 2009: 80), which was many more than could Canada, at least on short notice.

However, as the commissioners soon found out, this was not the only reason the Indigenous parties sought a meeting. They had two grievances, both associated with the HBC, which, to them, took precedence over negotiations. The first was that the company was acting as though it owned the land, notwithstanding that permission had not been granted. As one spokesperson declared: 'A year ago these people [the company] drew lines, and measured and marked the lands as their own. Why is this? We own the land; the Manitou [or Great Spirit] gave it to us. There was not [a] bargain; they stole from us'[13] (Hunt 1876:

179–80). The second was that the HBC had been paid £300,000 for the land, a sum that the Indigenous parties viewed as belonging to them. As Saulteaux Chief Pis-qua (Pasqua) said to Commissioner Morris, 'pointing to Mr. McDonald of the Hudson's Bay Company,' 'You told me you had sold your land for so much money 300,000 pounds. We want that money' (Morris 1880: 106). It is was only after these griev-ances had been aired and explanations given, a process that took place over the first four days, that negotiations began in earnest.

The Common Intention – Extinguishment or Sharing?

The case for the common intention being 'extinguishment' originates in the 'cede and surrender' clause in the treaty text. The Indigenous elders and leaders of Treaty 4 do not agree. Commissioner Laird reports that the Indigenous parties read a translation of the written treaty during negotiations (Laird 1874: 4, 5) and, on their insistence, at their conclu-sion, at which time he says 'the New Treaty was … read and explained to them' (ibid.: 7). Evidence to confirm this is found in the shorthand transcript which spells out the terms that were conveyed in detail on the third day (Morris: 1880: 92–3), the assertion that these terms were repeated on the next day (ibid.: 96), and the comparison made with another treaty on the afternoon of the sixth day (ibid.: 204–9). However, on none of these occasions is there evidence that the extinguishment clause was mentioned. Nor is there evidence that the commissioners even broached this matter at any other time, much less that the Indigenous parties had agreed to cede and surrender their lands.

It may well be that both parties already assumed that the Crown had sovereignty, and thus it was not necessary to address the issue during negotiations. Certainly, the written text took that view for it identified the Indigenous party as 'Her Indian subjects.' It is also clear that Commissioner Morris held it as well, for he addressed the Indigenous leadership as 'the Queen's subjects' (e.g., Morris 1880: 93, 94). However, there is nothing in the transcript to confirm that the Indigenous party shared this view.[14] On the contrary, on the few occasions when they re-fer to the queen, Indigenous leaders speak of her as though she did not have sovereignty over them. The best example of the difference in out-look is the contrasting statements of Commissioner Morris, who says, 'The lands are the Queen's under the Great Spirit' (ibid.: 102), and a spokesperson for one of the Indigenous parties (probably the Gambler), who says: 'We own the land; the Manitou [or Great Spirit] gave it to us'[15] (Hunt 1876: 179). This tends to support the position of Treaty 4 elders and leaders, who argue that 'our forefathers entered into Treaty exercising all the powers of sovereignty and nationhood' (Treaty 4 Chiefs Council 1999: 1). On this point, then, there appears to be no shared understanding: the parties entered into negotiations agreeing to disagree.

Yet the transcript also indicates that, whether or not they considered the Indigenous parties to be 'subjects of the Queen,' the commissioners negotiated with them as members of autonomous political communities whose standing equalled that of the Settlers. That is, when it comes to identifying individuals, Morris is careful to use terms designating Settlers and Indigenous peoples as 'equals' in status, as when he employs the word 'men' to describe all the participants in the negotiations (Morris 1880: 99); and the word 'friend' or 'friends' to describe the relationship between members of the Indigenous and Settler communities after negotiations – for example, he says, respecting the Lake of the Woods Treaty, that 'the white *man* and the red *man* made *friends* forever' (ibid.: 88; emphasis added). He also uses terms designating kin of the same generation and gender to describe members of these communities after negotiations, as in the following language concerning the relationship he seeks in Treaty 4 (ibid.: 109): 'The red man and the white man must live together, and be good friends, and the Indians must live together like brothers with each other and the white man.' In fact, he invokes a generationally hierarchical arrangement (mother to child) only when designating the relationship intended with the queen, but even in that case he equates the relationship to that between the queen and Settlers, saying, for instance, 'She cares for you as much as she cares for her white children' and referring to 'the Great Mother of us all' (ibid.: 96).[16] This is language that, with one exception, he never uses to describe his own relationship with First Nations, even though he makes it clear that he represents the monarch.[17] In this, his wording mirrors that found in the portion of the treaty text, cited above, which describes the 'Chiefs and Headmen' as having the same status to conclude a treaty on behalf of their peoples as do the commissioners on behalf of the Crown.[18] In other words, these sources support the understanding that the Indigenous parties were 'autonomous nations' (Treaty 4 Chiefs Council 1999: 2): there is no hint in the negotiations that the treaty agreement would change this status.

Furthermore, Commissioner Morris declared repeatedly (and daily on the first five days) that negotiations were with the Crown (Morris

1880: 88, 90, 91, 97, 109), and that the Indigenous leaders could take his words as coming from 'the Queen' herself. Typical was his statement on the second day that 'what I want is for you to take the Queen's hand, through mine, and shake hands with her forever' (ibid.: 15). He also represents himself as her 'messenger' (ibid.: 88) and 'servant' (ibid.: 97), as well as someone 'high in her Councils' and 'trusted by her,' a person, therefore, whom the First Nations were fortunate to have as their negotiating partner (ibid.: 96).[19] All things considered, the record substantiates the elders' assertions that Morris and the First Nations shared the understanding that Treaty 4 was negotiated with the queen, not the Dominion of Canada. There is no hint in the transcript that the commissioner conveyed the possibility that the status of the Indigenous parties as peoples who negotiate directly with the queen would be altered by the treaty agreement.

In summary, there is virtually nothing in the transcript that supports an interpretation of the extinguishment clause as resulting in the political subordination of the Indigenous parties to the government of Canada. Rather, it is more consistent with the evidence to conclude that the shared understanding of Treaty 4 resulted in a direct political alliance with the queen. In this sense, the treaty put the Indigenous parties in the same jurisdictional relationship with the Crown as other autonomous political entities within the Empire, such as Canada and New Zealand – that is, 'brothers to each other' and 'children of the Queen.' And just as Canada's jurisdiction did not extend to its 'brother' New Zealand, so did it not extend to this new partner (the newly adopted child of the queen and brother of Canada), Treaty 4 First Nations.[20] As I have come to understand it, that is the political relationship Elder Musqua evokes with these words: 'The Queen has adopted (First Nations) as children … a joint relationship will come out of that. And so we have a joint relationship with the Crown because the Queen is now our mother.' This interpretation is also consistent with the image that appears on the Treaty 4 medal (for a representation of a similar image, see the cover photograph of the Treaty 6 medal). On one side is the depiction of a representative of the Crown shaking hands with an Indigenous leader; in the background are teepees and a rising sun. On the other side is an image of Queen Victoria. That is, the medal conveys the message that the parties to the treaty are brothers to each other children of the queen.

Thus, it looks as though the extinguishment clause provides a less accurate picture of the shared understanding than does the one conveyed by the Indigenous elders and other leaders. However, another possible interpretation of this clause arises when one takes into consideration Elder Musqua's use of the word 'adopted' to describe the relationship with Indigenous parties to Treaty 4. In contrast, Canada and New Zealand (for example) are the queen's 'natural' children. So the question becomes, how does the adoption take place? This clause reads: 'The Cree and Saulteaux Tribes of Indians, and all other the [sic] Indians inhabiting the district hereinafter described and defined, do hereby cede, release, surrender and yield up to the Government of the Dominion of Canada, for Her Majesty the Queen, and Her successors forever all their rights, titles and privileges whatsoever, to the lands included within the following limits ...' If the Dominion of Canada and the queen are the same party, then the phrase 'yield up to the Government of the Dominion of Canada, for Her Majesty the Queen' means that First Nations agree to subordinate themselves to the authority of the Dominion, which we know is not faithful to the shared understanding. However, if they are separate parties, then it can be read as meaning that, as an already existing member of the alliance (as a natural child of the queen), the Dominion of Canada is acting as the conduit for an adopted child of the queen (a new ally) to connect with the head of that alliance. Read in this way, the surrender clause is accurate in that it affirms only that First Nations are entering into the same relationship with the queen as that between her and the Dominion, which, as constitutional convention has it, retains the authority to exercise forever all of its 'rights, titles, and privileges whatsoever,' notwithstanding that, symbolically speaking, these are held by the Crown; thus, they become 'subjects' of the Crown, but not 'subjects' of the Dominion of Canada.

That the common intent was that the Indigenous parties would retain such jurisdiction is supported, at least in part, by the wording of the clause in the written document that gives the chiefs and headmen, 'on their own behalf and on behalf of all other Indians' (within Treaty 4), the responsibility to 'maintain peace and good order between each other, and between themselves and other tribes of Indians and between themselves and others of Her Majesty's subjects, whether Indians, Half-breeds, or white men.' The relationship, then, would be as adopted 'siblings of the same sex' (the term commissioner used is 'brothers') to each other, and children of the queen. As an adopted child, it would be expected that the Indigenous 'brother' would be culturally different from the brother who is the 'natural' child of the queen. It is a position I find reflected in this passage in the elders' statement: 'The Queen promised to rule her Dominions and her Indian nations according to their traditions, customs, and their laws' (Treaty 4 Elders 1983: 4).

The Common Intention – Sharing the Land or Taking It Over?

The 'extinguishment' clause also suggests that the common intention was that the Indigenous parties would 'surrender' their rights, titles, and privileges with respect to the land itself. Their contemporary elders and leaders disagree. They suggest that their forebears 'didn't give the land, they didn't say, we give you this land. They just gave permission to use the land'[21] (Elder Kay Thompson, qtd. in Cardinal and Hildebrandt 2000: 62f). This permission, it is explained, does not expressly limit the economic activities of the Settlers, except with respect to the use of the land itself, about which the treaty specifies that the grant of land limits the right to food production, including both farming and ranching (Cardinal and Hildebrandt 2000: 22), a restriction referred to commonly by the phrase 'the depth of the plow' (Treaty 4 Elders 1983: 4; Cardinal and Hildebrandt 2000: 42, 22). More precisely, these sources are clear that no permission was granted for economic activities respecting the subsurface. This position, which is repeated by Elder Gordon Oakes (Cardinal and Hildebrandt 2000: 42, 22, 64), is expressed in categorical terms in the 1994 'Proclamation and Convention': 'We retain our inherent birthright and interest in all arable and non-arable lands, mines and minerals and royalties derived there from and all other natural resources that were bestowed on us by the Creator for our livelihood' (Treaty 4 Chiefs Council 1999: 2). It can be inferred from the context that the shared understanding of the terms did not exclude the building of either a telegraph line or a railway line, even though these activities used the surface of the land in non-agricultural ways.

The transcript and other sources provide little information on this matter. However, what there is clearly supports Elder Thompson's interpretation in that, on at least two occasions during the negotiations, Commissioner Morris says his request is to share in the use of the land. The first occurred during the discussion on the fourth day respecting the HBC's claim to own the land:

THE GAMBLER – When one Indian takes anything from another we call it steal-
    ing, and when we see the present we say pay us. It is the Company I mean.
MORRIS – What did the Company steal from you?
THE GAMBLER – The earth, trees, grass, stones, all that which I see with my eyes.
MORRIS – Who made the earth, the grass, the stone, and the wood? The Great
    Spirit. He made them for all his children to use. It is not stealing to use the
    gift of the Great Spirit. The lands are the Queen's under the Great Spirit.[22]

> The Chippewas (Saulteaux) were not always here. They come from the East. There were other Indians here and the Chippewas came here, and they used the wood and the land, the gifts of the Great Spirit to all, and we want to try to induce you to believe that what we are asking is for the good of all. (Morris 1880: 102)

As I take it, this means that, even though the commissioner claims that the Crown has the underlying title to the land, the Settlers are requesting only that they be able to join those already here in using the gifts of the Creator[23] (and that, in so doing, all will benefit – a point I will address below). Other than the assertion that the queen is the custodian of these lands, it is a representation that dovetails with the understanding of Elder Musqua: 'Because, if any man owns a piece of the Earth, then he no more respects Mother Earth. He no longer respects the Earth, because he believes he can do what he wants with that Earth and he can destroy it, he can do what he wants. That's the reason why we don't own the Earth, because it belongs to all the people. For the purposes of that we cannot own the Earth. We are willing to share it' (Cardinal and Hildebrand 2000: 62).

The second occasion was on the fifth day, when Commissioner Morris, in his opening remarks, emphasized that his interest was in sharing land, not owning it:

> We have two nations here. We have the Crees, who were here first, and we have the Ojibbeways (Saulteaux), who came from our country not many suns ago. We find them here; we won't say they stole the land, and the stones and the trees; no, but we will say this, that we believe their brothers, the Crees, said to them when they came in here: 'The land is wide, it is wide, it is big enough for us both; let us live here like brothers,' and that is what you say, as you told us on Saturday, as to the Half-Breeds I see around. You say you are one with them; now we all want to be one.
> (Morris 1880: 108)

The treaty text also suggests that the Indigenous parties agreed to restrict their foraging to certain lands and to permit this activity to come under the legislative authority of the government of Canada. The clause reads: 'And further, Her Majesty agrees that Her said Indians shall have right to pursue their avocations of hunting, trapping and fishing throughout the tract surrendered, subject to such regulations as may from time to time be made by the Government of the country, acting

under the authority of Her Majesty, and saving and excepting such tracts
as may be required or taken up from time to time for settlement, mining
or other purposes, under grant or other right given by Her Majesty's
said Government' (Treaty 4 1966: 7). Morris does mention the first restriction, explaining that 'you will have the right of hunting and fishing
just as you have now until the land is actually taken up' (Morris 1880:
96). At the same time, this is modified by the statement immediately before that 'we have come through the country for many days and we have
seen hills but little wood and in many places little water, and it may be a
long time before there are many white men settled upon this land' (ibid.).
Further, there is no indication in the transcript that he mentions that
these activities will be subject to regulation by 'the Government of the
country' (unless he means by the Indigenous governments already in
place), nor is there any mention of the subject of subsurface rights.

The Common Intention:
Fixed Terms or Open-Ended Sharing Relationship?

As discussed above, the written treaty declares that the common intention was that the Crown would fulfil specific and fixed commitments,
such as providing a certain number of farm implements, a school, and
a one-time allocation of reserved land of specified size. On the other
hand, the elders and leaders of the Indigenous parties today suggest
that, while these commitments are indeed laid out, they were merely a
tangible expression of a larger commitment to ensure that they would
benefit, not suffer, economically as a consequence of settlement. Their
position is often encapsulated in the statement 'What I [the queen] offer
you is on top of what you have' (Treaty 4 Elders 1983: 2), and, in particular, they maintain that the offer of ammunition and fishnets in perpetuity was intended as support for their foraging activities (ibid.) and
that the offer of cattle, ploughs, and other productive tools was designed to assist those who chose to take up agriculture (Cardinal and
Hildebrandt 2000: 66). Underlying these specific promises, then, was
the intent by the queen to do what she could to protect Indigenous
peoples' economic well-being. In that regard, her intention was to provide assistance in times of need so that they would be 'free from hunger' (Treaty 4 Elders 1983: 2, 3), to ensure that they would be as 'wealthy'
as the Settlers (Cardinal and Hildebrandt 2000: 47), and, perhaps most
important of all, to make certain that their economic security would not

require that they be required by the Crown to change their way of life (Treaty 4 Elders 1983: 2).[24] As well, among the other promises found in the written text, the Indigenous elders and leaders say that, as a token of 'good faith' and as an assurance that 'the treaty would never be broken,' the queen pledged to give every citizen of the First Nations a gift of five dollars annually, in perpetuity (ibid.: 4).

There is much in the transcript that supports this position. For one, Commissioner Morris referred repeatedly to the queen's concern about the current economic situation of the Indigenous parties, and her desire to assist them (Morris 1880: 88, 92, 94, 95, 113, 117, 118). He began by declaring that 'the Queen loves her Red children; she has always been friends with them; she knows it is hard for them to live, and she has always tried to help them in the other parts of the Dominion' (ibid.: 88). Then, in the midst of outlining the commitments specified in the text, he stated: 'The Queen cares for you and for your children, and she cares for the children that are yet to be born. She would like to take you by the hand and do as I did for her at the Lake of the Woods last year' (i.e., Treaty 3) (ibid.: 92). And then on the fifth day, when it appeared that the negotiations would fail, Morris made the following appeal: 'The Queen and her Councillors may think that you do not want to be friends, that you do not want your little ones to be taught, that you do not want when the food is getting scarce to have a hand in yours stronger than yours to help you. Surely you will think again before you turn your back on the offers' (ibid.: 113). Indeed, he intimated that the queen had already provided economic security to those who made treaties: 'More than a hundred years ago, the Queen's father said to the red men living in Quebec and Ontario, I will give you land and cattle and set apart Reserves for you, and will teach you. What has been the result? There the red men are happy; instead of getting fewer in number by sickness they are growing in number; their children have plenty. The Queen wishes you to enjoy the same blessings' (ibid.: 95). 'All we can do,' he concluded, 'is to put money in your hands and promise to put money in the hands of those who are away, and give you money every year afterwards, and help you to make a living when the food is scarce' (ibid.: 118). There were many other pledges to the effect that the terms of treaty were offered with the best interests of the First Nations in mind and in a loving spirit (ibid.: 90, 92, 95, 97, 104, 107, 109, 117).

Just prior to reaching agreement, Kanooses, spokesperson for the Cree, asked for this assurance:

KAN-OO-SES: Is it true you are bringing the Queen's kindness? Is it true you are bringing the Queen's messenger's kindness? Is it true you are going to give the different bands the Queen's kindness? Is it true that you are bringing the Queen's hand? Is it true you are bringing the Queen's power?

MORRIS: Yes, to those who are here and those who are absent, such as she has given us.

KAN-OO-SES: Is it true that my child will not be troubled for what you are bringing him?

MORRIS: The Queen's power will be around him. (Morris 1880: 117–18)

In the context of what the commissioner has already said, I take Morris's words as confirming Kanooses' understanding that the promises are intended to establish an open-ended relationship, for, as I interpret it, to have the queen's power around Kanooses' child is to say that the she will always treat those who belong to his family and his descendants (writ large) in the way a loving mother treats her children. That is, it confirms that the queen accepts the relationship that, as the Gambler explained earlier, Indigenous peoples have already extended to her family and their descendants. As the Gambler says to the commissioner:

Look at these children that are sitting around here and also at the tents, who are just the image of my kindness. There are different kinds of grass growing here that is just like those sitting around here. There is no difference. Even from the American land they are here, but we love them all the same, and when the white skin comes here from far away I love him all the same. I am telling you what our love and kindness is. This is what I did when the white man came, but [referring to how the HBC acted in surveying the land] when he came back he paid no regard to me how he carried on. (Morris 1880: 100)

And that, as I understand it, is the economic aspect of the common intent of the treaty relationship evoked by the statement 'the Queen adopted us as children.'

Conclusions

I think the evidence clearly shows that, on the balance of probabilities, the interpretation of the terms of Treaty 4 offered by our Indigenous partners today more accurately reflects the agreement we reached than does the version transmitted to us through the written text. That is, to gain their permission to settle on lands we recognized as belonging to them, we asked only to share the land with them (not take it over as by purchasing it). In return, we promised to do our utmost to ensure that our presence on these lands would result in benefits to them, and certainly would cause them no harm. Furthermore, whether or not we believed we had sovereignty, we treated our partners as independent political actors with their own leaders and with a right to make the final decision on our request, and there is nothing in the evidence to substantiate the proposition that, either in our minds or in theirs, the treaty terms were such that they would change the nature of our relationship. In fact, as mentioned above, there is some support for my position even in the text of the treaty. Put succinctly, but perhaps too mechanically, the agreement was this: they would share the land, and we would treat them like our own brothers and sisters.

But does this not seem absurd? Isn't it more reasonable to believe, the Supreme Court's dictates notwithstanding, that, as Chief Hardisty put it for Treaty 11, the Treaty 4 commissioners lied to the 'Indians' either by telling them falsehoods intended to get them to sign at any cost or by making promises which they personally felt to be honourable but which they knew they had no authority to make; and that they then lied to the government of Canada by claiming that the signed text represented the common intent of the treaty they had negotiated? There is reason to conclude that Commissioner Morris did not lie to our partners nor exceed his authority, but that is a topic I will address later. On the other hand, what is clear is that he did not hide from the government of Canada the terms of Treaty 4 that he had negotiated, for he made public what had transpired in a book that was published only six years after that agreement had been reached.

So, for a moment, let us set aside disbelief and accept the possibility that the version of Treaty 4 as explained by the Indigenous elders and other leaders was the product of good-faith negotiations. When looked at through this lens, Treaty 4 (and certain other numbered treaties) is a remarkable achievement. It says that, notwithstanding the indisputable cultural differences, the parties were able to come to a shared understanding that, at least from the perspective of the Indigenous party, endures today, despite what has occurred in the century and a half since the treaties were first negotiated. And that also may well mean that, as the Gambler's reference to property in Western terms and Commissioner Morris's to the idea of land sharing rather than ownership indicates, each party at that time had sufficient knowledge of the other's cultural ways to communicate with each other with reasonable fluency.

But more than that, the terms of Treaty 4 offer us a path to move beyond colonial relations as defined by the international community, for through them we come into substantive compliance with the United Nations Declaration on De-Colonization. Here is how. As discussed in chapter 4, Resolution 1541 (which implements that declaration) specifies that one way to achieve decolonization is through the creation of an independent state. What is less well known is that the resolution specifies two other ways to achieve decolonization ('Free Association with an Independent State' and 'Integration with an Independent State'). While neither maps the agreement reached in Treaty 4, they do indicate that decolonization can occur without the establishment of a new state. What this requires, as the resolution states in the relevant clause respecting Free Association, is that the result be a product of 'a free and voluntary choice by the peoples of the territory concerned.' It is impossible to be certain that Treaty 4 was such a product. On the one hand, Settlers already knew that we were 'here to stay,' and I think it fair to say that the Indigenous parties were well aware that we would not leave. In fact, as Cardinal and Hildebrandt observe: 'Both the arrival of the White man to First Nations' territories prior to the signing of treaties and the knowledge derived from First Nations belief systems enabled the First Nations to anticipate and prepare for the time when formal relations would have to be created between them and the arriving non-Aboriginal peoples' (Cardinal and Hildebrandt 2000: 31f). However, I think it is also clear that the terms proposed by Commissioner Morris as mitigation against this inevitability are of a kind that it cannot be assumed the Indigenous party would not have chosen voluntarily to accept, rather than insist that no settlement take place.

And it is evident from statements of the Indigenous elders and other leaders today that what they seek is that we now live up to the treaty provisions as they have fairly represented them. As one source notes: 'The Elders state that the Indians were promised Crown protection and assistance to develop and prosper. The promise is described in general terms, with reference to a continuing and comprehensive, Crown responsibility, and also in specific terms with respect to economic development' (*Saskatchewan Indian* 1986: 10). I therefore think it reasonable to believe that, had we honoured the treaties at the time they were negotiated, we may well have long passed the point where the legitimacy of our settlement on these lands might be in question.

If we take the view that we lied, the treaties become worthless pieces of paper and we are back to square one. But if we take the view that we meant what we said, they become transformative, for through them we became permanent partners sharing the land, not thieves stealing it, people who are here to stay not because we had the power to impose our will but because we forged a permanent, unbreakable partnership with those who were already here when we came. Treaties, then, and not the constitution, are our charter of rights, for they give us what is necessary before any form of self-governance can become legitimate: the legitimacy to be living in a place. Harold Cardinal says: 'Treaties represent an Indian Magna Carta.' That is also true for us.

But here is a problem. In return for this gift we vowed to keep certain promises in perpetuity. As Commissioner Morris put it in words often repeated back to us: 'The Queen has to think of what will come long after today. Therefore the promises we have to make to you are not for today only but for tomorrow, not only for you but for your children born and unborn, and the promises will be carried out *so long as the sun shines above and the water flows in the ocean*' (Morris 1880: 96; emphasis added). We know full well that we have not kept our word. That is a legacy with which we will have to deal, just as we will have to deal with the fact that we violated the principle of temporal priority and settled on lands without first gaining the consent of those already living on them. It is a matter we will need to address, for we cannot wish it away. And in my view it is principally for this reason, and not because Settlers have the power to impose their will, that it is fair for the Royal Commission on Aboriginal Peoples to declare that 'after 100 years of relying on a treaty that has been assumed to be about extinguishment, the parties cannot turn back the clock and begin again.'

Karl Marx once said: 'Men make their own history, but they do not make it as they please; they do not make it under self-selected circumstances, but under circumstances existing already, given and transmitted from the past. The tradition of all dead generations weighs like a nightmare on the brains of the living' (Tucker 1978: 595). Still, I have come to the conviction that, to get our bearings on how to move forward, it is helpful to imagine that we are living in the period in which we negotiated Treaty 4, and are considering for the first time how we might go about 'sharing the land' were we now ready to implement that treaty's provisions in good faith.

Chapter Six

Treaties and Coexistence

The only possibility of a just relationship between Onkwehonwe and the Settler society is the conception of a nation-to-nation partnership between peoples, the kind of relationship reflected in the original treaties of peace and friendship consecrated between indigenous peoples and newcomers when white people first started arriving in our territories. And the only way to remove ourselves from the injustice of the present relationship is to begin to implement a process of resurgence-apology-restitution and seek to restore the pre-colonial relationship of sharing and cooperation among diverse peoples.

(Alfred 2005: 156)

Introduction

It certainly would be easier to build an honourable relationship with our partners in Treaty 4 were we now at the moment when we first gained their permission to settle on their lands. But we cannot erase time. There is Canada, there are provinces, there has been mass migration, we have already visited much harm on our partners, and our failures to implement in full even those promises written into the treaty text are manifest, like, for example, the fact that a century and a quarter after we agreed to set aside lands for reserves in that treaty, we have yet to complete the process.[1] We have travelled too far to ignore that history. However, I am convinced it would be helpful to discuss what implementation in good faith would constitute were we to assume that today we are at the beginning and, having just negotiated Treaty 4, are now planning on implementing the political relationship to which we agreed.

The kind of relationship to which I am referring is frequently characterized by the phrase 'nation-to-nation,' as when John Borrows informs
us that, at the 1764 Treaty of Niagara gathering, 'a nation-to-nation relationship between settler and First Nations peoples was renewed and
extended' (Borrows 1997: 61); or by the word 'coexistence,' as when
Sharon Venne explains that, 'in entering into treaties with the British
Crown, Indigenous peoples agreed to coexistence understandings'
(Venne 2002: 51); or by a combination of both, as when the Assembly of
First Nations reminds us that 'the Royal Proclamation of 1763 and
Treaties entered into between the Crown and First Nations embody a
nation-to-nation relationship, based on the right of self-determination
and the principles of peaceful coexistence and sharing' (Assembly of
First Nations 2012: 4).

The relationship I have in mind is one I often associate with the Two
Row Wampum agreement between the Haudenosaunee and first the
Dutch and then the British Crown in the seventeenth and eighteenth
centuries. It has been described this way: 'We will not be like father and
son, but like sisters and brothers. These two rows will symbolize vessels, travelling down the same river together. One will be for the canoe
of the Onkwehonwe and their laws, their customs. The other will be for
the sailing ship of the European people and their laws and customs. We
will each travel the river together, but each in our own boat, and neither of us will try to steer the other's vessel'[2] (Mohawk Nation Council
of Chiefs 1996: 1).

This is the kind of relationship I described in chapter 5 as akin to that
between New Zealand and Canada at the time Treaty 4 was negotiated,
and that I have often heard portrayed as the sort of relationship we
might have arrived at had we substituted an unfounded belief in our
superiority with the understanding that Indigenous peoples are equal
in political standing to ourselves in our interactions with them. What I
will suggest is that, while the relationship expressed in these ideas
sounds reasonable, it would be impossible for us to implement it based
on how political relations are currently organized internationally and
domestically.

The Modern State and Relations between States

To state the obvious, the world as we have created it is organized into
territorial states each of which has 'sovereignty' or, to use the definition in Black's Law Dictionary, 'the supreme political authority of an

independent state' (1430) with 'jurisdiction' or 'a government's general power to exercise authority over all persons and things within its territory' (867). Relations between states have been governed since the 1648 Peace of Westphalia on the principles of 'mutual recognition,' an acceptance that each state is equal in political and legal standing, and 'coexistence,' based on the understanding that no state has the right to interfere in the internal affairs of another.

That these principles apply today is confirmed in the United Nation's 1970 Declaration on Principles of International Law Concerning Friendly Relations and Cooperation among States in Accordance with the Charter of the United Nations (2625 XXV). This Declaration makes a number of points, among them:

1) All States enjoy sovereign equality. They have equal rights and duties and are equal members of the international community, notwithstanding differences of an economic, social, political or other nature.
2) In particular, sovereign equality includes the following elements:
    (a) States are juridically equal.
    (b) Each State enjoys the rights inherent in full sovereignty.
    (c) Each State has the duty to respect the personality of other States;
    (d) The territorial integrity and political independence of the State are inviolable.
    (e) Each State has the right freely to choose and develop its political, social, economic and cultural systems.
    (f) Each State has the duty to comply fully and in good faith with its international obligations and to live in peace with other States. (UN 1970: Principle 6)

That is, states are to treat each other in a manner that is respectful of their equality of standing and their right to develop their systems without interference. It is to this kind of relationship that terms like 'nation-to-nation,' 'coexistence,' and 'mutual recognition' are usually applied. Thus, were the relationship we established in Treaty 4 truly parallel to that between Canada and New Zealand, we would have a framework for beginning treaty implementation. And, let me add, it would have been possible for the Treaty 4 commissioners to have imagined such a relationship if they accepted that our partners had the standing of states. This way of framing international relations had been in place for over two hundred years at that time, having been established in the Peace of Westphalia.

Here is the problem to which I am drawing attention. To be an 'equal in standing' in this system requires a party to have the status of a territorial state. There is no question that the British Crown had this standing when it negotiated Treaty 4. However, that standing derives unequivocally only from the fact that Britain is a territorial state in Europe. As Loron, spokesperson for the Penobscot people, wrote to the British authorities in the early eighteenth century: 'When you have ask'd me if I acknowledg'd Him for King I answer'd yes butt att the same time have made you take notice that I did not understand to acknowledge Him for my king butt only that I own'd that He was king in His kingdom as the King of France is king in His' (Wicken 1994: 111f). The Crown did not have the standing of a state in North America, for, as James Tully points out, 'the only valid way [we] could acquire sovereignty in North America was by gaining the consent of the sovereign nations that were already here, as would be the case anywhere else in the world' (Tully 2008: 234). Unless the result of negotiations was to carve out for us a *portion* of what is now Canada over which we had sovereignty and jurisdiction so that we were living like one state among many (as in Europe), the principles regarding international relations would not apply. Or, to put it another way: were we to imagine that the 'river' described in the Two Row Wampum agreement represents an international border separating the Onkwehonwe and 'the European people,' then we could imagine a relationship in which we were 'like sisters and brothers,' each travelling in our own canoe, following our own laws and customs, never trying to 'steer each other's vessel.' In fact, I would suggest that this image appears to represent well the kind of relationship framed by the UN Declaration. But of course that did not happen at Treaty 4. Nor does it appear as a possibility today. We do not see the land mass that is now Canada as comprising a number of states of which one is our own. No matter how seductive is the apparent similarity between our relationship with Indigenous peoples and the one that governs relations between states, the framework provided by the UN Declaration does not apply.

So now let me turn to the alternative: the relationship that applies when the parties are both within the same state.

Nations within States

To mention another obvious fact, in the ideal a state is imagined as being composed of at least two 'singularities.' The first is a collectivity often referred to as 'the civic nation,' by which is meant, to use Tully's description, a group of 'undifferentiated individuals' who are understood to be equal citizens of the state. The second is the collectivity often referred to by Tully as the 'culturally defined nation' and by Anthony Smith as 'the ethnic nation' or 'a named human population sharing an historic territory, common myths and historical memories, a mass, public culture, a common economy and common legal rights and duties for all members' (Smith 1991: 14).

And so in the ideal (and I admit this may be a bit controversial), each state is imagined as a single civic nation that is at the same time a single ethnic nation. For that reason, modern states are often referred to as 'nation-states.' This ideal was considered so fundamental by the mid-nineteenth century that John Stuart Mill called it 'in general a necessary condition of free institutions that the boundaries of governments should coincide in the main with those of nationalities' (Mill 1947: 294). In other words, as with international relations, from the perspective of the internal composition of the state, the ideal would be to divide the territory that is now Canada into a number of nation-states, with the governance of each in the hands of a single ethno-national community. But again that did not happen.

Of course, one of the most, if not the most, frequently recognized weakness of this framing of the ideal is that in reality states do not conform to Mill's 'necessary condition.' Nation-states actually most often include more than one 'ethnic nation,' and so the question becomes how to reconcile the heterogeneity of the reality with the homogeneity of the ideal.

Given that treaties did not result in the division of the continent into separate nation-states, this situation applies to the relationship established between Indigenous peoples and ourselves. Thus, the frame governing our way of thinking about relations with Indigenous polities is the one that exists among nations that find themselves within a single state; and here the idea of a 'nation-to-nation' relationship based on 'coexistence' and 'mutual respect' does not apply. Instead, it becomes an intractable problem that is 'managed' in one of two ways: by refusing to recognize that members of the non-dominant (generally minority) ethnic nations are anything other than citizens of the state, or by finding ways to accommodate recognition of some degree of 'special status.'[3]

To return to the Two Row Wampum analogy, if one imagines that the Onkwehonwe, the European Settlers, and the river are all in the same nation-state, we no longer see them as being in a relationship that is like that of 'sisters and brothers,' with each of us travelling in our own canoe, following our own laws and customs, never trying to 'steer each other's vessel.' Rather, the image is one in which we are travelling in the canoe of one of the parties, likely on a river named by that party, with the other party granted certain limited rights to follow its own laws and customs so long as they do not contradict those of the dominant one. This is a relationship akin to, but likely harsher than, the hierarchical one rejected by the Haudenosaunee when they declared that 'we will not be like father and son.'

Relying on colonial-era arguments as well as a faith in the unmitigated factuality of statements such as those in the numbered treaties regarding the extinguishment of the sovereignty and jurisdiction of Indigenous peoples, we act as though we could legitimately implement our relationship by regarding ourselves as the singularity that constitutes Canada. At one time we implemented policies that overtly sought to have Indigenous peoples abandon their canoes; and now, still consistent with how that understanding is framed in modern political thought, we seek to ensure that, whatever recognition and affirmation we give to 'Treaty and Aboriginal rights,' they are ultimately subordinated to law and custom as we have defined them.

An example of this kind of thinking is found in the Royal Commission on Aboriginal Peoples report *Treaty Making in the Spirit of Co-Existence* (RCAP 1993). Here, although the word 'co-existence' appears in the title, it does not mean the same thing as it does when it is applied to international relations. Rather, although the goal is to create 'harmonious co-existence' through 'an agreement that … recognizes Aboriginal and Crown rights with respect to land, and allocates rights of governance among the parties' (ibid.: 59, 60), the report describes 'harmonious co-existence' as being the result of Indigenous peoples limiting their exercise of political authority to such matters as (internal) citizenship, education, health, and social services (RCAP 1996: II, 167), that is, matters that '(1) … are vital to the life and welfare of a particular Aboriginal people, its culture and identity; (2) do not have a major impact on adjacent jurisdictions; and (3) are not otherwise the object of federal or provincial concern.'[4] Rather than characterizing a relationship between equals, here 'co-existence' is a term that only means existing in relation to another that exists independently of it, and it is therefore appropriately applied (as is the case with the royal commission) only to the subordinate party in the relationship.

The so-called British Columbia Treaty Process is another case in point. Established in 1993, it has as its goal the resolution of outstanding claims to 'land title' that resulted from the fact that, unlike most of Canada, the Crown did not generally negotiate treaties with Indigenous peoples in British Columbia prior to settlement on their lands (British Columbia Treaty Commission 2003: 3). Following from the principle of 'coexistence' as described by the royal commission, the British Columbia Process requires the parties to begin on the understanding that Canada and British Columbia already have sovereignty and jurisdiction on these lands, and that, moreover, Settlers are in legitimate occupation of the lands they already occupy: 'The BC treaty process has always been guided by the principle that private property [fee simple land] is not on the negotiating table, except on a willing seller – willing buyer basis' (ibid.: 16). Therefore, no provision is made for Indigenous parties to address the issue that they never consented to the original transfer of title required to set up the land-titles regime that now benefits Settlers, much less how Canada and British Columbia acquired sovereignty and jurisdiction absent their consent. As is consistent with this vision of 'coexistence,' they are limited by the terms of the process to finding ways to accommodate their interests within the political and legal regime imposed by the Settlers.[5]

These examples confirm that here the 'nation-to-nation' relationship is one in which it is one nation over another. It results in what Kiera Ladner aptly calls 'Negotiated Inferiority' (Ladner 2001), a relationship that, with all deference to Cairns for whom it is clear this was not intended, is well described by the term 'Citizens Plus.'

On Cede and Surrender

Of course there are many places in Canada where treaties were not negotiated, and there, as Tully points out, Indigenous peoples had every right to recognize the Europeans as immigrants subject to their laws (perhaps granting them some sort of minority status) (Tully 2008: 234). That would also be the case in those parts of Canada, such as in Treaty 4, where treaties were negotiated, unless the agreements stipulated that we acquired sovereignty and jurisdiction over the territories concerned. And, in fact, there are good grounds to conclude that what holds for Treaty 4 also holds generally: there is no place in Canada in which we acquired the standing of a state with sovereignty and jurisdiction over Indigenous peoples and their lands. Consequently, our status is that of immigrants subject to the laws of their nations every-where in Canada.

Let me underscore this point with examples from other treaties, be-ginning with some of the numbered ones. The first of these is Treaty 11, which, because it is the one with which I have the most familiarity, I will discuss most fully (Asch 2013). Like Treaty 4 (and the other num-bered treaties), Treaty 11 contains a cede and surrender clause. It reads: ' ... the said Indians do hereby cede, release, surrender and yield up to the Government of the Dominion of Canada, for His Majesty the King and His Successors forever, all their rights, titles, and privileges what-soever to the lands included within the following limits ...' It also stip-ulates, as in Treaty 4, that foraging will be regulated through the legislative authority of 'the Government of the Country acting under the authority of His Majesty.' At the same time, the Dene, the collective term for the Indigenous party with whom the Crown negotiated, are resolute that neither provision reflects what transpired.

Because the treaty was negotiated in 1921, much of the evidence to support the Dene's understanding comes from witnesses to the nego-tiations who were interviewed in the 1960s and early 1970s. Among these is Julian Yendo, chief at Wrigley, Northwest Territories, at the time of negotiations, whom I interviewed in 1970 when I was living there with my wife and doing research for my doctorate. On the same occa-sion, I also interviewed Philip Moses, a witness to the negotiations as well as the nephew of the Old Moses, the elder who advised Yendo. What follows is a brief excerpt from the interviews as translated by Edward Hardisty, who was chief at Wrigley at that time.

With regard to the cession, Philip Moses informed me that his uncle (whom he calls 'The Old Man') 'heard these rumors about treaties, that people had a hard time after that. Old Man wanted to see if they were after land or something. But they said "no."' Yendo also said that 'there wasn't anything mentioned about land.' With regard to the hunting provision, Philip Moses told me the elder 'asked the treaty party about everything. The Old Man asked all the questions. He asked about game laws and all that.' The reason, he continues, is that 'The Old Man ... wanted to make sure that no laws would be made about what they used to do. Move around, hunt here and there. The Commissioner said there wouldn't be any changes so long as the sun rises up.'

As recorded in René Fumoleau's book *As Long as This Land Shall Last*, Moses and Yendo's report of what occurred at Wrigley is similar to the testimony of numerous Dene witnesses from six of the eight communi-ties[6] along the Mackenzie River in which negotiations took place in the summer of 1921 (and for which Fumoleau had accounts).[7] Thus, for example, with respect to the land cession, Jimmy Bruneau (born in 1881 and chief at Fort Rae from 1936 to 1969) (Fumoleau 1973: 245), said 'we made an agreement, but land was never mentioned ... a person must be crazy to accept five dollars to give up his land' (ibid.: 248); and Noel Sotchia repeated: 'Land was never mentioned and we did not take the treaty to give our land to the Crown. If such was the case we would not have accepted the treaty money' (ibid.).

The evidence from the Dene respecting the promise of freedom to hunt is echoed in a series of affidavits organized by Bishop Gabriel-Joseph-Élie Breynat, who was enlisted by the Crown to be a member of the treaty party. These affidavits all assert that the Dene 'were promised that nothing would be done or allowed to interfere with their way of making a living as they were accustomed to and as their antecedents had done.' Indeed, the bishop was so incensed that the terms of the treaty as negotiated were not reflected appropriately in the written text that he went on a public campaign to pressure the government to honour them.

That the promise was made is echoed again in the judgment of Justice William G. Morrow in a trial in the early 1970s concerning the terms of Treaty 11. There, he says:

> Throughout the hearings before me there was a common thread in the testimony – that the Indians were repeatedly assured they were not to be deprived of their hunting, fishing and trapping rights. To me, hearing the witnesses at first hand as I did, many of whom were there at the signing, some of them having been directly involved in the treaty making, it is almost unbelievable that the Government party could have ever returned from their efforts with any impression but that they had given an assurance in perpetuity to the Indians in the territories that their traditional use of the lands was not affected. (*Re Paulette* 1973)

Morrow also argues that it is likely the Dene were not informed that the written treaty contained a cede and surrender clause, since 'the important phrase in respect of the surrender of the land,' by which 'the Indians were left nothing,' was 'camouflaged to some extent' by its position as 'one of the preambles in the text.' As Fumoleau says: 'Most official documents indicate that Treaty 11 was a cession of land. The Indians of the Mackenzie District contest this interpretation. They do not believe that their fathers ever intended to surrender the land to the Government' (Fumoleau 1973: 214).

The same can be said of other numbered treaties. Regarding Treaty 1, negotiated in 1871, Aimée Craft, who researched its terms for her master's degree in law, concluded that 'the Anishinabe have disputed that Treaty One is a surrender of their traditional territory, almost since the time pen touched paper. One hundred and forty years later, treaty implementation continues to be the subject of litigation and political tension' (Craft 2011: 3). In fact, she reports, 'the record does not mention discussions about concepts such as cession, release or surrender, terms that were later used in the treaty text to effect the purported surrender of land. The evidence shows that up until the last day of the negotiations, the Anishinabe were prepared to walk away from the treaty discussions. While it is unclear what was said, or what promises or assurances were delivered to entice them into signing the treaty on August 3, 1871, the fact remains that the Anishinabe were never recorded to have agreed to a complete surrender of land' (ibid.: 25). With regard to Treaty 7, it is reported that the Indigenous parties understood the agreement to be one of peace that would provide the stability required for Settlers to move onto Indigenous lands, and not a land cession (Treaty 7 Elders 1996: 111f); the latter point is underscored by Father Constantine Scollon's statement in an 1879 letter to Acheson Gosford Irvine of the Northwest Mounted Police that 'the First Nations did not believe they were agreeing to a land surrender,' which 'provides further evidence that the issue of "cede, surrender, release, and yield up" had never been discussed' (ibid.: 261). Similarly, with respect to Treaty 6, the Indigenous leaders say[8] that 'at no time did Treaty First Nations relinquish their right to nationhood, their Inherent Right to determine their own destinies, nor did they allow any foreign government to govern them.' And at Treaty 9, negotiated in 1905 in northern Ontario, John Long, who researched this treaty extensively for his book *Treaty No. 9: Making the Agreement to Share the Land in Far Northern Ontario in 1905* (2010), reports that, as with the Dene in Treaty 11, notwithstanding what is in the written document, the record of the negotiations indicates that 'at Osnaburgh they were also informed that they could continue to live as their forefathers, and at Fort Hope they were promised that their hunting and fishing would not be interfered with' (355); and, moreover there is no evidence that the cession clause was even discussed.

In short, there is good reason to agree with Henderson that, when it comes to the numbered treaties, what holds for Treaty 4 holds more generally: 'These treaties … did not transfer to the British sovereign blanket authority to govern First Nations or peoples. They did not grant to anyone any vast executive authority or legislative authority over Treaty First Nations' (Henderson 2007: 518).

Here are three illustrations from treaties negotiated prior to Confederation. The first, researched by Allyshia West for her MA thesis in anthropology, is from Treaty 45, negotiated with the Ojibwe (Ojibwa, Anishinabe) in Ontario. Regarding its terms, Ojibwe storyteller Esther Osche (Ojibwe Cultural Foundation) says that 'they did not surrender anything, they did not give up anything they just said, "we agree for the others to come"' (West 2010: 47). The second, also researched by West, is the treaty negotiated in 1862 in the same area. In this case, the evidence as to its terms includes the following excerpt from a petition written by the Indigenous party, the Wikwemikong (Anishinabe), and their allies four years later:

> We take occasion to protest again and to present to thee how displeased we were when the Ottawa (Manitoulin Island) was surrendered and how we grieve yet for it. What took place then [with] the treaty was not right at all. We repeat again that now we want our land. Please to the Great Spirit that we might own it yet. It does not look well to sell our land since it is only by intimidation that our land has been taken from us. Although we have protested, written to thee until now even that thou wouldst destroy and stop the sale of our land. It was on October 4th, to use English calcula-tion, 1862, that one great chief, a Commissioner W. McDougal[,] came to speak and made use of some Indians to ask them for their lands. But they all refused, loved their land on that day. It was on October 6th 1862 that some Indians having been spoken to again and when they had been in-timidated then only they surrendered their land. The Indians were not all pleased. Some few Chiefs only did the thing. But the majority a very great number were not willing at all and are not yet even now. We hope that when thou shalt see how things, the Treaty, took place it will suggest to thee some great determination for indeed we are very sorrowful for the loss of our land and truly we grieve much in our hearts. We shall never forget it, our Land. (West 2010: 68f)

Government at that time listened, and today many of the Wikwemikong live on what is officially called the 'Wikwemikong Unceded Indian Reserve.'

A century earlier, in 1744, the Haudenesaunee depicted the terms of their treaties in the same way. Onondaga Chief Canasatego (alternative spelling Canassatego), speaking to the person he called his 'Brother, the

Governor of Maryland' at the Treaty of Lancaster, stated: 'Brother: You came out of the Ground in a Country that lies beyond the Seas, there you may have a just Claim, but here you must allow us to be your elder Brethren and the Lands belong to us long before you knew any thing of them' (Henderson 2007: 163). And, at roughly the same time, the British superintendent of Indian affairs, William Johnson, informed his superior, Thomas Gage, about how Indigenous peoples viewed their status when he wrote:[9]

> It is necessary to observe that no Nation of Indians have any word which can express, or convey the Idea of Subjection, they often say, 'we acknowledge the great King to be our Father, we hold him fast by the hand, and we shall do what he desires' many such like words of course, for which our People too readily adopt & insert a Word verry different in signifiation, and never intended by the Indians without explaining to them what is meant by a Subjection. Imagine to yourself Sir, how impossible it is to reduce a People to Subjection, who consider themselves Independant thereof by both Nature & Scituation ... (Letter to Thomas Gage, 31 October 1764, qtd. in McNab and McNab 2009: n.p.)

That this point holds for treaties in general is underlined in the pleadings submitted by the Indian Association of Alberta, the Union of New Brunswick Indians, and the Union of Nova Scotia Indians in the legal action that they brought to the Judicial Committee of the Privy Council in Great Britain in an attempt to ensure that, notwithstanding Canada's intent to patriate its constitution, 'treaty and other obligations entered into by the Crown to the Indian peoples of Canada are still owed by Her Majesty in right of Her Government in the United Kingdom' (McNab and McNab 2009: n.p.). In other words, the relationship established by treaties was with Britain, not Canada – a position that Lord Denning (and the other justices) countered by asserting that in English law the Crown, once considered to be a 'unity,' was now understood to be 'divisible,' so that, even though the queen is one person, the term 'the queen' actually refers to separate entities (ibid.).

As I read the historical record, Indigenous peoples have spoken to us with one voice: using our conceptual frame, they had sovereignty and jurisdiction in their territories when we first arrived and they have not voluntarily relinquished this through treaties; and this is certainly the case as well where no treaties have been negotiated. Their word alone should suffice.[10]

But there is more to it than that. It is true that there are many scholars who take the position that treaties did dispossess Indigenous peoples. Yet there are few among them who also suggest that Indigenous peoples entered into such treaties voluntarily; and that fact alone, given the terms of my argument, invalidates these treaty provisions. At the same time, while the record shows that some of our own eyewitnesses saw the cessions as voluntary, there are many others, of whom I have named three – Father Scollon, Bishop Breynat, and Superintendent Johnson – whose words strongly support those of our Indigenous partners. There is sufficient evidence, not only to throw doubt on the proposition that we acquired sovereignty and jurisdiction anywhere in Canada, but also to confirm that 'on the balance of probabilities' what our partners say is faithful to the facts as we understood them even at that time.

From this conclusion, I wish to draw the following implication: if we want to move ahead in implementing the treaty relationship in good faith, it seems reasonable to start by accepting that, no matter where our partners reside, whether on rural reserves or in urban centres, they live on land that remains under their sovereignty and jurisdiction; and that we ourselves therefore live on 'unceded land,' or, as the Four Host First Nations at the Vancouver Olympics put it, on the 'traditional and shared traditional territories' of those who were here when we first arrived. This means that, rather than arguing over the point, we need to begin by determining the implications for us of accepting the reality of our status on Indigenous lands.

Conclusions: Moving beyond Westphalia

In such circumstances, according to our principles, the only path for us to take is to join Indigenous polities as immigrants, with perhaps the degree of autonomy associated with a level of 'negotiated inferiority' that I have attributed to the notion of 'Citizens Plus.' And there may be some truth to that representation, if, for example, Canassatego's remark, and others like it, that we are younger siblings is intended to identify our position as subordinates rather than describe the timing of our arrival on their lands – and the implications that flow from it. But frankly, though we are often reminded that we did not acquire sovereignty and jurisdiction from our partners, we seldom hear that our integration into their polities was the intent. Rather, over and over again, we are told that the goal has always been to establish the same 'nation-to-nation' relationship grounded in mutual respect and coexistence that

we conventionally ascribe as the ideal associated with relations between states rather than relations among nations within one. And that
means it stands outside the possibilities that we normally associate
with the organization of polities.

While I will explore this further in later chapters, I wish to conclude
here by pointing to the direction in which I am heading. To that end, I
will briefly discuss two iterations of the treaty relationship as it has
been explained to us. The first returns me to the passage in the Two
Row Wampum agreement that says: 'We will not be like father and son,
but like sisters and brothers. These two rows will symbolize vessels,
travelling down the same river together. One will be for the canoe of the
Onkwehonwe and their laws, their customs. The other will be for the
sailing ship of the European people and their laws and customs. We
will each travel the river together, but each in our own boat, and neither
of us will try to steer the other's vessel.' As I said, this passage suggests
that, in the ideal, our relationship is one that emphasizes our independence of each other. However, the Two Row Wampum agreement is
about more than adhering to the principles of 'peace, respect, and friendship – the principles by which we are to co-exist,' important as these
principles are. As Dale Turner puts it in this paraphrase of the agreement: 'Because we share the same space, we are inextricably entwined
in a relationship of interdependence – *but we remain distinct political entities*'[11] (Turner 2006: 54; emphasis in original).

To get at what this means, I find it useful to refer again to these sentences in the quote cited above (emphasis mine): 'These two rows will
symbolize vessels, *travelling down the same river together*'; and 'we will
each travel the river together, but each in our own boat, and *neither of us
will try to steer the other's vessel*.' In the first place, what is clear is that the
passages emphasize that we are on the same river, not that each of us is
on one side of it; we are 'sharing the same space,' as Turner puts it.
Thus, the fact that we are not trying to steer each other's vessel is not a
consequence of the fact that we are each on a different side of a line; we
remain distinct political entities no matter where we are on the river.
This view is supported by the fact that, among the Haudenosaunee, the
treaty is named Kaswehntha (or Guswhenta) or 'the river of life'
(Henderson 2007: 158). It therefore makes more sense to conceive of the
image as a reflection of our intent to form a relationship that will endure as long as life endures, rather than as a place represented on a map
where we may draw what is most important to our way of thinking: the
lines that separate us from each other.

As I see it, the phrase that we are 'inextricably entwined in a relation-ship of interdependence' is indicated by the use of the word 'together' in the sentences cited above, or, as the Haudensaunee Confederacy put it in a 1983 presentation to a Canadian House of Commons committee, 'the Europeans at the 1664 conference said that their King would be a father to us, but the Haudenosaunee replied that there is only one fa-ther for us, and we call him Sonkwaiatisen, the Creator. The Iroquois said, this is how it will be: You and I are brothers. We will not make laws for you, but we will look after you, help you settle in this land, give you the medicines you will need to survive, and show you what you can plant, what animals you can hunt, and how to use this land' (qtd. in Richardson 1989: 110). That is, not only does the Two Row Wampum agreement guarantee that each of us governs our own vessel, there is also a commitment that (to be reciprocal) we are in a relation-ship in which we will do what we can to help each other as together we move along the river of life.

In other words, as derived from the Two Row Wampum, our status results from our agreement to adhere both to the principles represented in the two rows and to the fact that we have agreed to join with Indigenous peoples in travelling down the river of life. And that does not work if we begin our journey by taking a portion of the river from the Onkwehonwe or by insisting that we alone have the authority to steer the vessel. As the Mohawk chiefs explain: 'Partnership and sovereignty are only mutually-exclusive concepts when rights are for sale, and there is no reciprocal respect' (Mohawk Nation Council of Chiefs 1996).

I find another helpful explanation of what *travelling down the same river together* means in Cardinal and Hildebrandt's description of how elders in Treaties 4, 6, and 8 in Saskatchewan define the word 'Witaskewin':

'Witaskewin' is a Cree word meaning 'living together on the land.' It is a word that has multiple applications and multidimensional meanings. It can include or refer to individuals or nations who are strangers to one another agreeing to either live on or share for some specific purpose a land area with each other, or it can be applied to land-sharing arrangements between individual members of the nation.

However, in the context of treaty-making, 'witaskewin' refers to nations who are strangers to one another entering into agreements for the purpose of sharing land or territory with each other. (Cardinal and Hildebrandt 2000: 39)

Witaskewin, then, further clarifies that the relationship identified by the word 'together' is one based, as Turner indicates, on the ethic of 'sharing.' And that, it seems to me, is key. Were we now at the beginning, I am suggesting that, rather than framing our status in terms of our success (or failure) at acquiring sovereignty and jurisdiction, it would be more productive to do so by recognizing that we are here to stay because our partners agreed to share the land with us. 'Canada,' as James Tully aptly puts it,

> is founded on an act of sharing that is almost unimaginable in its generosity. The Aboriginal peoples shared their food, hunting and agricultural techniques, practical knowledge, trade routes and geographic knowledge with the needy newcomers. Without this, the first immigrants would have been unable to survive. As we have seen, the Aboriginal peoples formalized the relation of sharing in the early treaties in the following form: they agreed to share this land with the newcomers on the agreement that the newcomers would neither attempt to govern them nor use their land without their consent. The treaties involved other exchanges as well, such as trade, military, educational and medical benefits, and political and legal interrelations, but the sharing of land and trade on this understanding were at the heart of the relationship. (Tully 2008: 244–5)

In order to implement the treaties fully, then, we need first to conceptualize how to form a relationship that falls outside the range of possibilities offered to us in contemporary political thought. It is to this matter I now turn.

Chapter Seven

Treaties and Sharing

Kiciwamanawak [cousin] ... Under the law of the Creator, a student can spend a lifetime trying to understand three words: 'All My Relations.' The phrase is said at the end of a prayer, but it is also said whenever we take something from nature. It is used to signify when a person is finished speaking, and it is a prayer in itself. But who are my relations? How should I relate to them? Why should I remember them when I gather from nature? Why should I remember them when I finish speaking? There are simple answers to these questions, but not complete ones. I could spend a lifetime trying to understand and never know it all.

(Johnson 2007: 18f)

Introduction

As discussed in the last chapter, had negotiations resulted in our acquisition of sovereignty over a portion of the land in Canada or over it all, we would have known how to implement the treaties. Similarly, if, as is the case, we did not gain sovereignty over any land, we would have a clear expectation that treaty implementation required us to integrate into one or more of the political societies of our partners. Wherever we live, we are living on lands the sovereignty and jurisdiction of which are in the hands of Indigenous peoples. And we know that, following from the principles of contemporary Western political thought, this means that we ought to be working to assimilate our polity into theirs.

But that is not the path offered to us. Our partners explain that negotiations resulted in establishing a permanent nation-to-nation relationship among us based on sharing even though we do not have sovereignty over any territory. From this it follows that, using Western framing,

Indigenous peoples are using principles other than those derived from contemporary Western political thought to determine our status on their lands.

Furthermore, they make it clear that these are principles they have honoured for a long time. As Elder Danny Musqua of Treaty 4 says, 'we had agreements between one another, hunting territories that we shared, trapping lands that we shared, gathering lands that we shared, medicine lands that we shared, peace territorial lands that we designated for the shelter and safety of all people' (Cardinal and Hildebrandt 2000: 39). And, as Leanne Simpson explains, the same principles have been applied with respect to people who live in the same community as well as in situations like our own: 'Our ancestors knew that maintaining good relationships as individuals, in families, in clans, and in our nation and with other Indigenous nations and confederacies was the basis for lasting peace. This was the foundation of a set of ethics, values, and practices known as Bimaadiziwin or "living the goodlife." Bimaadiziwin is a way of ensuring human beings live in balance with the natural world, their family, their clan, and their nation and it is carried out through the Seven Grandfather teachings, embedded in the social and political structures of the Nishnaabeg' (Simpson 2008: 32). Equally, these principles in question are applied to communities that are other than human, for, as Simpson says (following John Borrows), there were 'diplomatic agreements between human and animal nations' (ibid.: 33). She continues:

In many instances, clan leaders negotiated particular agreements with animal nations or clans to promote Bimaadiziwin and balance with the region. In Mississauga territory, for example, the people of the fish clans, who are the intellectuals of the nation, met with the fish nations twice a year for thousands of years at Mnjikanming, the small narrows between Lake Simcoe and Lake Couchiching. The fish nations and the fish clans gathered to talk, to tend to their treaty relationships, and to renew life just as the Gizhe-mnido [Creator] had instructed them. These were important gatherings because the fish nations sustained the Nishnaabeg Nation during times when other sources of food were scarce. Fish were a staple in our traditional foodway. Our relationship with the fish nations meant that we had to be accountable for how we used this 'resource.' Nishnaabeg people only fished at particular times of the year in certain locations. They only took as much as they needed and never wasted. They shared with other members of their families and communities, and they performed the

appropriate ceremonies and rituals before beginning. To do otherwise
would be to ignore their responsibilities to the fish nations and to jeopardize the health and wellness of the people. (Ibid.)

In short, the treaties our partners made with us are the result of the application of principles they have applied more generally.

To implement our treaties in good faith means that we need to learn
how these principles apply to our situation, and that means we need to
learn what they are. To do so, we clearly need some guidance. Fortunately, we have been given some already, and in this chapter I will
explain what I have come to understand in Western terms about a
concept that I am calling 'the linking principle.' As I now see it, this
principle provides a means to begin to comprehend the shape of a political relationship consistent with the notion of sharing associated with
'Witaskewin,' as well as with the association between parties illustrated
in the Two Row Wampum agreement.

Kiotseaeton and the Linking Principle

My discussion is based on a powerful statement concerning an aspect
of the treaty relationship that was explained to us in the seventeenth
century. This statement suggests that the link we made by treaty with
Indigenous peoples is so secure that it alone is sufficient to bind us
together permanently. The concept is found in the title of Robert A.
Williams, Jr's *Linking Arms Together: American Indian Treaty Visions of
Law and Peace 1600–1800* (1997). Following this lead, I came to a passage
in the *Jesuit Relations* for 1645 that describes the actions of Kiotseaeton,
a Mohawk chief of the Six Nations, at the conclusion of a 'Treaty of
Peace between the French, the Iroquois, and Other Nations':

> (Kiotseaeton) took hold of a Frenchman, placed his arm within his, and
> with his other arm he clasped that of an Alguonquin. Having thus joined
> himself to them:
>
> 'Here,' he said, 'is the knot that binds us inseparably; nothing can part
> us ... Even if the lightning were to fall upon us, it could not separate us; for,
> if it cuts off the arm that holds you to us, we will at once seize each other
> by the other arm.'
>
> And thereupon he turned around, and caught the Frenchman and the
> Algonquin by their two other arms, – holding them so closely that he
> seemed unwilling ever to leave them. (Qtd. in Schweitzer 2006: 62)

I have come to believe that what Kiotseaeton says holds as a foundational principle in our treaties. The link binds us so tightly that 'even if
the lightning were to fall upon us, it could not separate us; for, if it cuts
off the arm that holds you to us, we will at once seize each other by
the other arm.' It helps us to understand that, even though they retain
sovereignty, it is still possible for our partners to say, in the words of
Harold Johnson: 'I will never suggest that you go back where you came
from, for I assure you *Kiciwamanawak* [cousin] that you have a treaty
right to be here' (Johnson 2007: 14). So we should rest assured that
the treaty relationship alone is sufficient to ensure that we are here to
stay, notwithstanding that we do not have sovereignty on any of these
lands. Two nations live together as partners even though there is but
one sovereign.

Saying that the linking principle has the power to bind us to this land
is one thing. Believing it to be possible is another. And while, at the end
of the day, I know that it is incumbent on us to take our partners at their
word, the idea that sovereignty over a territory takes precedence is so
fundamental in our thinking that it would be useful to attempt to conceptualize how linking could have that power in its absence. That is
what I intend to do in this chapter.

The Westphalia Model of the State System

The 1648 Peace of Westphalia is the agreement that ended the
Thirty Years' War, which was among the longest and bloodiest wars in
European history. As a central cause of the conflict was a struggle between Protestants and Catholics over which religion would have hege-
mony, it was thought that warfare in Europe might be ended (or at least
muted) were there an agreement by all parties to divide Europe into
territories, each ruled by a secular authority with boundaries accepted
by all (Malanczuk 1997: 11). As a result, a foundation was laid for what
is known as 'Westphalian sovereignty,' in which states with recognized
borders became foundational in political organization. And hence the
proposition that two nations (that have sovereignty) cannot occupy the
same territory.

Had this model been understood solely as a solution by Europeans to
a problem on their continent, it might not have spread throughout the
world. But in fact it became touted as a model that was applicable
universally. While the practice may have spread only with European
expansion, a set of theoretical premises to justify it that remains central

to our thinking appeared at that time. What I am referring to is Thomas Hobbes's 1651 treatise, *Leviathan*, which, in developing these premises, also provides a theoretical rationale for concluding that the kind of nation-to-nation relationship our partners offered us is simply not possible.

To get a purchase on the reasoning that gives rise to this conclusion, I have summarized Hobbes's argument, focusing in particular on the myth he invents (i.e., his thought experiment based on reason) to explain it. This myth describes how human beings must live in our 'natural condition' or what social-contract theorists call the 'state of nature,' which Glen Newey (on whose interpretation of the text I am relying[1]) defines as 'a situation in which human beings have no government, no political institutions, and no executive forces such as a police force or army'[2] (Newey 2008: 74). Hobbes's account, which remains credible to many today as an accurate depiction of how human beings would actually behave in such a condition, demonstrates that it is simply not possible for us to trust that treaties formed by linking are sufficient to ensure that we have a recognized right to stay here in perpetuity without subordinating our polity to others; and that, therefore, to be secure requires that we have sovereignty and jurisdiction over our own territory.

Hobbes on Linking

Leviathan posits that human actions in the state of nature result from the application of certain universal principles (which Hobbes calls 'Laws of Nature'). The important ones for us are the first two, which Hobbes puts in these words:

> The first branch of which rule containeth the first and fundamental law of nature, which is: to seek peace and follow it. The second, the sum of the right of nature, which is: by all means we can to defend ourselves.
>   [Thus:]
>   It is a precept, or general rule of reason: that every man ought to endeavour peace, as far as he has hope of obtaining it; and when he cannot obtain it, that he may seek and use all helps and advantages of war. (Hobbes 1996: 80)

It follows that, if the first law of nature dominated, there would be peace among us all and therefore no need to make any claims for territorial sovereignty. But in the story as Hobbes tells it, it does not, for this reason: nature may be bountiful, but it is not bountiful enough. There will always be shortages. It is a point that Newey phrases this way: 'Goods are in relatively short supply in the state of nature. There are not enough goods to go round. Some goods, like food, merely happen to be scarce some of the time. Other goods, like excellence at music or sport, are necessarily scarce because it is a part of what it is to excel in one of these pursuits' (Newey 2008: 76).

Hobbes also posits (and Nature has decreed) that we are all virtually equal in our abilities and strengths (Hobbes 1996: 76). Thus, it follows that, to survive as a species, we must subordinate the first law of nature to the second, which is: by all means do what we can to defend ourselves. The result is that we end up in a perpetual struggle for resources, since, in a world of scarcity, it is never possible to become so secure that we will have enough to cover all contingencies: 'Where nobody feels secure, each person will have a reason to attack another person, for fear of being attacked first. The thinking which dominates in the state of nature can be summed up in the old adage that attack is the best form of defence. And, because each person has roughly equal killing power everybody is both a potential killer and a potential victim' (Newey 2008: 77). Consequently, notwithstanding the primacy of the first law, we inevitably end up in perpetual wars and threats of war, a condition of horrific proportions that Hobbes describes in these memorable words:

> ... where every man is enemy to every man, the same consequent to the time wherein men live without other security than what their own strength and their own invention shall furnish them withal. In such condition there is no place for industry, because the fruit thereof is uncertain: and consequently no culture of the earth; no navigation, nor use of the commodities that may be imported by sea; no commodious building; no instruments of moving and removing such things as require much force; no knowledge of the face of the earth; no account of time; no arts; no letters; no society; and which is worst of all, continual fear, and danger of violent death; and the life of man, solitary, poor, nasty, brutish, and short. (Hobbes 1996: 78)

He then asks whether we could trust that any agreement would be kept under these circumstances and answers 'no.' He concludes that 'covenants being but words, and breath, have no force to oblige, contain, constrain, or protect any man' (Hobbes 1996: 109); and that is precisely what Kiotseaeton offers – words and nothing more. So, in the world Hobbes describes, we cannot trust what he says or what Harold Johnson says, for words alone cannot bind us to keep our promises. It must therefore be concluded that the linking principle is an ineffective means to ensure that we are here to stay.

Having put us in this predicament, Hobbes then suggests that there is but one way out of it. It is for individuals to transfer 'their [individual] right to *judge* what is and is not conducive to self-preservation' (Newey 2008: 132; emphasis in original) to a common authority. It is a point he puts this way:

> The only way to erect such a common power, as may be able to defend them from the invasion of foreigners, and the injuries of one another, and thereby to secure them in such sort as that by their own industry and by the fruits of the earth they may nourish themselves and live contentedly, is to confer all their power and strength upon one man, or upon one assembly of men, that may reduce all their wills, by plurality of voices, unto one will: which is as much as to say, to appoint one man, or assembly of men, to bear their person; and every one to own and acknowledge himself to be author of whatsoever he that so beareth their person shall act, or cause to be acted, in those things which concern the common peace and safety; and therein to submit their wills, every one to his will, and their judgements to his judgement. (Hobbes 1996: 105f)

Hobbes calls that common authority 'The Commonwealth,' 'The State,' or 'The Leviathan.' It comes into being when a particular 'multitude of men' undertake the surrender of their individual sovereignty voluntarily: 'A commonwealth is said to be instituted when a multitude of men do agree, and covenant, every one with every one, that to whatsoever man, or assembly of men, shall be given by the major part the right to present the person of them all, that is to say, to be their representative; every one, as well he that voted for it as he that voted against it, shall authorize all the actions and judgements of that man, or assembly of men, in the same manner as if they were his own, to the end to live peaceably amongst themselves, and be protected against other men' (Hobbes 1996: 107).

Under these conditions, according to Hobbes, contracts will be enforced, for, to return and expand on the passage quoted above, 'covenants being but words, and breath, have no force to oblige, contain, constrain, or protect any man, *but what it has from the public sword; that is, from the untied hands of that man, or assembly of men, that hath the sovereignty, and whose actions are avouched by them all, and performed by the strength of them all, in him united'* (Hobbes 1996: 109; emphasis added).

At the same time, Hobbes asserts that all of humanity (or at least those portions of humanity that in his estimation have done so) do not act as one 'multitude of men.' Rather, we belong to 'multitudes of men' who all act in the same way. As a result, we end up with a number of sovereigns, each authorized to govern only by that multitude of men who gave rise to its shape: hence the modern state system, consisting of individual states with borders between them.

What, then, is the relationship between states? Hobbes suggests that, because there is no sovereign authority to enforce agreements, it reverts to the kind of relations that prevail in the state of nature: 'In all times kings and persons of sovereign authority, because of their independency, are in continual jealousies, and in the state and posture of gladiators, having their weapons pointing, and their eyes fixed on one another; that is, their forts, garrisons, and guns upon the frontiers of their kingdoms, and continual spies upon their neighbours, which is a posture of war'[3] (Hobbes 1996: 79).

But Hobbes's views on this matter are somewhat extreme. There are states, such as the members of the British Commonwealth (and especially the European Settler states of Australia, Canada, and New Zealand), that do not have a 'posture of war' towards one another. The basic point, though, remains: the modern state system requires every state to have a border to separate it from another state, no matter how close is the relationship between them. Robert Frost says, 'Good fences make good neighbours,' and the Commonwealth to which Canada belongs takes exactly that approach. In other words, in the system we have constructed, the only people we can trust sufficiently to live together with in perpetuity are those with whom we share a sovereign, or, as political theorist R.B.J. Walker puts it, the modern state system acts to separate 'ethical community inside and contingent power outside' (Walker 1993: 71).

Leviathan clearly demonstrates that the nation-to-nation relationship as proposed by our partners simply cannot exist, for to live as two nations requires that we draw a border between us: to share the land, we must first divide it. Hence, even if we take Kiotseaeton at his word and concede that the linking principle exists, it is only secondary to sovereignty, because it does not become effective until sovereignty has determined the 'ethical community' within which it will apply. In short, to have any kind of relationship between nations necessitates a border between them; and that we do not have. In sum, in the world we have created, the nation-to-nation relationship proposed by our partners is a logical impossibility. And that, *Leviathan* would have us believe, is the inevitable result of Hobbes's argument that, in the absence of a sovereign to enforce agreements, people cannot be counted on to keep their word.

Kiotseaeton's Response

As I have come to see it, Kiotseaeton responded (although of course not directly) to this apparent conundrum at the 1645 treaty with these words at his departure: 'Adieu my brothers; I am one of your relatives' (Williams 1997: 53). While we might be inclined to read the words 'brother' and 'relatives' as loose metaphors, perhaps to the point of being mere figures of speech, it has become clear to me that they are not, at least when I think the implications through. In particular, as I see it, Kiotseaeton's use of the words 'brother' and 'relative' to describe the relationship is an indication that the treaty has transformed nations that were once apart from one another into close kin who are joined together no matter where they live. Or to put it this way, by becoming family members, all have become members of the same ethical community, that is, the community within which promises are kept.

What, then, does this change in status mean? One possibility is that, by linking arms together, we all became brothers in one family, thereby turning us into a 'single ethical community' under the authority of a single sovereign. However, it is clear this did not transpire. The expanded ethical community results, not from a merger of all nations into one, but rather through the link established between them, for Kiotseaeton says that 'I am (now) one of your relatives,' not that we have now become one. That is, the nations remain distinct 'multitudes of men.' Yet that seems to make no sense. After all, to our way of thinking, to be a 'brother' or a 'sister' is to be a member of the same nuclear family.[4]

Fortunately, our partners have also given us help in taking the brother relationship one step further. Here is one way the relationship is described in two of the Confederation-era treaties through which we gained permission to dwell permanently on Indigenous lands. In the negotiation of Treaty 4, Elder Musqua (as mentioned above) used the following expression to describe the relationship we established: 'The Queen adopted us as children' (Cardinal and Hildebrandt 2000:

34). Taken alone, this appears to reflect the idea that we all became members of one family: ours. But then Harold Johnson describes relations established in Treaty 6 this way: 'When your family came here and asked to live with us on this territory we agreed. We adopted you in a ceremony that your family and mine call treaty. In Cree law, the treaties were adoptions of one nation by another. At Treaty No. 6 the Cree adopted the Queen and her children. We became relatives' (Johnson 2007: 13). Here, it seems that, in contrast to the formula of Elder Musqua, it is we who joined their family. But, in fact, what makes sense is to join the two adoptions together. At the moment the treaty relationship was established, we became, in a manner of speaking, adopted members of their family and they became adopted members of ours. This means that we each became equal members of two families – one by birth and the other by adoption – and thus the ethical community is expanded to include us all without merging us together in one.

  In the way I understand it, then, we would be wrong to imagine that treaties result in all of us joining one of the pre-existing families: theirs, if we concede that they never ceded sovereignty to us; or ours, if we assert that sovereignty was transferred to us at that time. The relationship is more nuanced than that. What it means is that each of us is now a member of both families and share a responsibility to sustain them both. Furthermore, as we are now 'brothers' in both families, the two nations can establish a nation-to-nation relationship without first requiring a border between them. That, then, is how I am coming to understand more fully what Harold Johnson means when he says to us that through treaty 'we became relatives,' and what Kiotseaeton meant when he said over three and a half centuries ago that through treaty 'I am one of your relatives.'

On Linking as a Principle

There still is this concern to address. We know treaties do not always last. Indeed, the 1648 Peace of Westphalia itself did not long survive. It thus appears that, despite Kiotseaeton's elegant reassurances, Hobbes's admonition that 'covenants being but words, and breath, have no force to oblige, contain, constrain, or protect any man' remains: no sovereign, no peace. But this does a disservice to Kiotseaeton. To have sovereignty over a territory in the modern state system far from guarantees it in perpetuity. States come and go and their boundaries may shift from time to time. To take but two examples from the last century: we do not question the salience of sovereignty merely because the borders of Germany have shifted several times or because the state that was once Yugoslavia has now disappeared. For us, sovereignty is foundational to our way of organizing political relations. In that sense, it is the central tenet of the paradigm[5] that provides the lens through which we make sense of events in the world. It is not disconfirmed even though we know from experience that its application does not ensure the stability that people once thought the Peace of Westphalia would inevitably bring. Sovereignty is a principle and in that sense stands above (as does the sovereign) what it interprets.

I am suggesting that the linking principle can also be understood as a foundational element in a paradigm. As I see it, when Kiotseaeton says, 'Here is the knot that binds us inseparably; nothing can part us ... Even if the lightning were to fall upon us, it could not separate us,' he is describing linking as a principle. In that sense, just as the Peace of Westphalia is an exemplification of the sovereignty principle, so is the Treaty of 1645 an example of the linking principle. And, as with the former, implementing it is understood to be an aspirational goal, perhaps even an expectation, but, as with the existence of Yugoslavia, not a certainty. What is certain, I believe, is that, rather than sovereignty, it is the linking principle that joins peoples and provides the foundation for the relationship that follows from it.

Living as I do within a paradigm in which sovereignty is fundamental, I have found it difficult to accept the possibility that the linking principle alone can ever have sufficient force to hold us together in perpetuity; and I imagine that others share this sensibility. That is, somewhere deep down, I fear that Hobbes's myth touches a fundamental truth: without a power to enforce it, no agreement will stand the test of time. Therefore, if we are to be here to stay, our only security lies in ensuring that we have sovereignty and jurisdiction over our own territory, even if to do so means to take it from others.

My challenge, which is shared by many, is to find a way to counter such a worry. In this regard, the most popular solution, at least since the time of Herder (Bernard 1965), has been to use 'culture' as a substitute for the 'sovereign' with respect to peoples without states. Like sovereignty, each 'culture' imposes a set of rules on a specific 'multitude of men' that provides the force necessary for them to keep agreements among themselves, or as Emile Durkheim put, it, their enforcement is governed by the 'collective consciousness'[6] of its members. However, while this addresses how an ethical community can be established in the absence of a ruler, it in fact only intensifies the problem of contract enforcement between communities. That is, now agreements between 'multitudes of men' are not to be trusted, not because they have different leaders, but because they do not share a common culture.

In my experience the only Western scholar who offers an effective counter to *Leviathan* on this matter in its own terms is anthropologist Claude Lévi-Strauss.[7] His argument demonstrates that at least certain agreements between 'multitudes of men' will be kept faithfully even under the conditions Hobbes posits as existing in the state of nature. His position is laid out in detail in his seminal work on the origin and development of human society, entitled *The Elementary Structures of Kinship*, to which I turn briefly now.

Lévi-Strauss's Response to Hobbes and the Linking Principle

In fine (translating his argument into the terms of this discussion), Lévi-Strauss suggests that there is much insight to be gained in understanding the linking principle if we liken the relationship it establishes to a marriage.[8] And at a superficial level at least, this appears to hold, for, like a marriage, a treaty relationship is primary and intended to grow over time. However, like Kiotseaeton, Lévi-Strauss is not casting a loose metaphor. To explain how his account counters Hobbes's depiction of the status of agreements in the state of nature, I will now discuss it from a sociological point of view.

Although, in its popular representation, the state of nature is peopled by undifferentiated individuals (often imagined to be single, adult males), the fact is that *Leviathan* does not depict it in that way. Rather, as Philip Abbott (1981) has pointed out, people live in families. While Hobbes uses the term in many different ways, even including manifestations that are akin to small cities, in his most consistent rendering, the family in the state of nature is the 'nuclear family,'[9] that is, one composed of a couple and their children,[10] so that for him the minimum number is three: a father, a mother, and a child (Hobbes 1996: 126). Relations between family members are governed with (normatively speaking) the father as sovereign and the child as subject.[11] In fact, it would be fair to conclude that the 'multitudes of men' who make the social contracts that give rise to states are acting in their capacity as fathers of families, and not as individuals (Schochet 1967: 441). Hobbes also indicates that the relationship between the parents is stable, for it is based on an agreement that can be enforced. Finally (a point to which I will return below), while this is unstated, there can be no doubt that Hobbes takes the view that marriages are monogamous. Thus, as Abbott points out, 'the family is already a well-established social unit in the state of nature' (Abbott 1981: 251), one that provides a rule-governed, reasonably coherent institutional setting within which to live and raise children in relative safety. To return to Walker's terminology, in the state of nature an ethical community is limited to the members of one (nuclear) family.

The conditions Hobbes ascribes to the state of nature, then, apply not to relations within families but to relations between them. That is, as Abbott observes, the description 'warre of every man against every man in the state of nature' amounts to a 'warre of every father against every father' (Abbott 1981: 251); or, as I would put it, 'the war of Family against Family.' It is a point that Hobbes phrases this way: 'Where there is no Commonwealth, there is, as hath been already shown, a perpetual war of every man against his neighbour; and therefore everything is his that getteth it and keepeth it by force; which is neither propriety nor community, but uncertainty' (Hobbes 1996: 152).

The problem that gives rise to the Commonwealth is that families (or fathers) are unable to come to agreements among themselves without a sovereign to enforce them. In that sense, as Schochet points out, the family is the state in miniature so that all the social contract does is extend the mechanism that governs within families to relations between them (Schochet 1967). That is, while it is possible to imagine (if one does not take an extreme view of Hobbes) that families might form temporary alliances, it is sovereignty in the image of a family as a discrete unit that endures. The linking principle, then, must be secondary to it.

It is on this point that Lévi-Strauss intervenes. In effect, what he seeks to demonstrate is that, while Hobbes's contention may hold if one looks at relations between families with regard to almost every conceivable circumstance, there is one, core to the human condition, in which reason dictates that it will not. That condition is reproduction, and it is in the requirement to form marriages[12] for that purpose that Lévi-Strauss finds an agreement that is self-enforcing. Here is how.

As just discussed, for Hobbes, a marriage is a contractual agreement made between a man and a woman for the purpose of conceiving and raising children. However, he does not reflect on the process through which couples are formed (or the means by which partners find one another). In fact, as far as I can determine, he mentions it only in this passage: 'For the savage people in many places of America, except the government of small families, the concord whereof *dependeth on natural lust*, have no government at all, and live at this day in that brutish manner, as I said before' (Hobbes 1996: 89; emphasis added). In other words, Hobbes is suggesting that the sex drive alone is sufficient to organize individuals into couples. This might make sense at first blush, for he also posits that marriage is monogamous. Therefore, unlike other 'resources,' there is no scarcity in supply since, presumably, humanity comprises an equal number of males and females.

Yet, even if we accept his exception to the rule of scarcity, this reading elides a fundamental problem in distribution: in the state of nature there exists between families 'a perpetual war of every man against his neighbour; and therefore everything is his that getteth it and keepeth it by force; which is neither propriety nor community, but uncertainty.' Hence we are left with an image in which families are constantly raiding other families both to acquire partners and to retrieve those members of one's own family that others have taken, conditions that make it highly unlikely that families could have the stability Hobbes ascribes to them. Given this constraint, it becomes hard to imagine how we could find and keep marriage partners if we drew them from outside our own family, much less have the stability to raise families. The only secure place, in that scenario, to find a marriage partner would be from within one's own family. And here, speaking logically, the problem is that it is far from certain that a family as Hobbes describes it will include the personnel required. In short, relying on the sex drive alone would place the very survival of the human race into perpetual doubt.

The rational solution is to expand the pool of marriage partners to include those who belong to other families, but Hobbes offers us no way to get there in the state of nature. It is true that introducing the concept of culture would have that effect. However, this requires the arbitrary imposition of a concept into Hobbes's model that he does not include, for *Leviathan* does not assume that in the state of nature human beings belong to different cultural communities. In fact, to have done so would have undermined his argument on the necessity of a sovereign in its entirety.

In contrast, Lévi-Strauss offers a way out from within the very conditions that Hobbes imposes on the state of nature. What he argues is that, from a logical point of view, the issue can be resolved once a family is sufficiently secure that members of other families will honour marriage contracts made with it.[13] The way this is accomplished (which in Lévi-Strauss's mind is so fundamental that it arises at the moment when human beings achieve the level of consciousness that permits us to form societies) is by having each family voluntarily relinquish in perpetuity his or her right to choose a marriage partner from among the members of his family to all other families. The method by which this is accomplished is the incest taboo. As a result, marriage is governed by what Lévi-Strauss calls the 'rule of exogamy.' This means that families understand from the outset that they must cooperate with other families to survive; as Lévi-Strauss says, it generates the understanding that 'the biological family is no longer alone ... it must ally itself with other families in order to endure' (Lévi-Strauss 1969: 485). And this, as Abbott sagely observes, opens up the possibility of a state of nature in which, at minimum, 'family warfare is likely to have been muted by growing networks of kinship ties' (Abbott 1981: 251).

In short, Lévi-Strauss offers us a way to conceptualize the formative role that the linking principle plays from within Hobbes's characterization of the state of nature in at least two ways; first, by showing us that, even as Hobbes describes it, making connections between families is essential to our survival; and second, by demonstrating that, at a global level, there is a contract (the rule of exogamy) that is so fundamental to the self-interest of family members that it will be honoured by all, despite Hobbes's contention that 'covenants being but words, and breath, have no force to oblige, contain, constrain, or protect any man.'

Linking and Our Treaties

How, then, does linking as a principle help us to better understand that the treaty relationship we established here is an enduring one? To illuminate this matter, Lévi-Strauss's reflections on the role of marriage in linking families together have again been most helpful. Let me share an insight in this regard. I think it fair to conceive of treaties between Indigenous peoples and ourselves collectively (figuratively, of course) as something comparable to a marriage between two families. That is, a treaty links two collectivities just as a marriage joins two families together. Furthermore, as with our treaties, this marriage joins together two families that are living together on lands that originally belonged to one of them.

What, then, following the principles Lévi-Strauss describes, would be the nature of the relationship between the families? This is a matter that Lévi-Strauss discusses with reference to societies in the world today, which he calls 'Dual Organizations' (Lévi-Strauss 1969: 69–83).

First, the two cannot assimilate into one family notwithstanding where they are living, for the rule of exogamy requires that each marries into a different family (albeit in a form of marriage that is unfamiliar to most of us),[14] and in this circumstance that means only members of the other family. To survive, then, the two families would have to join together and yet remain distinct.[15] Thus, as in the Two Row example, they are together, yet separate, wherever they are on the river. Furthermore, even though one partner has sovereignty (to use our language), they are equal nations in that each remains autonomous and yet requires the other to survive.

This helps me to envision what is meant by the understanding that treaties provide 'the knot that binds us inseparably' as well as Harold Johnson's promise that 'I will never suggest that you go back where you came from, for I assure you *Kiciwamanawak* [cousin] that you have a treaty right to be here' (Johnson 2007: 14).

As well, this image helps me to better comprehend the relationship to land described as *witaskewin* or 'sharing the land together.' That is, under these circumstances the goal of the treaty relationship would not be to share the land by cutting it into 'parts' but, as the *Oxford English Dictionary* puts it, to share it in the sense of 'to participate in ... to perform, enjoy, or suffer in common with others.' Thus, in this context borders are drawn not to separate nations but to differentiate areas. As Elder Musqua says: '[The boundaries of] these lands were always laid out before these peoples ... That's how they set out things between one another. They understood the means by which land was used' (Cardinal and Hildebrandt 2000: 39).

That, then, is how Lévi-Strauss's reflections on the principle of linking have guided my thinking as I have sought to comprehend one aspect of the complex set of relations that has often been termed the nation-to-nation relationship.

Building a House Together

But there is a relevant aspect of the relationship that I find Lévi-Strauss's approach does not address. While the relationship between marriage partners is supposed to strengthen over time, in his discussion it remains static. The key insight that has led me to this view comes from words I heard spoken at a gathering of Dene and Métis leadership in Yellowknife in April 1990.[16] The leaders had assembled to discuss strategy for a meeting with the minister of Indian affairs and northern development to be held the following day.[17]

At this gathering, some leaders expressed their views regarding the results of a decade of negotiations with the federal government under the Comprehensive Claims Policy. In particular, while they had reached agreement in principle on a number of matters, there had been little progress in following through on what they understood to be a shared understanding that the principal objective of negotiations was to implement the political relationship proposed in the Dene Declaration, notwithstanding that the government policy expressly placed such matters outside its terms of reference. At one point, a leader (as I recall, it was George Kurszewski) chose to describe the situation in these words (which I can only paraphrase): 'We want to build a house with the White Man. The treaty is our foundation. The comprehensive claim was to be one of the walls. But all the government wants to do is destroy our house and remake us in their image.'

What struck me then and has remained with me ever since is the clarity with which these words express the option before us all. When we begin with the sovereignty paradigm, we imagine that living together means forcing us all into one house with a pre-configured shape. However, this statement made it clear that the alternative is not just for us to work together to ensure that both families thrive, although that is certainly necessary. It is also to build a house in which we both can live, the shape of which cannot be predetermined because it is the consequence of the steps we take in building it.[18]

But there is this caveat to add. We are not starting as though we all arrived at the same place at the same time. The families we are joining have been building houses here for a long, long time. As a result, as Leanne Simpson points out, they have already developed protocols through links they have established with others, including 'animal nations,' which provide a way of ensuring that human beings live in balance with the natural world, their family, their clan, their nation, and beyond. As new participants, then, it is our responsibility to take particular care in contributing to building lest we inadvertently damage the houses already here, for, whether or not we claim sovereignty, we have much to learn from Indigenous peoples about how to live on these lands, despite our predisposition to believe the opposite.

Conclusion

This chapter offers my best efforts to describe the nation-to-nation relationship between Indigenous peoples and Settlers. In that pursuit, I have touched on some central themes in Western political thought and ventured an interpretation of certain Indigenous political ideas that I have formulated through listening to our partners. I hope that I have not done violence to either, or have written so obscurely that I have helped clarify nothing. Still, I take comfort in Harold Johnson's observation that, when it comes to understanding the meaning of 'all my relations,' one can never know it all, even after spending a lifetime reflecting on it.

But what I can say with certainty is this. The way we make sense of political relations is so deeply ingrained in us that it would be very hard to embark on a different way were we at the beginning and prepared to approach the nation-to-nation relationship we have been offered with the utmost goodwill and a complete openness to learn from our partners. Furthermore, we are not now at the beginning (and in fact never could be). We are almost 150 years after Confederation and, as I said at the opening of chapter 6, there is Canada, there are provinces, there has been mass migration, we have already visited much harm on our partners, and our failures to implement in full even those promises written into the treaty text are manifest.

The question, then, is whether there is now a way forward even if we approached the matter with openness and goodwill. That is the topic I will address in the next chapter.

Chapter Eight

Spirit and Intent

Our people have always understood that we must be able to continue to live our lives in accordance with our culture and spirituality. Our elders have taught us that this spirit and intent of our treaty relationship must last as long as the rivers flow and the sun shines. We must wait however long it takes for non-Aboriginal people to understand and respect our way of life. This will be the respect that the treaty relationship between us calls for.

(Josephine Sandy, qtd. in RCAP 1996: II, ch. 2, pt. 3)

Introduction

I am thankful for Ms Sandy's forbearance. But, frankly, our partners do not need to wait any longer. It is long past time for us to act in good faith and begin building 'one of the walls' of the house of which George Kurszewski speaks. At the end of this chapter I will make a simple proposal: it is to fulfil the obligations we made in the numbered treaties, and to extend the same offer to all other Indigenous communities. But, first, I need to describe in more detail what I understand of the relationship between Settlers and Indigenous peoples established through treaties based on the linking principle.

On the Ethnie

In our understanding, as exemplified in Hobbes, each portion of humanity parcels itself into what R.B.J. Walker elegantly terms 'a spatial-cum-institutional container,' which holds 'the cultural and ethnic aspirations of a people' (Walker 1991: 450). In the political science tradition, the contents of these containers are seen to be of two kinds. There is a fundamental form that we often refer to as 'a culture' or 'an ethnic nation' (or a 'tribe'). A better descriptor in my view is 'ethnie,' a term Anthony E. Smith coined to identify those who share a collective name, a common myth of descent, a distinctive culture, an association with a specific territory, and a sense of solidarity, thereby endowing themselves 'with a definite identity, both in their own eyes and in those of outsiders' (Smith 1986: 22–9); and we imagine that each of us is associated with at least one. The second kind, political scientists call 'the civic nation,' which is conceived of as a community of equal, rights-bearing citizens adhering to common liberal and democratic values (Ipperciel and Woo 2009: 160). However, the civic nation does not replace the ethnic nation. Rather, it provides a container in the form of a state that enables more than one ethnie to co-exist in the same 'territory.' At the same time, we recognize that bringing two or more ethnies together in this way inevitably leads to 'problems of internal cohesion' (Nagata 2001: 11515–16) that may be 'accommodated' but not resolved. Thus, in this formulation, the 'ethnie' is the foundational form for it is the only one that we see as unproblematic (a point that is further underscored by the attention currently being paid to the presumed decimation of ethnies, as well as civic nations, through the processes of 'globalization').

Therefore, it would follow that our partners think in the same terms, especially since they are not living in states. Members of the ethnie we call 'Cree' would prefer to live among other 'Cree' in a 'Cree' territory and so on. If this is truly the case, then the previous chapter has taken us on a long detour, for all it has shown is that 'linking arms together' is a wonderful image of how we can join together that may work in a mythological world constructed by social-contract theorists but has no applicability to what we actually do.

But the fact is that this is not so. What follows is a brief account of how our partners lived at the time we negotiated the first numbered treaties. Because I believe it is the clearest way for me to convey this perspective, what follows will be based on findings of Western-trained academics in ethnohistory and anthropology. And because I have already referred to Treaty 4 and will be discussing Treaty 6, I will focus on the region covered by these treaties. The discussion will show that ethnie identity was not foundational in determining where people chose to live.

On Indigenous Political Relations in Treaties 4 and 6 in the 1870s

Conforming to our understandings, in our casual descriptions of it, the region covered by Treaties 4 and 6 is deemed to be the domain of an ethnie named 'The Cree.' This territory is vast, ranging from just west of Lake Winnipegosis in the east to the Rocky Mountains north of Red Deer, Alberta, in the west, south along the border near Weyburn, Saskatchewan, and north virtually to Lesser Slave Lake, Alberta. Within this territory, it is imagined that Cree lived principally with other Cree. Thus, regionally and locally, the ethnie was foundational. However, given their small population, there were no strictly demarcated borders, so that, on occasion, even their adversaries – as were the Blackfoot as time went on – might venture within (Milloy 1988).[1]

But this version does not take into account the well-reported fact that the region was home to two other ethnies – the Assiniboine or Stoney and the Plains Ojibwa (or Saulteaux) – and that these communities were 'interconnected' (qtd. in Sharrock 1974: 102), with members living in 'close contact' with one another for generations (Jenness 1932; Albers 2001). As Patricia Albers puts it, 'throughout much of the eighteenth and nineteenth centuries, these populations jointly occupied a large area of territory'[2] (Albers 1996: 91). The work of experts on the 'Plains Cree' (Darnell 2001), the 'Plains Ojibwa' (Albers 2001), and the Assiniboine (DeMallie and Miller 2010) makes clear that, long before treaties were negotiated, members of different ethnies were already living amongst one another in the same region.

Furthermore, relying on such sources as 'the journals, letters and reports of the missionaries, explorers, traders, and government officials who live among, observed, and wrote about [the people living in this region]' (Sharrock 1974: 103), ethnohistorians Susan Sharrock and Patricia Albers have shown conclusively that ethnie affiliation did not always determine with whom people lived.[3] While there were residential communities composed exclusively of Cree or Assiniboine or Ojibwa, a traveller could very easily come across members of different 'ethnies' living together in the same community: some containing Cree and Assiniboine, others Cree and Ojibwa, or the three together,[4] and still others that also included members of other ethnies.[5] To take one example of the latter, Albers describes a mid-nineteenth-century community in the future province of Saskatchewan that 'was predominantly Cree but mixed with Assiniboine and Ojibwa' and 'was led by a Crow-Hidatsa known as Sweet Medicine' (Albers 1996: 113).

Susan Sharrock also identifies three principal forms these 'multi-ethnie' communities took. Two of these overlap to some extent with the notion that 'ethnie' is foundational. The first, 'The Alliance Form' (which Albers calls the *polyethnic alliance formation*), consists of communities that are 'allied and bilingual' (Sharrock 1974: 103) but often 're-tain some level of residential and ethnic distinctiveness' (Albers 1996: 93). This leaves the impression that, while they may work and some-times assemble together, in their daily lives members of each ethnie reside in separate communities. The other, which Sharrock labels 'The Fused Ethnicity Form,' is described by Albers this way: 'Groups that were once distinct are now joined. Indeed, they become so intermin-gled that they are virtually indistinguishable from each other in a cul-tural and social sense. In the process, they not only form a political entity that is separate from their parent populations, but they also as-sume an ethnic identification that is distinctive as well' (ibid.).

The only example of this form familiar to most of us is the combina-tion of Plains Cree and French-speaking Settlers that the *Handbook of North American Indians* refers to as 'The Plains Métis.' Here, the parties developed a new language form 'based on Plains Cree and Canadian French with a distinctive Saulteaux or Ojibwa element' (Payment 2001: 661). But two other forms are mentioned in the literature: Cree-Assiniboine (who are sometimes referred to as 'The Young Dogs' [Sharrock 1994: 111]); and the 'Oji-Cree,' which represents a 'fusion' of Cree and Ojibwa (Relland 1998: 147–8).[6]

The third form, identified by Sharrock as 'The Intermarriage and Polyethnic Coresidence Form,' is quite different from what one might expect: 'Members of two ethnic units form polyethnic families and / or polyethnic coresidence units' (Sharrock 1974: 106). That is, here mem-bers of at least two ethnies are living together in the same community and speaking one another's language. What is more interesting is that people identified as 'Assiniboine' and 'Cree' commonly formed such communities even though the two languages are as dissimilar from one another as are English and Swahili. As Albers reports, in the Qu'Appelle region (where Treaty 4 was negotiated), Cree and Assiniboine were 'so intermixed that it was impossible to distinguish them. Local residence groups were bilingual and bicultural, and they held dual ethnic affilia-tions as well' (Albers 1996: 101).

But this does not exhaust the possibilities. The fact is that there were residential communities composed of what might be termed 'combina-tions of combinations,' such as, for example, Young Dogs with Métis,

Cree, and Ojibwa, or even combinations of ethnies we presume not to be associated with this 'territory,' such as the one led by Sweet Medicine mentioned above.

In fact, at least some of the communities with which we negotiated Treaty 4 included such a varied membership. Here are three examples:

- a community led by Kaneonuskatew (One That Walks on Four Claws or Gordon Gibson – Ka-ne-on-us-ka-tew in Morris's orthography) [(Morris 1880: 330)] that 'consisted of forty-seven families [approximately 375 individuals[7]] of Plains Cree, Swampy Cree,[8] Sauteaux, Scottish mixed-blood, and Métis' (Carter 1990: 46).
- a community led by Keeskee hew mus coo musqus (Little Black Bear – Kus-kee-tew-mus-coo-mus-qua in Morris's orthography [Morris 1880: 330]) that included Assiniboine, Saulteaux, Young Dogs, Dakota, and Calling River Cree (ibid.: 48); and
- a community led by Chief Cowessess and 'comprising five major groups – the Plains Cree, Saulteaux, Assiniboine, Métis, and English half-breeds, although individuals from other cultural groups were also part of the band.'[9] (Innes 2012: 123)

As Albers says:

The historic situation of the Plains Assiniboin, Cree and Ojibwa did not conform to the typical tribal models where territories were divided, claimed and defended by discrete ethnic groups, nor did it fit descriptions in which political allegiances were defined primarily in exclusive ethnic terms. Ethnicity in the generic and highly abstract sense of a 'tribal name' [i.e., 'ethnie'] did not always function as a marker of geopolitical boundaries. Given the pluralistic pattern of land use and alliance making, most of their ethnic categories did not have a high level of salience or any a priori power to organize and distribute people across geographical space.[10] (Albers 1996: 91)

The evidence, in short, clearly shows that in the region of Treaties 4 and 6 (and elsewhere) our partners were living at the regional level in the kind of multi-ethnie container we associate with the state, and at the local level in the kind we associate with the city. Yet there apparently was none of the friction we normally associate with people living together in multi-ethnie communities, even though there was no common sovereign or ethnie to bind them together.

Implications for Treaty Implementation

This finding confirms that, in this way of organizing communities and relations between them, ethnie affiliation is one of the attributes that, like one's abilities (or disabilities), one brings to building a community but does not determine either its shape or its contents. But in its absence what determines them? For that, the best answer I can give is that there may well be none. What seems to count is not an attribute held in common but a commitment by individuals who, for a myriad reasons, decide to link together – a finding that seems to confirm the applicability of the linking principle in the real world. One can readily imagine that our partners anticipated that we would adhere to the same principles; that is, we would not try to incorporate our partners into an 'institutional-cum-territorial' container of our making but would rather link arms with them to shape a container in which we could all live comfortably.

Looked at in this light, the treaties express our mutual commitment to that understanding. For many reasons, we decided to be here to stay in perpetuity. To that end, we negotiated treaties through which we gained permission to do so by linking with those already here to stay. As our partners often say, a treaty is a covenant, for, as with those made with the Creator, it binds us to 'an agreement that will survive forever' (Arnot 2010: 2). The provisions written into the treaties, then, represent some of the attributes we are bringing to the relationship. To fulfil them is to build on the foundation the treaties established. In that regard, they are a tangible expression of a much larger undertaking to contribute to the relationship that our partners often refer to with the phrase 'spirit and intent.' To honour the treaties is not merely to discharge an obligation. It is a step towards building a house together.

Because treaty implementation is an enduring process, it is impossible to ensure that all of us will get every step right every time. In fact, there may be times when one of the parties deliberately takes the wrong step. As a result, there may occasionally be frictions and tensions between us, as is inevitable in any enduring relationship. For this reason, if I understand correctly the Haudenosaunee explanation, there will be moments when it is necessary to 'polish the Covenant Chain' (Hill 2010: 21) and to apologize, as when Taminy Buck, a Shawnee chief, did when he asked for 'forgiveness for breaches of his tribe's treaty with the colony' at a treaty conference with Pennsylvania officials held in 1748 (Henderson 2007: 112). Since we are mortal, but treaties last forever, it

also means that, as Stumpee pointed out to Georgia's colonial authorities at a 1757 conference at Savannah, reminding ourselves of our commitments is essential for we need to be 'sensible that these treaties are
binding not only upon those who signed them but upon our whole
people and their posterity. Yet it would be well that that are renewed
and confirmed in our days, that the young men may be witnesses to
them and transmit a knowledge of them to their children' (ibid.).

As I have come to see it, whether we get it right or wrong at any particular moment, to act in accord with 'spirit and intent' is to act with
'kindness'[11] towards our partners, by which I mean 'having a gentle,
sympathetic, or benevolent nature; ready to assist, or show consideration for, others.'[12] I have chosen the term 'kindness' for two reasons.
First, Kanooses uses it in Treaty 4 when he enquires as to Morris's intent
by asking: 'Is it true you are bringing the Queen's kindness? Is it true
you are bringing the Queen's messenger's kindness? Is it true you are
going to give the different bands the Queen's kindness?'[13] Second, Dene
children in Wrigley (where I lived in 1969–70) use the same word when
speaking English to describe proper comportment.[14] Let me add that, in
my understanding, acting with 'kindness' does not mean giving anyone anything that they request for sometimes that may be unkind.
Kindness requires judgment, which means the intent to respond proportionately to the perceived needs of the other.[15]

So I am suggesting that, had we fulfilled our commitments when the
treaties were negotiated, we would by now have come some way in
building the relationship. But that is not what we did. In fact, we not
only did not act in accord with the spirit and intent of the treaties, we
did not even fulfil the promises as we had written them down in good
faith. Let me illustrate with two examples.

Implementing Our Commitments – Provisioning Seed and Tools

All of the numbered treaties, except for 9, contain clauses or undertak-
ings similar to this provision in Treaty 4:

> It is further agreed between Her Majesty and the said Indians that the fol-
> lowing articles shall be supplied to any band thereof who are now actually
> cultivating the soil, or who shall hereafter settle on their reserves and com-
> mence to break up the land, that is to say: two hoes, one spade, one scythe
> and one axe for every family so actually cultivating, and enough seed

wheat, barley, oats and potatoes to plant such land as they have broken up; also one plough and two harrows for every ten families so cultivating as aforesaid, and also to each Chief for the use of his band as aforesaid, one yoke of oxen, one bull, four cows, a chest of ordinary carpenter's tools, five hand saws, five augers, one cross-cut saw, one pit-saw, the necessary files and one grindstone, all the aforesaid articles to be given, once for all, for the encouragement of the practice of agriculture among the Indians.[16] (Treaty 4 1966)

What is the 'spirit and intent' of this clause? Is it to provide these specific items and nothing else or is it promised with an underlying objective in mind? The transcripts are unambiguous on this point: it is the latter. Here is how Commissioner Morris explained it during Treaty 4 negotiations:

What the Queen and her Councillors would like is this, she would like you to learn something of the cunning of the white man. When fish are scarce and the buffalo are not plentiful she would like to help you to put something in the land; she would like that you should have some money every year to buy things that you need. If any of you would settle down, she would give you cattle to help you; she would give you some seed to plant. She would like to give you every year, for twenty years, some powder, shot, and twine to make nets of. I see you here before me today. I will pass away and you will pass away. I will go where my fathers have gone and you also, but after me and after you will come our children. The Queen cares for you and for your children, and she cares for the children that are yet to be born. She would like to take you by the hand. (Morris 1880: 92)

In making this promise, Morris was responding to a request made by our partners. As Chief Sweet Grass put it in a letter he wrote in anticipation of Treaty 6 negotiations in 1871: 'We want cattle, tools, agricultural implements, and assistance in everything when we come to settle' (Morris 1880: 171). The provisions represent a response to the request; and that there is an expectation that other provisions might be provided should these prove insufficient is confirmed in the following: 'I said you would get seed: you need not concern yourselves so much about what your grandchildren are gong to eat; your children will be taught, and then they will be as well able to take care of themselves as the whites around them' (ibid.: 213). The expectation on both sides was that we would act 'to ensure that First Nations continued to have the means of livelihood, in return for agreeing to share the use of their territory with Euro-Canadian newcomers' (Ray, Miller, and Tough 2002: 188).

This does not mean that we had a complete meeting of the minds, for Morris's position was clearly infused with an evolutionary logic in conformity with which he expected that our partners would voluntarily adopt our way of life as they came to understand that it was better than their own. At the same time, there is no doubt that our partners did not share this view. However, Morris also anticipated this difference for he said: 'Understand me, I do not want to interfere with your hunting and fishing. I want you to pursue it through the country, as you have heretofore done; but I would like your children to be able to find food for themselves and their children that come after them. Sometimes when you go to hunt you can leave your wives and children at home to take care of your gardens' (Morris 1880: 204).

While there was no meeting of minds on this point, Morris made it clear that we were approaching the matter with 'kindness' and would be prepared to revise our position should our assumptions prove wrong. Similarly, our partners, who were concerned about the increasing scarcity of resources that sustained them, were willing to take up agriculture to see the extent to which it might provide a solution. While there is no evidence that our partners were fully invested in the future Morris laid out, they did recognize that their current way of making a living was under great stress and at least some of them were prepared to increase their reliance on agriculture as a response to these conditions. Therefore, there was a sufficient degree of mutual understanding to implement the provision regarding seed and tools, notwithstanding that our partners may not have agreed with our underlying reasons for making this commitment. There is every possibility that there would have been a positive outcome had we chosen to implement the promise in the spirit and intent with which it was negotiated. But that is not what we did.

For a number of reasons, not the least of which was the rapid demise of the buffalo that our partners feared, many of them quickly made the decision to take advantage of this clause in Treaty 4 and begin cultivation. And, of course, they had every reason to expect that, as it was a goal we shared and a provision we had proposed, our government would implement its commitment quickly and in full. However, we did not respond in that way. Instead, our government read this clause so closely that we would provide what was promised only to those few communities *already* living on reserves. When it came to the others, government did not see fit even to begin consultations regarding the selection of reserve sites for four years (Carter 1990: 58). It acted in the same way when it came to those living on reserves. It refused to provide ploughs and harrows to the community of Day Star, which by 1877 was already living on a reserve and working the land, because 'there were [not] as yet ten families cultivating as stipulated in the treaty' (ibid.: 67). Furthermore, government routinely provided seed too late for planting (ibid.: 65) or provided grain of such poor quality that it proved useless (ibid.: 65, 96); and until 1882, when it finally decided that no Canadian-made plough would work on the prairies, the ones provided had to be discarded (ibid.: 95).

Given the circumstances, government actions led to widespread hunger and even starvation. So the question is: How did government respond when our commitment 'to put something in the land' when 'fish are scarce and the buffalo are not plentiful' was not fulfilled?

Implementing Our Commitments – Disaster Relief

Our commitment to look after our partners in times of privation is certainly implicit in the treaties, as when, in Treaty 4, the commissioner said: 'The Queen cares for you.' Moreover, it is made explicit in the following clause in written into Treaty 6: 'That in the event hereafter of the Indians comprised within this treaty being overtaken by any pestilence, or by a general famine, the Queen, on being satisfied and certified thereof by Her Indian Agent or Agents, will grant to the Indians assistance of such character and to such extent as Her Chief Superintendent of Indian Affairs shall deem necessary and sufficient to relieve the Indians from the calamity that shall have befallen them' (Treaty 6 1964: 4).

A request to include such a clause was made as early as 1871 in the letter to which I referred above, when Chief Sweet Grass asked that government 'make provision for us against years of starvation, we have had great starvation this past winter, and the small-pox took away many of our people' (Morris 1880: 171). It was also the subject of much discussion during Treaty 6 negotiations. Initially, Morris rejected the proposal on the grounds that it was unnecessary: assistance would be provided as a matter of course. As he stated:

I know that the sympathy of the Queen, and her assistance, would be given you in any unforeseen circumstances. You must trust to her generosity. Last winter when some of the Indians wanted food because the crops had

been destroyed by grasshoppers, although it was not promised in the treaty, nevertheless the Government sent money to buy them food, and in the
spring when many of them were sick a man was sent to try and help them.
We cannot foresee these things, and all I can promise is that you will be
treated kindly, and in that extraordinary circumstances you must trust to
the generosity of the Queen. (Ibid.: 211)

He also expressed concern that the clause might lead to excesses (and
perhaps thus not be in keeping with the proportionality I associate with
the notion of 'kindness'). However, he was reassured on this point first
by the Badger, who said:

We want to think of our children; we do not want to be too greedy; when
we commence to settle down on the reserves that we select, it is there we
want your aid, when we cannot help ourselves and in case of troubles seen
and unforeseen in the future.
    I do not want you to feed me every day; you must not understand that
from what I have said. When we commence to settle down on the ground
to make there our own living, it is then we want your help, and that is the
only way that I can see how the poor can get along. (Morris 1880: 211)

Chief Mis-tah-wah-sis then offered the same reassurance:

It is well known that if we had plenty to live on from our gardens we
would not still insist on getting more provision, but it is in case of any ex-
tremity, and from the ignorance of the Indian in commencing to settle that
we thus speak; we are as yet in the dark; this is not a trivial matter for us.
    We were glad to hear what the Governor was saying to us and we un-
derstood it, but we are not understood, we do not mean to ask for food for
every day but only when we commence and in case of famine or calamity.
(Ibid.: 213)

The Beardy reinforced this point by saying, 'When I am utterly unable to help myself I want to receive assistance,' and then indicated that
the intent was reciprocal by adding, 'I will render all the assistance I can
to my brother in taking care of the country' (ibid.: 227).
    After ultimately agreeing to the provision, Morris used the following
language in explaining its meaning: 'In a national famine or general
sickness, not what happens in every day life, but if a great blow comes
on the Indians they would not be allowed to die like dogs' (Morris 1880:

228). But, unfortunately, a 'great blow' did soon come. During the late 1870s starvation was so great (Carter 1990: 69, 71) that in 1879 Dr D.W.J. Hagarty, medical superintendent for Manitoba and the North-West, reported: 'Hunger has shown its terrible effects upon them and scrofula and other kindred diseases are becoming deeply rooted' (Lux 2001: 33). Things became even more dire in the early 1880s. In 1882 Dr Edwards wrote that 'many of those [living on the reserves he visited] who have died this winter have died from absolute starvation' (ibid.: 44), a position confirmed by these shocking statistics: during the winter of 1883–4 three Treaty 6 reserves, the Mosquito, Grizzly Bear Head, and Lean Man, together lost over 25 per cent of their population (77 deaths in a population of 300), of which 50 (or nearly 17 per cent) were children (ibid.: 51). Lux pointed to a similar death rate in the Treaty 4 region. The causes, he said, 'can be directly linked to economic conditions' (ibid.: 4).

This graphic picture of conditions at Poundmaker's reserve in Treaty 6, written by schoolteacher Father Cochin, sums up the situation: 'I saw gaunt children, dying of hunger, come to my place to be instructed. Although it was 30–40 degrees below zero their bodies were scarcely covered with torn rags ... The hope of having a little morsel of good dry cake was the incentive which drove them to this cruel exposure each day... The privation made many die' (Lux 2001: 51).

There can be no doubt that, by the 1880s, our partners (in Treaty 6 and elsewhere) were suffering a general famine. Under these conditions, it would be expected that, even if the 'famine clause' had not been included in Treaty 6, common humanity or even the spirit and intent of the other treaties would have moved government to act to ensure that these human beings 'would not be allowed to die like dogs.' But that was not so.

In some cases, we deliberately withheld needed food even when we had full storehouses filled with resources intended for our partners, as when Allan MacDonald, agent for Treaty 4, stated in 1882: 'I know they are not getting enough flour, but I like to punish them a little. I will have to increase the rations but not much.' But, largely, the problem was the manifest inadequacy of what we provided. To take one example: in 1880 Dr John Kittson of the North-West Mounted Police reported that the daily ration offered to our partners was inadequate (Lux 2001: 38). To underscore the point, he compared it to amounts given to, among others, state prisoners in Siberia, who, he found, received more than twice as much (ibid.). In fact, the ration was so meagre that 'gaunt men and women with hungry eyes were seen everywhere seeking or begging for a mouthful of food – little children – fight over tid-bits. Morning and evening many of them would come to me and beg for the very bones left by the dogs in my yard. When I tell you that the mortality exceeds the birth rate it may help you to realize the amount of suffering and privation existing among them' (ibid.).

Moreover, the way we provided rations violated what we had promised. Government relied on public policy, not treaty obligation, to rationalize the support it did give. Under this policy, as Dennis Guest notes: 'An applicant for public assistance, unless he had a medical certificate excusing him from work, could be required to saw cordwood or break rock as a condition for receiving help' (qtd. in Shewell 2004: 355n69). This meant that our partners received rations only when they were prepared to work on projects approved by government officials, and even then only when those providing assistance determined that 'they had performed work of some value' (Carter 1990: 84). To add insult to injury, they 'were expected to work for rations when there were not enough tools, implements, or seed' and even when 'much of the necessary equipment was sitting (unused) in the government storehouse' (Lux 2001: 41). And worst of all, our actions were part of a deliberate policy to use their starvation as 'a tool for subjugating [them]' (Shewell 2004: 7).

Our partners did not take this lying down. They petitioned for redress. In 1883 the Treaty 6 chiefs in the Edmonton region wrote Sir John A. Macdonald, then both prime minister of Canada and the minister responsible for Indian affairs, requesting his help because the local officials under his authority had not acted to alleviate their 'dire poverty' and 'utter destitution' (Devine 2004: 149). Such appeals were to no avail. Matters came to a head at the Duck Lake Council in 1884, when our partners from across the region assembled to hammer out a united position, after which 'a delegation of Chiefs would travel to Ottawa where it was believed someone with sufficient authority could make some changes' (Stonechild 1986: 158).

But before that could happen, the North-West Rebellion broke out. While our partners, by and large, refrained from violating the treaty relationship by participating in the rebellion (Stonechild 1986: 168; Miller 2009: 193), they were dealt with as if they had. Further infringements were placed on their ability to fend for themselves, such as when government imposed the infamous 'pass system [that] in plain violation of treaty promises about mobility … required reserve residents to obtain a pass signed by the agent or farming instructor before leaving the reserve (Miller 2009: 193), and trumped-up charges of treason were laid against Big Bear and Poundmaker, although neither had not taken part in the rebellion (ibid.).

The government of Canada has never apologized for its part in causing the famine, much less been held to account for its actions and the
violence those actions did to our partners and to the relationship that
had been established by the treaties. In fact, it maintained similar policies until at least the 1960s. Emblematic of these are the residential
schools, which were intended to coerce the children of our partners to
assimilate into Canadian society by separating them from their parents
at an early age (RCAP 1996: I, 341). As misguided as this policy was,
one would assume that common humanity, if not the treaty relationship, would have made sure that sufficient funds were set aside to ensure that the policy would be implemented in such a way that the
material, if not the emotional, needs of the children would be met.

Again that was not the case. Government consistently chose to exercise the policy with such parsimony that the schools became places
where 'underfunding, short rations and overwork contributed ... to
the children's ill-health' (RCAP 1996: I, 360), leading to so many deaths
that in 1911 lawyer S.H. Blake concluded that government negligence
in avoiding 'preventable causes of death' brought it 'within unpleas-
ant nearness to the charge of manslaughter' (ibid.: 357f). As if this were
not bad enough, in order to make ends meet, school administrators
introduced a policy that, like the one imposed on those starving in the
late nineteenth century, required that children work half-days 'to produce revenue' for the schools. Nor did things improve in later years,
for, as a 1955 reviewer of the residential school in Fort Providence,
Northwest Territories, remarked: 'I would sooner have a child of mine
in a reform school than in this dreadful institution' (ibid.: 363). As reports of survivors confirm, the violence and abuse experienced at residential schools disrupted and destroyed many lives, leaving a legacy
that endures today.

Finally, in 2008, over a quarter of a century after the majority of the
residential schools were closed, the government recognized and apologized for the damage done to those who attended, their relatives,
and their descendants. In Prime Minister Stephen Harper's evocative
words:

> We now recognize that, far too often, these institutions gave rise to abuse
> or neglect and were inadequately controlled, and we apologize for failing
> to protect you.
>
> The Government of Canada sincerely apologizes and asks the forgive-
> ness of the Aboriginal peoples of this country for failing them so pro-
> foundly. (Government of Canada 2008)

But that was then. What about now? When measured against the actions of our government in the 1880s and during the period of the residential schools, there is no doubt a noticeable improvement, if only because deliberate starvation and forced assimilation are no longer acceptable as policy options. But, as newspaper headlines announce weekly, violations and abuses continue to be a very real presence in the lives of our partners. Among the most egregious of these is the harm caused, in the pursuit of resource development, by the sustained assault on the lands, waters, and communities of Indigenous peoples.

The situation with the Lubicon Lake Cree First Nation of northern Alberta is a case study of what has been taking place more generally. The Lubicon were supposed to be included in Treaty 8 but were missed during the negotiations in 1899. In the 1930s the community petitioned for inclusion in the treaty. Government agreed and, among other commitments, announced its willingness to honour the provision to set aside land for a reserve. The size of the proposed reserve was determined in 1940, with the location subject to survey. However, that survey was never undertaken.

After waiting decades, the Lubicon decided to make a legal claim to their land. In 1975, along with a number of other 'isolated communities,' they filed a caveat 'to serve notice of their unextinguished Aboriginal rights' (Lubicon Settlement Commission 1993). Unfortunately, at that time sizable oil and gas reserves were also discovered on the same lands (Martin-Hill 2008). The Alberta Court of Appeals, which was hearing an appeal of the Paulette case, mentioned in chapter 6, expressed its view in passing that, owing to the way in which the Alberta land titles legislation was written, this caveat would be held to be valid should the matter ever reach it. In response, rather than respecting that decision, the government of Alberta passed extraordinary legislation that retroactively changed the terms of the land titles act so that the Lubicon's case would fail.

As a result, industry was allowed to develop non-renewable resources even on lands that had been set aside for the Lubicon's reserve. Between 1979, when development began in earnest, and 1983, over four hundred oil wells were drilled within a twenty-kilometre radius of the Lubicon's community of Little Buffalo (Lubicon Nation n.d.). This had a dramatic, negative impact on the community's ability to maintain economic self-sufficiency. In that same period the number of moose harvested dropped from 200 to 19, and trapping income declined from $5,000 to $400 (1983$). The Lubicon were forced by circumstances to turn to the modern-day equivalent of rations, welfare, to survive, so that by 1989 over 90 per cent of the population relied on it, up from 10 per cent ten years earlier. Meanwhile, during these years, the oil wells pumped out what is estimated to be $1 million a day (1984$), with none of the benefits going to the Lubicon. Despite repeated attempts to address the matter, the situation remains unresolved, and we continue to permit non-renewable-resource development on the lands on which the Lubicon live and work, and on the lands of others, with no acknowledgment of the devastating effects.

Conclusion: Taking a First Step Today

So where do we start today? We are no longer in the 1870s, when Confederation was new. We have travelled down the path I have described for so long, and caused so much damage, that we cannot wish the past away. Indeed, we cannot even assume that, given our record and our current actions, our partners would be willing to let us polish the Covenant Chain no matter how sincere our intentions. And then of course there are those with whom we did not reach agreements. Would they be willing to negotiate knowing how we have acted up to now? Treaty rights may now be in our constitution, but, as with Aboriginal rights in general, recognition serves only 'to reconcile pre-existing Aboriginal sovereignty with assumed Crown sovereignty' (Chief Justice McLachlin, *Haida* 2004: para 20). Our sovereignty comes first; their rights come second.

Nonetheless, I believe that returning to the promises we made in the treaties gives us a purchase on where to begin now. Doing so will transform what our constitution frames as Indigenous 'rights' into Settler 'obligations,' and obligations must be honoured whether or not we claim sovereignty. While they are certainly much more than that, treaties are also contracts, and even the sovereign must obey the terms of a contract into which he/she enters, for our law says that 'in matters of contractual liability, the Crown is not governed by any special provision: the Crown is bound by a contractual obligation in the same manner as an individual' (*Pratte* 1979). And that is as true now as it was when Lord Watson, speaking for the Privy Council, stated in his 1882 judgment in *Windsor and Annapolis Railway Company*: 'Their Lordships are of the opinion that it must now be regarded as settled law that, whenever a valid contract has been made between the Crown and a subject, a petition of right will lie for damages resulting from a breach of that contract by the Crown' (*Windsor and Annapolis Railway Company* 1882: 44). So, sovereign or not, we are bound to these agreements – that is how rights are reconciled in our law; and especially so now that we have given treaties constitutional protection.

The place to begin is no different today than it was at the time the treaties were negotiated. We must fulfil the terms of those agreements as negotiated, in good faith and with their spirit and intent in mind, and then extend the same offer to those with whom we have yet to make agreements. In taking this view, I find support from our partners.

Let me give one example. In October 2011 the Treaty 9 community of Attawapiskat in northern Ontario declared a state of emergency owing to the immediate health threat faced by families living in tents and makeshift sheds. In January 2012 Chief Theresa Spence followed this up by writing a letter to Indian Affairs Minister John Duncan in which she outlined a series of chronic challenges facing members of the community. These range from soil contamination at the community school (known by the department to have existed since 1977) and unresolved water problems (known to have existed since 1992) to the 'deplorable state of our housing stock' (also known since 1992), as reported in a study the volumes of which 'when stacked upon each other would reach four feet in height.'

The government's response was predictable. Initially, it was negative and condemnatory, but as the public became more aware of the situation, it responded minimally, by fulfilling some of the promises it had made. Chief Spence was central in this effort, keeping the pressure on the government. But beyond those tactics was an understanding that she conveyed at a meeting of Assembly of First Nations leaders:[17] 'We must go together and tell the government: this is our land, this is our life. We need to say "enough is enough." Respect our treaty and follow our treaty, *as we did.*'

So I am suggesting that we begin by taking up that challenge. Of course, where there are still promises written into treaty texts that remain outstanding, these commitments ought to be fulfilled fully and promptly. But that is not all. We also must act in accord with the spirit and intent of the treaties as they were negotiated. That is, when it comes to the agricultural clause, we should understand that its intent is to 'ensure that First Nations continued to have the means of livelihood, in return for agreeing to share the use of their territory with Euro-Canadian newcomers' (Ray, Miller, and Tough 2002: 188).

Even more than that, I think that our commitment at the time the treaties were negotiated was to ensure, as best we could, that our coming onto these lands would be beneficial, not harmful, to our partners. In that regard, I think we could take guidance as to how to fulfil our obligations from the so-called 'famine' or 'famine and pestilence' clause in Treaty 6, for it provides a general orientation regarding how to deal with our treaty partners, at least when the language is modified slightly to read like this: 'When we and our partners come to an understanding that a "calamity" has befallen them, and particularly when our actions are its cause, we will not fail to provide what is necessary and sufficient to assist them in overcoming it.' That is, at the very least, we should seek to live on these lands in a manner that best ensures that no calamity befalls Indigenous peoples; and *that* we surely have not done.

So this is my suggestion. Let us agree that in the future we let this understanding orient not only how we interpret all clauses in all treaties but also our interactions with those with whom we have yet to negotiate agreements or have negotiated so-called modern treaties. And, furthermore, let us undertake to strictly observe the same understanding when it comes to calamities that our actions may cause, whether that means making sure that our roads do not damage the gravesites of our partners' ancestors (*Vancouver Sun*, 31 August 2011) or taking care that our developments do not produce the kind of environmental degradation visited on the Lubicon and so many others.

I admit that my suggestion does not take us far down the path, but it is a step in the right direction. So if, after consultation, our partners agree to give us that chance, I propose that this would be a good place to begin building the foundation that will enable us to say that it is by agreement, not by imposition, that we too are here to stay. The question then is how to encourage us to move in that direction, a matter that I take up in the final chapter.

Chapter Nine

Setting the Record Straight

To the Indians of Canada, the treaties represent an Indian Magna Carta. The treaties are important to us, because we entered into these negotiations with faith, with hope for a better life with honour. We have survived over a century on little but that hope. Did the white men enter into them with something less in mind? Or have the heirs of the men who signed in honour somehow disavowed the obligation passed down to them? The Indians entered into the treaty negotiations as honourable men who came to deal as equals with the queen's representatives. Our leaders of that time thought they were dealing with an equally honourable people.

(Cardinal 1969: 28)

Introduction

My thesis comes down to this. Treaties offer us the means to reconcile the fact that we are 'here to stay' with the fact that there were people already here when we first arrived. I rely on the terms of Treaty 4 as negotiated to illustrate the obligations we entailed in coming to that kind of agreement. In chapter 8 I suggested that, had we acted in accord with what we promised at that time, we might now well be on the way to establishing a good relationship with our partners. I also concluded that (with the consent of Indigenous peoples) this path still offers us a way forward notwithstanding the negative way in which we have dealt with our obligations in the past. This chapter seeks ways to encourage our governments to act in the manner I believe they should.

To that end, for reasons I will discuss below, I focus on how treaty making in general and treaties negotiated at Confederation in particular are presented in the dominant narrative history of this country. In this regard, how this narrative deals with two elements of the quote by the late Harold Cardinal cited above will be central to orienting my approach to encouraging governments to act differently: the claim that 'treaties represent an Indian Magna Carta,' and Cardinal's belief that his forebears, when it came to those with whom they negotiated Treaty 6, 'were dealing with ... equally honourable people.' I begin by summarizing the dominant account of our history and of the role played by treaty making in it.

From Colony to Nation: A Story of the History of Canada

As recounted in leading English-language Canadian texts (Blake et al. 2011; Finkel and Conrad 2002; Francis et al. 2004; Granatstein et al. 1990), the history of Canada as a civic nation is a 'Coming of Age' story with Canada and the United Kingdom as the two principal protagonists, and the path to our full maturity as a state the central theme. In contrast to the United States, another child of Britain, we represent our passage *From Colony to Nation* (as it is described in the title of one famous history text) to be incremental, a growing to maturity, not a radical departure as with the rebel child to the south. The point is put this way in Robert Kroetsch's 'Canada Is a Poem': 'We cannot find our beginning. There is no Declaration of Independence, no Magna Carta, no Bastille Day. We live with a terrible unease at not having begun. Canada is a poem. We dreamt a poem, and now we must try to write it down. We have a gift of languages, and now we must make the poem' (Kroetsch 1977: 13). And, as historian Daniel Francis wrote twenty years later: 'Canada is a country without an independence day' (Francis 1997: 17).

Nonetheless, there is a major transition point in our history, called 'Confederation,' that is demarcated by the passage in 1867 of the British North America Act, which provided us with our present institutional form, federalism. From this we derive the two major periods of Canadian civic history. The first is 'Pre-Confederation.' Here, the key events include the fall of Quebec in 1759 and the consequent Treaty of Paris in 1763 by means of which Britain gained authority over what is now Canada; and the quest for 'responsible government,'[1] its establishment in principle with Lord Durham's Report of 1839 and, in practice (depending on the reading), no later than 1859. It concludes with the struggle for Confederation, which is seen as a solution to the dysfunction of the existing form of legislative association.

The second period, which is called 'Post-Confederation,' begins with Confederation itself. It is immediately followed by an era of consolidation and expansion, especially to the west, so that in just four years, with the purchase of Rupert's Land in 1869 (and Manitoba's joining of Confederation one year later) and the incorporation of British Columbia in 1871, Canada became a country of virtually the same size as it is today. What follows is a period in which Canada incrementally gains recognition as an equal in political status of the United Kingdom, and thus acquires permission to take its place as a state equal in standing to all others. However, the key moment of transition comes only some fifty years later with the passage of the Constitution Act of 1982 by the British Parliament.

For many, what reinforces this as a pivotal moment in our history is the fact that, in contrast to the British North America Act, in which the only reference to Indigenous peoples was a statement specifying that 'Indians and lands reserved for Indians' are the responsibility of the federal government, the new constitution recognizes and affirms 'aboriginal and treaty rights of the aboriginal peoples of Canada.' For this reason, among many others (of which constitutional protections for 'rights' and an amending formula are frequently represented as the most significant), there is a sense that, whether or not a new label should apply, a new ('post-Confederation') period begins with the passage of the Constitution Act of 1982.

Relations with Indigenous peoples play a minor part in this account, taking a role beyond mere mention only in conjunction with the period of western expansion in the immediate aftermath of Confederation. Here, the Riel Rebellion in 1869, the negotiation of the numbered treaties on the plains, and the North-West Rebellion of 1885, along with the completion of the Canadian Pacific Railway that same year, are recognized as the most noteworthy events. Generally speaking, treaties are represented as nothing more than a convenient way in which we could took control over the land (Francis et al. 2004: 36; Blake et al. 2011: 37), a point explained by Granatstein et al. in this way: 'Before the new social order could be created, the old had to be displaced. Arrangements were made to extinguish Indian title to most of the fertile lands of the southern Prairies' (Granatstein et al. 1990: 24). That is, the treaties are important only as evidence of the country's maturation after Confederation.

The texts all specify that the treaties contained provisions for the benefit of our partners (e.g., Finkel and Conrad 2002: 31). They also indicate that we failed to fulfil our treaty promises, and make it plain that our partners were aggrieved (Granatstein et al. 1990: 38; Blake et al. 2011: 67f; Finkel and Conrad 2002: 46; Francis et al. 2004: 88). However, the dominant narrative uses these facts to reinforce its focus on the story of westward expansion, for they are discussed in the context of Canada's gaining political supremacy in the aftermath of the failed North-West Rebellion. Afterwards, the continuation of Indigenous peoples' problems is attributed to government policy under the Indian Act rather than to violations of treaty promises (e.g., Francis et al. 2004: 292).

In short, this narrative creates the impression that treaty making was a momentary event in our history, merely one small step in the story of our development as a civic nation. It also reinforces the view that we are less than honourable people, for there is not even a hint that we are obligated to fulfil our commitments once we have the power to ignore them.

Recounting the History of the Numbered Treaties on the Plains

This rendering also reflects the dominant interpretation of treaty making at the time of Confederation. In the academic literature, our goal in treaty making is depicted as a means to gain control over the land (e.g., Tobias 1983). It is explained that Indigenous peoples were sufficiently powerful militarily and sufficiently numerous relative to the Settler population to impede our nation-building ambitions (ibid.; Miller 2009: 153–7). Therefore, achieving our objectives required that we either subdue them militarily or negotiate peaceful access to their lands by making treaties. We chose the latter option on pragmatic grounds, of which cost-effectiveness loomed large, a point that Jean Friesen puts this way: 'That the government persevered so long in some of the negotiations is a testimony not to humanitarianism but to the desire for a *cheap* Indian administration' (Friesen 1986: 212; emphasis in original). J.R. Miller quantifies the government's motivation by using this often-cited statistic: 'In the 1870s, when the United States was spending $20 million a year on Indian wars, Ottawa's entire budget was only $19 million' (Miller 2000: 210). The explanation for our failure to live up to our obligations follows the same reasoning. Once our partners no longer posed a threat, we made the pragmatic decision to dispense with our commitments. And it was that decision, consciously taken, that led to the starvation, the grievances, and everything else that followed. As John Tobias suggests:

As [then Indian Affairs Commissioner in the North-West Territories Edgar] Dewdney admitted in 1885, the treaties' promises and provisions were not being fulfilled, and Dewdney himself had taken steps to assure Canadian control over the Cree, which were themselves violations of the treaties. Thus, he had refused to grant the Cree the reserve sites they selected; he had refused to distribute the ammunition and twine the treaties required. His plans for dealing with the Cree leaders were based on a political use of the legal and judicial system, and ultimately he made use of the military, the police, and the courts in a political manner to achieve his goals of subjugating the Cree. (Tobias 1983: 548)

As a result, this scholarship frames what on the surface appear to be binding obligations as policy options to be fulfilled to the extent that we alone determine, based on what we ourselves, and no one else, believe is prudent politically as well as fiscally. It is a point that Miller captures vividly in the following passage:

Once treaty-making was concluded in the 1870s, the self-interested and at times insensitive nature of federal treaty-making was revealed. There were numerous problems with treaty implementation because a distant government had little interest in the welfare of western peoples. Even when the collapse of the bison economy by 1879 created conditions of extreme hardship, Ottawa showed little concern. In fact, that collapse made it easier to ignore First Nations' protests ... Some later commentators – especially undergraduates, who tend toward cynicism – suggest that this heartlessness 'proves' that Canada never intended to honour its treaty promises. There is no evidence from the treaty negotiations themselves to sustain such an interpretation. Rather, once setbacks in the West weakened the peoples there, it became all too easy in a parliamentary democracy in which votes – something First Nations did not have, of course – were what counted for politicians to drop treaty obligations down the priority list when it came to allocating resources. (Miller: 2009: 296)

While Harold Cardinal may consider treaties to be a Magna Carta, that is a view not universally shared; as Friesen puts it: 'To the commissioners as to most Canadians then and now, the treaties were considered a "once and for all" way of clearing the land of the legal obligations of Indian title' (Friesen 1986: 210). And so there is every reason to conclude that our partners were not dealing with 'an equally honourable people.'

But that is not the last word. This account would be accurate only were there in fact a unity of purpose between those who negotiated these treaties on our behalf and those who implemented them; and that is a rendering that does not fit well with the evidence available to me when it comes to the treaties Morris negotiated. This evidence shows that the commissioners with whom Harold Cardinal's forebears negotiated Treaty 6 were honourable people in that they honestly believed that the commitments they made in return for permission to settle on those lands would be kept. What happened, however, is that those who implemented that treaty (and others negotiated by Morris) transformed those solemn obligations into policy options to be fulfilled at the government's whim; although in my view the term 'policy options' is hardly appropriate. To deliberately starve people into submission, to rip children from families, and to despoil the lands on which they live and work for our benefit are not policy options. They are inhumane, criminal acts worthy of harsh punishment.

So let me now turn to the evidence on which I have drawn this conclusion. It is a matter I will address from four perspectives: Did Morris mean what he said? Was he authorized to say it? Did he expect that governments would keep the commitments he made on behalf of the Crown? How did he react when they did not?

Morris and the Numbered Treaties

With regard to the first question, there is strong evidence that Morris's position reflected a well-established conviction held by many of his contemporaries that, regardless of where we imagined Indigenous peoples to be in 'universal history,' we could not settle on their lands without their permission. One of its principle proponents was the Aborigines' Protection Society (Heartfield 2011). Founded in 1836 by prominent members of the British political community in the wake of their successful efforts through the Anti-Slavery Society to abolish slavery, this organization proved to be highly influential in the formulation of policy on relations with Indigenous peoples throughout the Empire, Canada included.

For example, as noted in the Prologue, the APS's 'Outline of a System of Legislation,'[2] drawn up at its request by lawyer Standish Motte, took the position that among 'the indefeasible rights of every people, (not under allegiance to any other power,) to the natural rights of man ... [are] their rights as an independent nation.' Furthermore, it avowed that 'no country or people has a right by force or fraud to assume the sovereignty over any other nation.' Instead, the APS insisted that 'such sovereignty can be justly obtained only by fair treaty, and with their consent' (Aborigines' Protection Society 1840: 14). Furthermore, the model legislation asserted that 'no treaty or agreement with any aboriginal inhabitants of our colonies, on the part of he British Government, or by British subjects, shall be valid, *unless it secures an adequate reserve of territory for the maintenance and occupation of the aborigines and their posterity*' (ibid.: 15; emphasis added).

The proposal also made it plain that it would be wrong for Settlers to impose their ways on Indigenous peoples even if they took the view that these were superior, for it said: 'to help, and not oppress, should be our object; – so as to cultivate and promote that mutual dependence and reciprocal good-will, which should make them view us as brothers and patrons, and not as intruders or hard task-masters – and which by arousing and enlisting their sympathies, would infallibly lead them to be moral, intelligent, peaceful, and happy, – attached friends, and faithful allies' (Aborigines' Protection Society 1840: 9).

That the APS's view of treaty making did not entail removal of Indigenous peoples from their lands is confirmed in its 1839 report on the situation in Canada (Aborigines' Protection Society 1839: 17, 24). And I should note that in this case the APS's words had a direct effect on policy in that Lord Glenelg, then colonial secretary, embraced this view (ibid.: 20f) and that as a result in Canada (in contrast to the United States) the practice of expelling Indigenous peoples from their land was discontinued.

In short, by the 1840s, there was a prominent organization in Britain which took the position that:

1. Indigenous peoples have sovereignty and jurisdiction in their territories;
2. treaties are the only legitimate means to acquire sovereignty and jurisdiction (or, by implication, to create conditions to permit settlement on these lands);
3. treaty provisions should benefit Indigenous peoples and must include sufficient land for them to live in perpetuity; and
4. while 'civilization' is the object, it should be encouraged by example and not imposed.

The necessity of treaty making prior to settlement at the time Morris negotiated the treaties was shared by Lord Dufferin, then governor general of Canada. As noted in chapter 1, in his 1876 'Speech at Government House, Victoria, British Columbia,' he stated: 'In Canada, no Government, whether provincial or central, has failed to acknowledge that the original title to the land existed in the Indian Tribes and the communities that hunted or wandered over them, [therefore] ... not until [we negotiate treaties] do we consider that we are entitled to deal with a single acre.'[3] Furthermore, his view that treaties prior to settlement are required even though we may claim sovereignty and jurisdiction was evident in the same speech when he chastised the government of British Columbia for erroneously assuming that it had the authority to permit settlement because 'the fee simple title in, as well as the sovereignty over the land, resided in the Queen.'

Lord Dufferin also made it clear that he did not believe it was right to impose our ways on Indigenous peoples. In his 'Speech at the Indian Reserve, Tuscarora,' in 1874, he said: 'It is to be hoped that in the course of time a more settled mode of existence will gradually be extended among all the Indian subjects of the Canadian Government, but at the same time I wish it to be understood that it is by no means the desire of the Government unduly to press upon its Indian subjects a premature or violent change in their established habits. To have done this would have been, in my opinion, a great mistake' (Dufferin 1882: 155f).

In short, there is solid evidence to support the proposition that Morris's position as treaty commissioner reflected a stance of long standing that he likely shared.[4] Thus, there is every reason to suppose that, when Morris represented that 'one of the gravest of the questions presented for solution by the Dominion of Canada ... *was the securing of the alliance of the Indian tribes, and maintaining friendly relations with them*' (ibid.: 9; emphasis added) – not clearing them from the land or reneging on our obligations – he meant what he said.[5]

Moving to the second question, there is also solid evidence supporting the view that Morris had the authority to represent the treaty relationship in the manner that he did. First, it is clear that in practice his authority was not limited to what was vested in him prior to negotiations, for the Dominion government accepted the validity of all clauses in all treaties as Morris negotiated them, including such wide-ranging promises as the 'famine provision' that were not included in the version of Treaty 6 given to him (Talbot 2009: 151f). Second, it is also clear that, although he was appointed by the government, he was (as he stated) authorized to negotiate by the Crown. (That this still holds is illustrated by the fact that in 1999 Jane Stewart of the federal government signed the Nisga'a Agreement on behalf of 'Her Majesty the Queen in Right of Canada,' as well as in her capacity as 'Minister of Indian Affairs

and Northern Development' [Nisga'a Nation 1999]). While this may
now be a mere formality, given the relationship between the government and the Crown at that time, it was not necessarily the case when
Morris negotiated the numbered treaties. As Lord Dufferin stated during his speech in Victoria, Indigenous peoples had a direct relationship
with the Crown rather than with the Dominion government: 'You must
remember that the Indian population is not represented in Parliament,
and, consequently, that the Governor General is bound to watch over
their welfare and especial solicitude' (Dufferin 1882: 209–10). Lord
Dufferin's position was not necessarily inaccurate, for he noted to Lord
Carnarvon, then secretary of state for the colonies, that the extent of his
authority as governor general was not spelled out, and he took a rather
broad view of it. In fact, Barbara Mussamore suggests that Dufferin's
disagreement with the Dominion government on this point was one of
the reasons for Canada insisting that the regal representative's authority be laid out in writing before the next governor general was appointed (Mussamore 2005: 453–83; also see Blake et al. 2011: 52f).[6] In other
words, at the time Morris negotiated the treaties, it was arguable that,
since he was lieutenant governor of Manitoba and thus in a direct relationship with Lord Dufferin, he was acting on behalf of the queen as an
agent independent of the Dominion government.[7]

To this let me add the informal authority that may well have vested in
Morris on account of his stature. He was certainly not an underling who
was hired by the government to negotiate treaties on behalf of the
Crown. At that time, he was the sitting lieutenant governor of Manitoba
(and recently had also been its de facto premier) as well as the province's
former chief justice. Prior to that, he had served as a minister in Canada's
first post-Confederation cabinet. He was also a confidant of our first
prime minister, an ardent supporter of Confederation, who, as a good
friend of both George Brown and Sir John A. Macdonald, brokered the
'Great Coalition' that was key to making the new union possible (Talbot
2009: 47). He was also one of the leading advocates, if not the leading
one, for including Manitoba and Rupert's Land within Confederation.
In brief, his status as, if not a father of Confederation, at the very least
one of its leading architects, may well have given him sufficient standing to take the initiative in shaping the treaty relationship with
Indigenous peoples within the newly formed Canadian union.

Turning to the third question, there is good evidence indicating that
Morris had every reason to believe that government would honour the
commitments he made on behalf of the Crown. The reason is simple;
that is what the Dominion government guaranteed it would do when it

requested permission from Britain to annex Rupert's Land. In a letter written in the year of Confederation, the Senate and House of Commons stated: 'We, your Majesty's most dutiful and loyal subjects ... in Parliament assembled, humbly approach your Majesty for the purpose of representing ... *that, upon the transference of the territories in question to the Canadian Government, the claims of the Indian tribes to compensation for lands required for purposes of settlement will be considered and settled in conformity with the equitable principles which have uniformly governed the British Crown in its dealings with the aborigines'* (Cauchon and Cockburn 1867: 412; emphasis added). It was thus fair for Morris to take parliamentarians at their word when they stated that, as 'dutiful and loyal subjects,' they would fulfil the commitments made on the queen's behalf, including the famine provision. Further, he apparently was of the view that government would do so because 'he knew from his legal background and experience with land titles that any breach of the treaties would threaten the legitimacy of Canada's claim over the territory' (Talbot 2009: 120).

As for the last question – How did Morris react when the Crown's promises to Indigenous peoples were not kept? – the evidence is unequivocal. During his tenure as lieutenant governor of Manitoba, Morris 'advocated tirelessly for the faithful implementation of the *spirit* of the treaties, arguing that oral promises, from specific agricultural implements to general principles of reciprocity and mutual assistance, should be honoured' (Talbot 2009: 121; emphasis in original). However, government was not receptive, and Morris's 'approach was increasingly at odds with Ottawa' (ibid.). By 1876, the Department of Indian Affairs had taken steps to reduce his involvement in treaty implementation, and by 1877 his authority in that sphere was taken from him completely (ibid.).

But Morris did not leave without a struggle. He 'increasingly protested against what he perceived to be a breaking of the treaties and the violation of the treaty relationship, especially the direct link between the First Nations and the Crown embodied in the office of the Lieutenant-Governor' (Talbot 2009: 149). In fact, as Talbot points out (ibid.: 160), it was only in 1878, after Macdonald returned to power, Morris had been pushed out as lieutenant governor, and Edgar Dewdney had been appointed 'to the newly created and all-powerful position of Commissioner of Indian Affairs for the North West Territory,' that policies such as deliberate starvation and the withholding of rations as well as farm implements began in earnest. As Morris wrote towards the end of his life: 'I warned [David] Mills [minister of the interior from 1876 to 1878] as to breach of faith concerning Indian Treaties. I had two years of fighting with Mills and would have resigned but for Lord Dufferin who stood by me and advised me not to do so' (ibid.: 2009: 164f).

That our partners did not hold Morris responsible for the privations they suffered at that time is indicated by the fact that, on his death in 1889, a number of chiefs from Manitoba and the northwest made the long journey to Ontario to attend his funeral. Among them was Chief John Prince of Clandeboyne, Manitoba, who explained that he had come because 'the Great Spirit called me here to be by the side of my friend' (Talbot 2009: 165).

This evidence leads me to conclude that Commissioner Morris acted honourably in at least these respects. He negotiated on the understanding that treaties are required before settlement, and that their purpose is to build relationships with those already here, not impose our ways on them.[8] As he said: 'I see them retaining their old mode of living with the Queen's gift in addition' (Morris 1880: 231). That, then, as I understand it, was the purpose of treaty implementation as Morris saw it.

Keeping Our Promises

Writing into our history the disjuncture between those who negotiated and those who implemented treaties such as Treaty 6 is important if only for the sake of accuracy. But there is more to it than that. First, it offers evidence to support Harold Cardinal's contention that his forebears negotiated with 'equally honourable people' who shared the hope that the agreements would lead to 'a better life with honour,' whatever the shape that each party believed this life would take. Of equal importance is what this story tells us about our own history. And in this regard I believe that reporting on the disjuncture between promises and implementation can influence governments to act in conformity with the commitments that we made. Here is how.

If governments were motivated to act honourably, then setting the record straight on this point would be sufficient to ensure that they would fulfil the commitments they made. But that is unlikely to happen. Governments run on expediency, and the driving force behind decisions is a cost-benefit analysis of the consequences of any action taken. And, as Miller rightly suggests, their level of commitment to address this matter derives from that calculus. To bring about a different way of thinking requires that we change the outcome of that analysis, and the only sure way to do that is to change Settler opinion, since, as the Aborigines' Protection Society declared, 'a local legislature, if properly constituted, should partake largely in the interests, and represent the feelings or the settled opinions of the great mass of the people for whom they act' (Parliamentary Select Committee 1837). This is as true today as it was in 1837.

Unlike our predecessors, however, we are hobbled today by the fact that the local legislature is controlled by the executive branch of government. The Crown may be a separate institution, but it is a puppet of the government, for what it says, and how it acts, is dictated by the latter. Courts may be helpful, but they cannot be decisive. What Trudeau says still holds: 'It will be up to all of you people to make your minds up and to choose for or against it' [self-determination]. For better or worse, government will be persuaded to act only when it is pressured to do so, and the best way I know to bring government to change its mind on an issue is to gain public support.

That is where Harold Cardinal's reference to the treaties as a 'Magna Carta' comes in. What I understand him to be saying is that all peoples have principles so fundamental that to violate them is virtually unthinkable. For Settlers, one of the most basic of these, the origin of the rule of law, is embodied in the Magna Carta. As least for us, it is, as Lord Denning of the Privy Council said, 'the greatest constitution document of all times – the foundation of the freedom of the individual against the arbitrary authority of the despot' (qtd. in Pallister 1971: 1). To respect the rule of law is a core principle of our governance system. It is assumed that governments will adhere to it, regardless of cost.

Right now, Settlers do not see treaty making in the same way as Indigenous peoples do. It is considered to be relatively insignificant in the story of our country, something worthy of mention only in the context of what is far more important: the establishment of Confederation, and the passage of the British North America Act of 1867 that gave the new union political life. As is reflected in our monuments on Parliament Hill, the 'Fathers of Confederation' were those, like George Brown and Sir John A. Macdonald, who propelled us in that direction.

But that is an artifact of the way we tell our story. Here is what I mean. The history of Canada is embedded in the history of British colonialism. From our first settlement, we have had to address how to reconcile the fact that we are here to stay with the fact that there were already people here to stay. Today, as in the 1870s, the 1830s, 1763, and even the seventeenth century, we have taken two positions on what this means. One is that, from the outset, we have had the authority to govern this land and

the people already living here in whatever way we see fit. The other is
that to settle here required making and respecting agreements with
Indigenous peoples. This debate is no longer of moment in most of the
world, where colonists have either left or have become absorbed into
the polities of those present when they arrived. But in Canada it remains as alive for us now as it was in times past. This is true whether
we arrived yesterday or descend from those who arrived a century ago
and more. On this matter there are no 'new immigrants,' for we are all
here to stay.

When we tell our country's story as we now do, we privilege only
the first perspective on our history, for fulfilling our treaty obligations
counts for little only when we assume that we need not do so to legitimize our presence on these lands. This narrative encourages governments today as much as at the time of Confederation to discount the
importance of keeping our promises. However, when we include in
our history the position on the importance of treaty making offered by
Commissioner Morris and Lord Dufferin, a different picture emerges.
What then becomes clear is that, at the time of Confederation, the view
taken by those who controlled treaty implementation was contested
by a prominent leader in building Confederation and by the queen's
official representative. They believed that in Canada to be 'here to stay'
would mean making treaties amenable to all before settling on new
lands and adhering to them. In this rendering, treaties become like
a Magna Carta for us, for they are the foundation that legitimizes our
settlement on these lands. As Morris suggested, to dishonour our obligations would be to call into question that legitimacy. And I think it fair
to say that, were Settlers by and large to come to that view, then governments would be encouraged to act on the understanding that our treaty
obligations are solemn commitments and not policy options. But this
cannot happen so long as this debate is written out of our history. What
I suggest is that, at the very least, we incorporate the perspective of
Dufferin and Morris on treaty relations into the story we tell of
Confederation and the settling of the west.

Conclusion

Of course, the evidence I have on this point is not definitive. At the
same time, I am not resting my case on the veracity of Lord Dufferin
or Commissioner Morris. After all, their words only expressed principles we have long held. To dwell on land we know already belongs to

others requires their consent and our faithful keeping of the commitments we made in obtaining it. It also requires that, to the extent that we fail to do so, we seek to do what is necessary to rectify any harm our actions have caused.[9] What I am suggesting, therefore, is that we need to ensure that, whether or not he meant what he said, the treaties Morris negotiated keep faith with these principles. That is a foundation on which we can build today even if his intent was less than honourable.

There is no question that, for the last century and more, we have lived here as though these principles do not apply; that, for one reason or another, Indigenous lands were ours for the taking. The question before us is whether we are now prepared to keep faith with the principles on which Morris's actions rested. I am convinced that this is the direction to take. It is my hope that laying out the reasons that led me to this conviction will assist others in finding a different place to stand.

Proportionality

To act with kindness, in my understanding, is to act proportionately. This comes from my interpretation of a story told to me by Mrs Jessie Hardisty.

To set the context, let me turn to the source in Western thought that I found most helpful in gaining an insight into what Mrs Hardisty is explaining: French anthropologist Marcel Mauss's 1921 publication *The Gift*, and in particular his discussion of a set of practices associated with the establishment and fulfillment of agreements between certain societies that have neither a state form of organization nor a common culture.[1]

Mauss suggests that in these societies connections are established through a set of practices associated with 'gift giving' that can be analytically separated into two phases. The first, associated with the initiation of a relationship, can be reduced to a simple choice: between giving and receiving, and refusing to give and receive: 'To refuse to give, to fail to invite, just as to refuse to accept, is tantamount to declaring war; it is to reject the bond of alliance and fellowship'[2] (Mauss 1954: 11; Mauss 1990: 13).

If the parties agree to give and receive, then the relationship is confirmed by a set of practices associated with what Mauss calls 'returning the gift given.' In this phase, the roles are reversed so that the party that received now gives, and the party that gave now receives. In his understanding, performing these practices does more than complete a cycle. It establishes a permanent relationship between the parties by setting up, as Mary Douglas suggests, 'a perpetual cycle of exchanges within and between generations'[3] (Douglas 1990: viii).

Transferring that to our circumstances, we came here; we had the choice of declaring war or making peace. We chose the latter by making a promise to give certain gifts to Indigenous peoples (treaty obligations).

Establishing our relationship, then, depends in the first instance on making our offer real, and their accepting it. In this view, the *act* of fulfilling our promises constitutes the first step.

Superficially, Mrs Hardisty's account illustrated the point Mauss was making. Using the perspective of a relationship between a host and a guest who arrives at the host's camp, she made it clear that when the intent is to establish or maintain 'the bond of alliance and fellowship,' the host offers food, which the guest eats. That is, the establishment of a relationship is signalled by the giving and receiving of gifts. Equally, she explained that rejection of the relationship is associated with a refusal to accept a gift given. However, her account was more nuanced, for she also took into account how a member of a party intending to 'declare war' might get away alive by pretending to eat the food while hiding it in his/her hand, and then dropping it on leaving, to be later discovered by the host.

However, it was her illustration of this practice in a particular story that provides a whole new perspective on what the obligation to give entails, and what fulfillment means. This story concerns a 'medicine war' between some Mountain Dene and Dene from the Yukon that begins around 1905 and ends in the 1930s. It was told to me in the context of giving me some information on the 'Old Timers' alive at the time Treaty 11 was negotiated in 1921, one of whom was named 'Kleng' in Dene but was also called 'Bavard' or 'The Talkative One' and later became better known as 'Mbe Cho'[5] or 'Big Stomach.' Let me tell the whole story and then return to the incident with which the conflict began.

At some point (around 1905 I believe) some people Mrs Hardisty identified as 'Yukon Dene' sought to initiate a contest with some 'Mountain Dene' (with whom she was living) to see whose medicine was stronger. The Yukon Dene tried to use the protocol regarding 'refusal' to provoke a war; they did so through the way in which they treated 'Kleng,' then a young man, when he arrived at a Yukon Dene camp. Here is her description (transcript):

> The mountain Indians from Norman had trouble, a long time ago, with the Yukon mountain Indians. Bavard went to their country and was given lots to eat. If he didn't eat it all, well, then there would be trouble. They gave too much to eat but luckily he was MBE CHO.[4] So he ate it all and licked the plate. Those men they ate almost nothing.

...

When [Bavard] finished they came back, anyway. They wanted to see whose medicine was stronger. But the Norman Indians they always got the best. The old men were alive then. Yatsule's dad and the other old men. The way that they beat them was, to first, take things like shells from a breech loader, flint and other things. For example, an old woman who was Yendo's mother ... and Yatsule's father's wife ... said to her sons one night 'I feel something hot in my hand, Can you take it out?' and it was a bullet and that is how they took lots of bullets from them. By medicine. Those Yukon Indians had to watch the camp all the time. It was just awful, they said. And then there was a big fog too. They couldn't see good so they had to beat it back to their country.

...

Long after the Norman Indians went back there and took two of those Yukon Indians back with them. They were good friends then. One man, Simon Yukon [the other man's last name is Yukon too] they married two girls from Norman. Some of the people from Norman too, went to the Yukon. Some of these married whites; perhaps some Indians too. At the end they were good friends. It was only at the beginning when they were strangers that there was trouble.

Let me return to the encounter that initiated the 'war.' It is clear that, in contrast to Mauss, intent cannot be reduced to a choice between giving and receiving and the refusal to give or receive, for here the intent to refuse is signalled by giving too much. Therefore, to establish a relationship means to give 'proportionately' – not too little, not too much – so as not to encourage the recipient to 'refuse,' as was clearly the intent of the hosts in the Mbe Cho story.

The Post-Confederation Numbered Treaties

Notes

Preface

1 These are estimates based on Susan Hume's article in the *Edmonton Journal* (Hume 1971), which gives Mrs Hardisty's birthday as early December and her age as eight-six on Christmas Day, and my personal knowledge that she died one day before her 100th birthday.

1. Overview

1 I came to focus on Treaty 4 through my work with Alison DuBois, then a doctoral student at the University of Victoria. In my study of this treaty, I began to realize that, as had been explained to me many times previously, the numbered treaties negotiated immediately following Confederation are key to an understanding of how to reconcile our presence on Indigenous lands with our principles.

2 For a discussion of my reasons for choosing 'Indigenous' rather that 'Aboriginal,' see Asch 2001.

3 This book does not address the matter of individual identity directly. However, to the extent that it is relevant to determine the group to which an individual belongs, I propose to include as members of the Settler community individuals who can trace their ancestry to those who were here when Settlers first arrived, but who, on honest reflection, conclude that, nonetheless, they are not members of the Indigenous community. At the same time, my view is that, regardless of the community with which one identifies, to be here to stay also entails identification with both. This is a topic that I will discuss in chapters 7 and 8. Suffice it to say here, by way of preliminary explanation, that, while we can define

ourselves as members of a community in an either/or sense, identity will
also depend on our need to sustain the existence of (and in that regard
identify with) both.

4 In this book, I am taking the view that the Métis in general and the historic
Métis Nation in particular are not part of the Settler community notwithstanding that, at the time of Confederation, the Crown, while accepting
they had land rights, apparently did not hold that Métis had the same
standing as First Nations in negotiations on land settlement. I believe
the Crown was wrong. The Métis were a collectivity of the kind that had
the standing to be represented by leaders of their own choosing. The
fact is that, since the inclusion of Métis as an Aboriginal people in the
Constitution Act of 1982, Canada has gone a long way towards accepting
that view as well.

2. Aboriginal Rights and the Canadian Constitution

1 *Black's Law Dictionary* definition of 'sovereignty.'
2 *OED* definition of usufruct: '1.a. *Law.* The right of temporary possession,
use, or enjoyment of the advantages of property belonging to another,
so far as may be had without causing damage or prejudice to this.'
3 It is also clear from this judgment that Tysoe was sympathetic to Davey's
view.
4 For a general discussion on this matter and the role played by anthropology in these disputes, see Hancock 2007.
5 Taken from (Hancock 2007: 80f). As Hancock says on p. 80: 'The English
translation of the judgment is unreported; this chapter is based on a copy
of the translation in the James Bay cabinets of the Canadian Indian Rights
Collection of Library and Archives Canada … The judgment in French is
reported as *Gros-Louis et al. v. la Société de développement de la Baie James et al.*
(1974) Que. P. R. 38.'
6 These are the Assembly of First Nations, the Native Council of Canada,
the Métis National Council, and the Inuit Committee on National Issues.
7 In contrast to the Accord, there are no provisions in this document
guaranteeing Aboriginal representation in the Senate (II-9) or representation at any first ministers' conferences that directly affect them (22-D),
though it does state (V-60) that 'there should be Aboriginal consent to
future constitutional amendments that directly refer to Aboriginal peoples.' See: http://www.solon.org/Constitutions/Canada/English/
Proposals/CharlottetownLegalDraft.html (accessed 23 December 2011).

8 The full list includes 'jurisdiction and authority to act' with regard to 'all, some, or parts of the following: governing structures, membership, marriage, adoption and child welfare, Aboriginal language, culture and religion, education, health, social services, administration/enforcement of Aboriginal laws, policing, property rights, land management, agriculture, hunting, fishing and trapping on Aboriginal lands, taxation, transer and management of group assets, management of public works, housing, and local transportation' (INAC 1995: 3).

9 The full list includes: divorce, labour, administration of justice, penitentiaries, environmental protection, fisheries co-management, migratory birds co-management, gaming, and emergency preparedness (Tsawwassen First Nation 2007: 4).

10 For this anthropologist, the division of authority raises a question. Laws respecting those who belong to the category 'marriageable' are within the jurisdiction of the federal government, while those specifying who can officiate at ceremonies are in the provincial domain. The policy uses the word 'marriage' (indeed, agreements use this word alone as well as in conjunction with solemnization). Does this mean that Indigenous governments would have the authority to determine who belongs to the 'marriageable' category?

11 Established in 1991 with four Indigenous and three non-Indigenous commissioners, the commission was mandated to 'investigate the evolution of the relationship among aboriginal peoples (Indian, Inuit and Métis), the Canadian government, and Canadian society as a whole. It should propose specific solutions, rooted in domestic and international experience, to the problems which have plagued those relationships and which confront aboriginal peoples today' (RCAP 1996: I, ch. 1, s. 1).

12 The report specified: 'To give a partial list, it seems likely that an Aboriginal nation with an exclusive territory would be entitled as a matter of its core jurisdiction to draw up a constitution, set up basic governmental institutions, establish courts, lay down citizenship criteria and procedures, run its own schools, maintain its own health and social services, deal with family matters, regulate many economic activities, foster and protect its language, culture and identity, regulate the use of its lands, waters and resources, levy taxes, deal with aspects of criminal law and procedure, and generally maintain peace and security within the territory' (RCAP 1996: II, pt. 1).

13 I realize that the date at which our sovereignty presumably supersedes the sovereignty of those who were here already is a matter of consequence in legal proceedings. It is not my intention to engage in that speculation here,

and that is why I use the parenthetical phrase. However, I take the position that I do not only because the quote says 'from the outset' but also because this is reinforced in *Van der Peet*, where the Court says:

> 'The fact that the doctrine of aboriginal rights functions to reconcile the existence of pre-existing aboriginal societies with the sovereignty of the Crown does not alter this position. Although it is the sovereignty of the Crown that the pre-existing aboriginal societies are being reconciled with, it is to those pre-existing societies that the court must look in defining aboriginal rights. It is not the fact that aboriginal societies existed prior to Crown sovereignty that is relevant; it is the fact that they existed *prior to the arrival of Europeans in North America*. As such, the relevant time period is the period prior to the arrival of Europeans, not the period prior to the assertion of sovereignty by the Crown' (*Van der Peet* 1996, para. 61; emphasis in original).

14 In drawing this conclusion, Chief Justice Lamer relies on an article I co-authored with Patrick Macklem in which we say that Aboriginal rights 'inhere in the very meaning of aboriginality.' While the text does support the interpretation that Aboriginal rights are held by indigenous peoples alone, it also supports the view that these rights include a right of self-determination in that it states: 'The production and reproduction of native forms of community require a system of rights and obligations that reflect and protect *unique relations that native people have with* nature, themselves and *other communities* (Asch and Macklem 1991: 502; emphasis in original). And First Nations sovereignty is the means by which 'identity' (which in my view includes political identity and is thus one of the functions of governance) 'pre-existed the settlement of Canada and continues to exist notwithstanding the interposition of the Canadian state' (ibid.: 503).

15 http://www.duhaime.org/LegalDictionary/D/DeFacto.aspx (accessed 19 May 2012).

16 The *OED* definition of 'de jure': 'of right, by right, according to law. Nearly always opposed to *de facto*.'

3. Aboriginal Rights and Temporal Priority

1 It should be added that Montesquieu begins *The Spirit of the Laws* by disagreeing explicitly with Hobbes's assertion that war dominates the State of Nature, arguing instead that humans are naturally cooperative

and have a natural desire to join with others to form society (Montesquieu
1989 [1748]: 6).

2 Lawmentor: http://www.lawmentor.co.uk/glossary/T/time-immemorial/
(accessed 20 May 2012).

3 I am referring to section 16 (official languages) of the Canadian Constitution
Act, 1982; section 23 of the Charter of Rights and Freedoms; and the fact
that Canada is organized in a manner that ensures that an ethno-national
minority within its borders has jurisdiction with respect to many matters
based on the fact that it forms a majority within a provincial jurisdiction.

4 http://www.catholic/forum.com/saints/pope0214a.htm (accessed
20 February 2012).

5 *Stanford Encyclopedia*: 'An act is morally right if and only if that act maxi-
mizes the good, that is, if the total amount of good for all minus the total
amount of bad for all is greater than this net amount for any compatible
act available to the agent on that occasion.'

6 http://plato.stanford.edu/entries/colonialism/#LibEmp

7 I am referring here to Lévi-Strauss (1960) 'hot,' 'cold' society distinction.

8 http://www.panarchy.org/mill/stationary.1848.html.

4. Aboriginal Rights and Self-Determination

1 According to Ashcroft, as opposed to 'occupation colonies' in which colonials
resided temporarily, 'settlers tended to stay permanently in settler colonies.
In taking possession of the land and cultivating it, there was never much
thought to returning home.' Imperial Archive n.d., http://www.qub.ac.uk/
schools/SchoolofEnglish/imperial/key-concepts/Settler-Colony.htm.

2 For a general discussion on colonialism, see the entry in the *Stanford
Enclyclopedia of Philosophy*. It reads as follows: 'This entry uses the term
colonialism to describe the process of European settlement and political
control over the rest of the world, including Americas, Australia, and parts
of Africa and Asia.'

3 There is no one community that forms a majority population in the world,
and, even when taken as a whole, the largest fragment of the world's
population, the Chinese, constitute only 20 per cent of it. Therefore, when
the world is considered as a single entity, self-determination cannot be
established for any country on the basis of majority rule.

4 Article 2 of the 1960 Declaration states: 'All peoples have the right to
self-determination; by virtue of that right they freely determine their political
status and freely pursue their economic, social and cultural development.'

5 Karin Pierce, the United Kingdom representative, was quite explicit on this point: 'She emphasized that the Declaration was non-legally binding and did not propose to have any retroactive application on historical episodes. National minority groups and other ethnic groups within the territory of the United Kingdom and its overseas territories did not fall within the scope of the indigenous peoples to which the Declaration applied' (UN 2007b).

6 http://www.supremecourt.gov/publicinfo/speeches/viewspeeches. aspx?Filename=sp_05-23-03.html (accessed 29 October 2011).

5. Treaty Relations

1 Two recent books discuss the corpus of treaties: Miller's *Compact, Contract, Covenant* (2009), which provides a thorough historical survey of treaty making in Canada, and Henderson's *Treaty Rights in the Constitution of Canada* (2007), which goes into significant depth on the legal and constitutional aspect of treaty making in various regions of the country. These are texts I relied on extensively in preparing this chapter.

2 There were also territorial treaties in Nova Scotia, New Brunswick, and Prince Edward Island in the period before 1763. See http://www.kstrom .net/isk/maps/novascotiatreaties.html (accessed 28 July 2009).

3 I gratefully acknowledge the role of Aimée Craft, Alison DuBois, Allyshia West, and Kelsey Wrightson as well as John Borrows, Rob Hancock, Marc Pinkoski, Brian Noble, Conrad Sioui, and Sharon Venne in overcoming my reluctance to research the treaties. In fact, I can say with confidence that, through their work, I have learned that there is much of value to be gained in pursuing this avenue.

4 When two parties to an agreement (contract) both have the same understanding of the terms of the agreement. Such mutual comprehension is essential to a valid contract. http://legal-dictionary.thefreedictionary.com/ meeting+of+the+minds.

5 In fact, a meeting of the minds can be reached even if one of the parties says one thing but means another, for *Halsbury's Laws of England* states: 'Where one party (A) expresses an apparent intention (objective intention) which does not express what he actually means in his own mind (subjective intention), an apparent *meeting of the minds* of the parties may suffice for a binding contract' (5th ed.: vol. 22, s. 2[i], s. 233; emphasis in original).

6 For an extensive discussion of the reasons courts have rejected textualism, see Henderson 2007: ch. 4.

7 While these statements appear in a dissent, Justice McLachlin makes it clear that her perspective is based on the majority opinion in previous leading judgments, and its authority is supported in subsequent ones.

8 For a full list with appropriate transliterations, see Ray, Miller, and Tough (2002: 223).

9 Hunt describes this encampment and the formal structure of its organization (Hunt 1876: 176, 178–9).

10 It is clear that the Saulteaux chiefs did not participate, but not whether other members of that community did.

11 The text indicates that groups identified as Stoney (Stonie) and as Assiniboine adhered to Treaty 4.

12 '14. Any claims of Indians to compensation for lands required for purposes of settlement shall be disposed of by the Canadian Government in communication with the Imperial Government; and the Company shall be relieved of all responsibility in respect of them.' http://en.wikisource.org/wiki/Rupert's_Land_and_North-Western_Territory_Order/Schedule_8 (accessed 25 August 2009).

13 These words are reported as follows in the transcription: 'The company,' said the Gambler, 'have stolen our land' (Morris 1880: 101).

14 As discussed in chapter 9, Morris's use of the term sovereignty permits a more nuanced interpretation.

15 This may well be a shorthand version of the following remark by the Gambler as reported in the transcription: 'The Indians were not told of the reserves [for the HBC] at all. I hear now, it was the Queen gave the land. The Indians thought it was they who gave it to the Company' (Morris 1880: 104).

16 Also see Morris 1880: 92, 107.

17 Indeed, even in the case where he uses the term 'father,' Morris is speaking as though he were the queen (Morris 1880: 95).

18 If this is not sufficiently clear, here is the text to which I am referring: 'ARTICLES OF A TREATY made and concluded this fifteenth day of September, in the year of Our Lord one thousand eight hundred and seventy-four, between Her Most Gracious Majesty the Queen of Great Britain and Ireland, by Her Commissioners, the Honourable Alexander Morris, Lieutenant Governor of the Province of Manitoba and the North-West Territories; the Honourable David Laird, Minister of the Interior, and William Joseph Christie, Esquire, of Brockville, Ontario, of the one part; and the Cree, Saulteaux and other Indians, inhabitants of the territory within the limits hereinafter defined and described by their Chiefs and Headmen, chosen and named as hereinafter mentioned, of the other part' (Treaty 4 1966: 5).

19 He uses the word 'Dominion' to describe where Christie lives (Morris 1880: 88), and 'government' in relation to alcohol control (ibid.: 93) as well as to differentiate between it and the Hudson's Bay Company (and in that regard appears to conflate government with the queen) (ibid.: 93). While he does not specify to which government he is referring, it is clear from the context that he means the Dominion government (ibid.: 111). Canada is not mentioned at all.

20 In the research for her MA thesis on the Manitoulin Island treaties, Allyshia West cites the following statement by Governor Bond Head at the negotiation of Treaty 45, which to my mind provides an excellent example of the kind of relationship suggested: 'Children – Your Great Father the Lieutenant Governor, as a token of the above Declaration, transmits to the Indians a Silk British Flag, which represents the British Empire. Within this flag, and immediately under the Symbol of the British Crown, are delineated a British Lion and a Beaver, by which it is designated that the British Peoples and the Indians, the former being represented by the Lion and the latter by the Beaver, are and will be alike regarded by their Sovereign so long as their Figures are represented on the British Flag, or, in other Words, so long as they continue to inhabit the British Empire' (qtd. in West 2010: 61).

21 Treaty 4 elders Gordon Oakes and Danny Musqua put it this way: 'Our land is plentiful' (Cardinal and Hildebrandt 2000: 36) and 'we were willing to share' (ibid.: 62).

22 It is, of course, a point on which the Indigenous party disagreed (Hunt 1876: 179).

23 For a similar representation regarding treaties with Ojibwa in southern Ontario in the latter part of the eighteenth century, see Schmalz 1991: 124.

24 These are in fact commitments Commissioner Morris explicitly makes in Treaty 6 where he says: 'What I have offered you does not take away from your way of living, you will have it then as you have it now, and what I offer now is put on top of it. This I can tell you, the Queen's Government will always take a deep interest in your living.'

6. Treaties and Co-Existence

1 For a detailed discussion of unfulfilled treaty obligations, see Office of the Treaty Commissioner (2007: ch. 4).

2 Another version, by the late Elder Ray Fadden, reads: 'We will not be like Father and Son, but like Brothers. [Our treaties] symbolize two paths or two vessels, travelling down the same river together. One, a birch bark canoe, will be for the Indian People, their laws, their customs and their

ways. The other, a ship, will be for the white people and their laws, their customs and their ways. We shall each travel the river together, side by side, but in our own boat. Neither of us will make compulsory laws nor interfere in the internal affairs of the other. Neither of us will try to steer the other's vessel' (qtd. in Anonymous n.d.).

3 Of course, when these fail, there is a third option: carving states out of a territory that once constituted a single state.

4 Thus, it explicitly excludes such matters as environmental management 'that have a major impact on adjacent jurisdictions or that attract transcendent federal or provincial control' (RCAP 1996: II, 167).

5 I hasten to add that I am not passing judgment on the wisdom of Indigenous parties who make agreements on these terms, for there are circumstances when any agreement is better than none at all. At the same time, it strikes me as unreasonable for the government of British Columbia to take upon itself the authority to determine the terms of these negotiations, and then offer them on a take-or-leave-it basis.

6 In the records I have available to me, there is no eyewitness evidence on the promises regarding the freedom to hunt at Fort Good Hope and Arctic Red River. Similarly, there is no eyewitness evidence in the record of discussions regarding land cession at Fort Good Hope and Fort McPherson.

7 Further information on what transpired appears in Shirleen Smith's 1999 doctoral dissertation 'Dene Treaties, Anthropology and Colonial Relationships' (Smith 1999).

8 http://www.treatysix.org/about_principals.html (accessed 26 July 2010).

9 http://www.inverhuronrate.com/history-inverhuron-1-main.html (accessed 21 October 2012).

10 The UN special rapporteur on the human rights of Indigenous peoples, Miguel Alfonso Martínez, indicates in his report that what holds in Canada holds elsewhere too: 'Indigenous parties to treaties have rejected the assumption held by State parties, that treaties provided for the unconditional cession of indigenous lands and jurisdictions to settler States' (Martínez 1999: para. 118).

11 This is a paraphrase because I replaced 'they' with 'we.' The original reads: 'Because they share the same space, they are inextricably entwined in a relationship of interdependence – *but they remain distinct political entities.*'

7. Treaties and Sharing

1 I have chosen Newey principally because he discusses the relationship between the state of nature and the family as a form of government in a

way that I find simplifies matters. However, having read numerous commentaries, I am convinced that the variations in opinions on this subject do not alter my conclusions.

2 Let me add that I have also chosen it in part because, as Larry Johnston says, 'the Hobbesian conception of the state of nature as a state of war is one of the most powerful images of political thought' (Johnston 2001: 103).

3 Newey puts it this way: 'Hobbes' main point here is clear: national leaders are in a state of war against one another "because of their independence" – because there is no world government which wields supreme power over them' (Newey 2008: 241).

4 What I mean is that we separate ourselves into nuclear families and so it makes no sense to us. On the other hand, it might well make sense to those who organize themselves based on clans and relations between them, or, indeed, to those in other systems (such as those based on lineages).

5 *OED*: 'A conceptual or methodological model underlying the theories and practices of a science or discipline at a particular time; [hence] a generally accepted world view.'

6 'The shared mental and moral orientations of societies' (Coser 1997: xix).

7 Lévi-Strauss' approach aligns with the tradition in Western philosophy in which the human being, as Tzvetan Todorov describes, is conceptualized 'as a being who *needs others*' (Todorov 2001: 10; emphasis in original). It includes Charles Taylor's understanding that 'we define our identity always in dialogue with, sometimes in struggle against, the things our significant others want to see in us' (Taylor 1994: 32f), and Martin Buber's idea that the Self has no existence except in the relation to an Other (Buber 1970: 53–6). Particularly helpful in translating the philosophical into the political are Tully's reflections on relationality and ancient constitutionalism in *Strange Multiplicities*.

8 Kendall defines marriage as 'a legally recognized and socially approved arrangement between two or more individuals that carries certain rights and obligations and usually involves sexual activity' (Kendall 2011: 359). Like Lévi-Strauss, I am defining it as a legally sanctioned union between a man and woman for the purpose of reproduction. However, of course, while I am going to argue that the treaties are like a marriage, relations between nations are not gendered.

9 Abbott describes this form as 'the Patriarchal Empty Shell Family.' He contrasts this with one, which unfortunately he calls 'group marriage,' that imagines a family 'without any real conception of parenthood' so that it 'fits only a borderline definition of the family' (Abbott 1981: 253). This

other form, which Abbott calls 'the autistic family,' yields a conceptualiza-
tion of the community that is so unstable that it appears to make survival
of the human race impossible even in the short run. While he cites a
putative example, the Ik as described by Colin Turnbull, the fact is that
Turnbull's representation has been refuted by subsequent ethnographic
research (cf. Abrahams 2002).

10 Definition in Kendall (2011: 436; emphasis in original): 'A *nuclear family*
is a family composed of one or two parents and their dependent children,
all of whom live apart from other relatives.'

11 At the same time, Hobbes allows for the fact that children may be born
outside marriage and in this case argues that 'if there be no contract, the
dominion is in the mother' (Hobbes 1996: 124). This is the remark that
leads Abbott to the view that Hobbes might imagine a form of the family
that is based on group marriage. However, there is little other support
for it in *Leviathan*, and so Hobbes was likely pointing to a variant of the
dominant form.

12 Lévi-Strauss defines marriage androcentrically. As a result, he says that
women are a resource to be given to and received from other men.
However, this is not only wrong, it is superfluous to his argument, for it
works as well if not better when, as indicated by the term 'marriage
partner,' both genders are accorded the same status. For further discussion
on this point, see Asch 2005.

13 It is important to note that Lévi-Strauss accepts the proposition that
'scarcity' extends to marriage partners, and yet demonstrates that his
solution still holds (Lévi-Strauss 1969: 37). He bases his claim on the
assertion that males are naturally polygynous (Martínez 1999: para. 118).

14 I mean cross-cousin marriage or marriage between persons who are
classified as children of opposite sex siblings.

15 To act in this way requires a form of relating to one another that is so
foreign as to appear to be impossible, so let me illustrate one possibility
with this clumsy (and, for the purposes of treaty, likely not appropriate)
example drawn from Lévi-Strauss's discussion of Dual Organizations.
Suppose we imagine that, in the universe of two families, one must always
be the colour Blue and the other Yellow. The rule of exogamy, then, would
require members of the Blue family to marry members of the Yellow
family. That means that the parental generation is composed of a member
of each. Yet, for the rule of exogamy to apply, the children must always be
either Blue or Yellow. This result (in the case I am drawing on) is achieved
by assigning all the children in both families the colour of the family of the

same sex parent. That is, if it is through the father, the children of a father from the Blue family will be Blue and vice versa. This means that maintaining both families requires the cooperation of members of both (one Blue parent and one Yellow parent) to ensure the survival of each.

16 While this meeting was not attended by the public (as were the negotiations sessions), I was permitted to attend as a member of the support staff. However, I was not present at a portion of the meeting that was 'private.'

17 At the meeting the next day, which I did not attend, the minister presented this ultimatum: 'My plane is on the tarmac, and the engine is running. If we don't have a deal by 6 p.m. I am getting on that plane and will not return.' That is, accept a settlement that subordinates your political rights or I will unilaterally end negotiations. The Dene leaders' decision, which was difficult to make, ended up splitting their nation, with some regions, likely because they were fearful of the consequences of not agreeing to the deal on the terms offered, making separate claims and others holding out for an agreement that recognized and affirmed their political rights as a self-determining people (some are still holding out to this today). The experience left me convinced that my goal as an anthropologist would be to understand a way of thinking that forces people into making such a choice.

18 While the focus is on deliberativeness in our actions, we also need to recognize that, as John Ralston Saul points out, the shape of what we do is also affected by unconscious processes (Saul 2009: 279).

8. Spirit and Intent

1 Flanagan represents it this way: 'A party of Cree might ride for days in Blackfoot territory without encountering any Blackfoot. If they met, they might fight, or they might establish friendly relations and the Blackfoot might allow the Cree to hunt without opposition' (Flanagan 2008: 115).

2 While Albers's study focuses on the 'northeastern plains,' there is nothing in what either she or others have written to indicate that what took place there is unique.

3 They found that members of different ethnies cooperated across ethnie lines economically by forming multi-ethnie work groups, such as when hunting buffalo and supplying provisions for fur traders, and by working on 'complementary activities' in the same territory, just as, for example, in the early nineteenth century the Ojibwa 'were primarily trappers of small game, whereas the Assiniboine and Cree were mostly big game hunters' (Albers 1996: 92, 99).

4 I came across no record in the literature I examined of Ojibwa-Assiniboine communities.
5 These included communities of Settlers such as French and Scots/Irish.
6 Here is how Elder Musqua, a self-identified 'Oji-Cree,' describes himself:

> We come from the Padiwami but Naconini is what we are termed by the Crees and this is what we call ourselves, Naconiniwak. So that is what we call ourselves ... So we are Ojibwa in a sense in terms of where we came from historically, but we changed when we came to these prairies. We began to associate through our marriages with the Crees. In some places we are called the Oji-Cree but we just call ourselves Saulteauxs. We intermarried with the Crees for five hundred years, maybe more. This occurred much more so when we came to these prairies because the Crees were already here. So being a brother tribe we allied with them and we protected one another. They were protective toward us. We lived in close proximity. We intermarried with one another. So the Naconiniwak is what we want to be known as ... We are an offspring of both the Cree and the Eastern Indians that came from Ontario, Wisconsin, Michigan and that area. The old people tell us that we are a distinct tribe to ourselves. We want to be a distinct tribe. [There] is only eight thousand of us. We are a very small group. Some of the old people are worried that we are going to be swallowed up by the Cree or swallowed up by the Ojibwa. We want to be who we are and who we believe we are, a child of both and to say that we are one or the other would be to profess our destruction ... We call ourselves the Anishanabe. We are just human beings. We are made of the earth and spirit.' (Relland 1998: 147–8)

7 Based on Hudson Bay Company trader William McKay's estimate that the camp of Big Bear (Mistahimaskwa) comprised 520 people in 65 lodges (Wiebe 1982).
8 In fact, to complicate matters further, Western observers used many terms to identify the Cree, some, like 'Swampy,' having to do with geography, and others, like Calling River, referring to a particular location.
9 While I have no specific evidence regarding the residence groups associated with the first two, Innes makes it clear that the members of Cowessess' band remained together after Treaty 4 was negotiated.
10 In fact, as Witgen's recently published study shows, the term 'Cree' is an Ojibwe word that was used to designate one regional variant of that

language, and 'emerged as a "national" identity in the context of the fur trade, rather than as a form of self-designation for the indigenous peoples of the … region' (Witgen 2011: 87). In other words, the people living in a particular region became identified by the ethnie term 'Cree' because those labelling them (the fur traders) took the view that this was an appropriate (and universally valid) way to categorize collectivities.

11 The closest equivalent I have found in academic discourse is in Habermas's description of consensus decision making, where 'everyone is required to take the perspective of everyone else, and thus project herself into the understandings of self and world of all others.'

12 *OED* definition of 'kind' (adj.): http://www.oed.com.ezproxy.library.uvic .ca/view/Entry/103445?rskey=xmKhtA&result=2#eid (accessed 15 April 2010).

13 Morris replies: 'Yes, to those who are here and those who are absent, such as she has given us.' I interpret the last clause as referring to the queen's power. However, it may refer her kindness as well.

14 In this regard, it is akin to the Gambler's usage during these negotiations: 'Look at these children that are sitting around here and also at the tents, who are just the image of my kindness. There are different kinds of grass growing here that is just like those sitting around here. There is no difference. Even from the American land they are here, but we love them all the same, and when the white skin comes here from far away I love him all the same. I am telling you what our love and kindness is' (Morris 1880: 100).

15 I take this from a story that I was told. It is about someone who, with hostile intent, gave another person so much to eat that it was hoped he would be unable to finish it. For a detailed discussion on this point, see appendix I.

16 Treaty 6 contains an enrichment of these provisions in which the number of hoes, spades, axes, and scythes for each family was doubled. As well, there was an increase in the supply of plows and harrows, a quadrupling of the number of oxen, and an increase in the number of cows; each band was also provided with two carts. Treaty 6 included too a grant of $1,000 per year for three years 'to assist and encourage in such cultivation' (Treaty 6 1964: 4) once a band settled on a reserve, and a promise to set aside reserves or, as Morris puts it, 'a home of your own' within which 'to build and to plant' (Morris 1880: 171). Its specific terms were the same as those in Treaty 4, including the clause, cited above, concerning the crown's desire to 'help you make your home there' (ibid.: 206).

17 *Toronto Star*, 6 December 2011 (accessed online the same date).

9. Setting the Record Straight

1 'a government responsible to the representatives of the people, i.e., an executive or Cabinet collectively dependent on the votes of a majority in the elected legislature' (Careless n.d.).

2 Full title: *Outline of a System of Legislation for the Securing of Protection to the Aboriginal Inhabitants of All Countries Colonized by Great Britain: Extending to the Political and Social Rights, Ameliorating Their Condition, and Promoting Their Civilization.*

3 Furthermore, an 1878 judgment cited an order-in-council affirming that 'the crown has no constitutional jurisdiction to grant lands prior to an Indian treaty' (Clark 1999: 307).

4 As Talbot says: 'Morris's approach to treaty making was informed by precedent. He took pride in British conceptions of justice an the rule of law, and long before moving to the North West he had recognized that the First Nations had, in British law and practice, an inherent claim to the land' (Talbot 2009: 65).

5 Indeed, it is also conceivable that, in Morris's understanding, the intent of the cede and surrender clauses was not to subordinate our partners to our rule but to cement an alliance. Here is how he put the relationship between Britain and Canada that he presumed would result from Confederation in an 1865 speech in support of the project and the annexation of the northwest:

> We have either to rise into strength and wealth and power by means of this union, *under the sheltering protection of Britain*, or we must be absorbed by the great power beside us.
>
> We will have the pride to belong to a great country still attached to the Crown of Great Britain, in which, notwithstanding, *we shall have entire freedom of action and the blessing of responsible self government.* (Qtd. in Talbot 2009: 47f; emphasis added)

If the rationale for Confederation was that Canada would gain protection from Britain and yet retain full self-government, then it is not far-fetched to conclude that this was also the intent of the cede and surrender clause in the numbered treaties.

6 In fact, it has come to light in recent years that, at least in the United Kingdom, the Crown has vetoed an act of Parliament (Booth 2013).

7 This apparently was also the position that Prime Minister Macdonald took, for he insisted, counter to Morris, that Morris reported to the queen

through Lord Dufferin rather than directly, so he should be addressed as 'Your Honor' rather than 'Your Excellency' (Beal 2007: 156).

8 At the same time, I do not mean to suggest that Morris's vision of that future is one to accept uncritically, for in many ways it fails to resonate with contemporary understandings. For example, it is offensive to our sensibilities to justify our commitment on the grounds that the higher purpose is to bring 'Christianity and civilization to leaven the mass of heathenism and paganism among the Indian tribes' (Morris 1880: 296). But, when these words are read in the context of the times, what becomes crucial is that to Morris and those like him, the 'benefits of civilization' were seen as 'gifts,' for 'to help, and not oppress, should be our object.' The intent is for us to become their allies, not their bosses.

9 This is my idea of how these principles translate into section 35(1) rights: 'Aboriginal rights' or perhaps more explicitly 'Aboriginal title' (or, as Lord Dufferin called it, 'the title of the original owners of the soil') is our guarantee that we will obtain the consent of Indigenous peoples before we encroach on their lands; and 'Treaty rights' is our guarantee that we will keep the commitments we make in gaining that consent.

Appendix I: Proportionality

1 That is, societies he would define as of the 'Kula type.'

2 This is my re-rendering of the Halls translation (Mauss 1990). The original reads: 'L'obligation de donner est non moins importante; son étude pourrait faire comprendre comment les homees sont devenus exchangistes. Nous ne pouvons qu'indiquer quelques. Refuser de donner, négliger d'inviter, comme réfuser de prendre, équivaut à faits déclarer la guerre; c'est réfuser l'alliance et la communion' (Mauss 1950: 162f).

3 While it is not relevant for this discussion, I will note that, in Mauss's view, the motivation to continue is contained in the notion of 'obligation,' which he sometimes likens to indebtedness and at other times to a force of nature, as when he says: 'What imposes obligation in the present received and exchanged, is the fact that the thing received is not inactive, but is animated by what might fairly be called a spiritual force, it seeks to return to its birthplace' (Mauss 1990: 11f). Perhaps it is for this reason that he calls his book *Essai sur le Don*, for in French 'don' is associated with a spirit that compels its motion (like, for example, the English phrase 'the gift of music,' which compels the possessor to play music for others); an alternative would be 'cadeau,' but this, as in English, identifies a gift as an inert object. It is also associated with the idea of giving a donation.

4 This is my informal orthography. In the South Slavey Dictionary, stomach is rendered as 'gombé' (South Slave Divisional Education Council 2009: 27). I would guess that the 'go' refers to 'one's,' so that it is actually 'one's stomach.' However, I wrote it down as 'mbe' in my casual orthography (perhaps because to my ears Mrs Hardisty's pronunciation was closer to the Dogrib form [Dogrib Divisional Board of Education 1996: 33]). In Dogrib, 'Cho' as a suffix refers to something that is big (ibid.: vii).

References

Abbott, Philip. 1981. The three families of Thomas Hobbes. *Review of Politics* 43(2), 242–58. http://dx.doi.org/10.1017/S0034670500029740.

Aborigines' Protection Society. 1839. *Report on the Indians of Upper Canada by a sub-committee of the Aborigines Protection Society.* London: William Barr, Arnold and Co. http://eco.canadiana.ca/view/oocihm.35802/2?r=0&s=1

Aborigines' Protection Society. 1840. *Outline of a system of legislation for the securing of protection to the Aboriginal inhabitants of all countries colonized by Great Britain: Extending to the political and social rights, ameliorating their condition, and promoting their civilization.* London: John Murray, etc. http://eco.canadiana.ca/view/oocihm.47266/3?r=0&s=1

Abrahams, Curtis. 2002. The Mountain People revisited. *New African* 01 (February).

Albers, Patricia C. 1996. Changing patterns of ethnicity in the northeastern plains, 1789–1870. In Jonathan D. Hill, ed., *History, power, and identity: Ethnogenesis in the Americas, 1492–1992*, 90–118. Iowa City: University of Iowa Press.

Albers, Patricia C. 2001. Plains Ojibwa. In Raymond J. DeMallie, ed., *Handbook of North American Indians Vol. 13: The Plains, Part 1*, 652–60. Washington, DC: Government Printing Office.

Alfred, Taiaiake. 2005. *Wasáse: Indigenous pathways of action and freedom.* Toronto: University of Toronto Press.

Anaya, S. James, and Siegfried Weissner. 2007. The UN Declaration on the Rights of Indigenous Peoples: Towards re-empowerment. *Third World Resurgence* 207 http://www.twnside.org.sg/title2/resurgence/206/cover3.doc

Anonymous. n.d. Haudenosaunee history and the legend of the peacemaker. Retrieved from <http://www.earth-treaty.com/ts_iroqhst1.html>

Arnot, David. 2010. The honour of First Nations — The honour of the Crown: The unique relationship of First Nations with the Crown. Paper presented at the Crown in Canada: Present realities and future options. Ottawa, ON: 9–10 June. http://www.queensu.ca/iigr/conf/Arch/2010/ConferenceOnTheCrown/CrownConferencePapers/The_Crown_and_the_First_Nations.pdf

Asch, Michael. 1984. *Home and native land: Aboriginal rights and the Canadian constitution*. Toronto: Methuen.

Asch, Michael. 1999. From *Calder* to *Van der Peet*: Aboriginal rights and Canadian law, 1973–1996. In *Indigenous peoples' rights in Australia, Canada, and New Zealand*, ed. Paul Havemann, 428–46. Melbourne: Oxford University Press.

Asch, Michael. 2001. Aboriginal Rights. In *International encyclopedia of the social and behavioral sciences*, ed. N. Smelser and P. Baltes, 1–5. Oxford: Pergammon. http://dx.doi.org/10.1016/B0-08-043076-7/02842-4.

Asch, Michael. 2005. Lévi-Strauss and the political: *The Elementary Structures of Kinship* and the resolution of relations between Indigenous peoples and settler states.' *Journal of the Royal Anthropological Institute* 11(3), 425–44. http://dx.doi.org/10.1111/j.1467-9655.2005.00244.x.

Asch, Michael. 2013. On the land cession provisions in Treaty 11. *Ethnohistory* 60(3), 451–67.

Asch, Michael, and Patrick Macklem. 1991. Aboriginal rights and Canadian sovereignty: An essay on *R. v. Sparrow*. *Alberta Law Review* 29(2), 498–517.

Assembly of First Nations. 2012. *First Nations plan: Honouring our past, affirming our rights, seizing our future*. Ottawa: Assembly of First Nations.

Avalon Project. 2008. The Covenant of the League of Nations (including amendments adopted to December, 1924). Connecticut: Lillian Goldman Law Library. Electronic document, http://avalon.law.yale.edu/20th_century/leagcov.asp#art23.

Banting, Keith, and Richard Simeon, eds. 1983. *And no one cheered: Federalism, democracy, and the Constitution Act*. Toronto: Methuen.

Barnard, Frederick M. 1965. *Herder's social and political thought: From Enlightenment to nationalism*. Oxford: Clarendon.

Beal, Robert. 2007. An Indian chief, an English tourist, a doctor, a reverend, and a member of Parliament: The journeys of Pasqua's pictographs and the meaning of Treaty Four. *Canadian Journal of Native Studies* 27(1), 109–88. http://www2.brandonu.ca/library/CJNS/27.1/05beal.pdf

Bennett, Gordon. 1978. *Aboriginal rights in international law*. London: Royal Anthropological Institute in association with Survival International.

Berger, Thomas R. 1977. *Northern frontier, northern homeland: The report of the Mackenzie Valley Pipeline Inquiry*. Ottawa: Minister of Supply and Services.

Black's Law Dictionary s.v. 'jurisdiction,' 'sovereignty'

Blake, Raymond, Jeffrey Keshen, Norman Knowles, and Barbara Messamore. 2011. *Narrating a nation: Canadian history post-Confederation*. Toronto: McGraw-Hill Ryerson.

Booth, Robert. 2013. Secret papers show extent of senior royals' veto over bills. *The Guardian*, 15 January 2013. http://www.theguardian.com/uk/2013/jan/14/secret-papers-royals-veto-bills.

Borrows, John. 1997. Wampum at Niagara: The Royal Proclamation, Canadian legal history, and self-government. In *Aboriginal and treaty rights in Canada: Essays on law, equity, and respect for difference*, ed. Michael Asch, 155–72. Vancouver: UBC Press.

British Columbia Treaty Commission. 2003. *What's the deal with treaties? A lay person's guide to Treaty making in British Columbia*. 3rd ed. Vancouver: British Columbia Treaty Commission.

Buber, Martin. 1970. *I and thou*. Trans. Walter Kaufmann. New York: Touchstone.

Cairns, Alan. 2000. *Citizens plus: Aboriginal peoples and the Canadian state*. Vancouver: UBC Press.

Cairns, Alan. 2005. *First Nations and the Canadian state: In search of coexistence*. Kingston, ON: Institute of Intergovernmental Relations, School of Policy Studies, Queen's University.

Canada. 1969. Statement of the Government of Canada on Indian policy. Ottawa: Queen's Printer.

Cardinal, Harold. 1969. *The unjust society: The tragedy of Canada's Indians*. Edmonton: Hurtig.

Cardinal, Harold, and Walter Hildebrandt. 2000. *Treaty elders of Saskatchewan: Our dream is that our peoples will one day be clearly recognized as nations*. Calgary: University of Calgary Press.

Careless, J.M.S. n.d. Responsible government. The Canadian Encyclopedia Online.

Carter, Sarah. 1990. *Lost harvests: Prairie Indian reserve farmers and government policy*. Montreal: McGill-Queen's University Press.

Castellino, Joshua, and Steve Allen. 2003. *Title to territory in international Law: A temporal analysis*. Farnham, U.K.: Ashgate Publishing.

Clark, Bruce. 1999. *Justice in paradise*. Montreal: McGill-Queen's University Press.

Cochon [Cauchon], Joseph, and James Cockburn. 1867. Address to Her Majesty the Queen from the Senate and House of Commons of the Dominion of Canada.' In *British and foreign state papers 1869–1870*, vol. 60.

London: William Ridgway.

Condorcet, M. de 1795. *Outlines of an historical view of the progress of the human mind*. London: J. Johnson.

Corntassel, Jeff. 2008. Toward sustainable self-determination: Rethinking the contemporary indigenous rights discourse. *Alternatives: Global, Local, Political* 33(1): 105–32. http://dx.doi.org/10.1177/030437540803300106.

Coser, Lewis. 1997. Introduction. In Emile Durkheim, *The division of labor in society*, ix–xxiv. New York, NY: The Free Press.

Craft, Aimée. 2011. *Breathing life into the Stone Fort Treaty*. LL.M. Thesis, University of Victoria.

Cumming, Peter A., and Neil H. Mickenberg. 1972. *Native rights in Canada*. Toronto: Indian-Eskimo Association.

Darnell, Regna. 2001. Plains Cree. In *Handbook of North American Indians Vol. 13: The Plains, Part 1*, ed. Raymond J. DeMallie, 638–51. Washington, DC: Government Printing Office.

Dehcho First Nation. 2011. Dehcho process report, June 2011. Retrieved from < http://www.dehcho.org/documents/negotiations/2011%20Dehcho%20 Process%20Report.pdf>.

DeMallie, Raymond J., and David Reed Miller. 2010. Assiniboine. In *Handbook of North American Indians Vol. 13: The Plains, Part 1*, ed. Raymond J. DeMallie, 572–95. Washington, DC: Government Printing Office.

Devine, Heather. 2004. *The people who own themselves: Aboriginal ethnogenesis in a Canadian family, 1660–1900*. Calgary: University of Calgary Press.

Dogrib Divisional Board of Education. 1996. *A Dogrib dictionary*. Retrieved from http://www.tlicho.ca/sites/default/files/A_Dogrib_Dictionary.pdf.

Douglas, Mary. 1990. Preface. In *The Gift: The form and reason for exchange in archaic societies*, trans. W.D. Halls. New York: W.W. Norton.

Dufferin, Earl of. 1882. *Speeches and addresses of the Right Honourable Frederick Temple Hamilton, Earl of Dufferin*. Henry Milton, ed. London: John Murray.

Duhaime's law dictionary, s.v. 'de facto'

Finkel, Alvin, and Margaret Conrad. 2002. *History of the Canadian peoples, Vol. 2: 1867 to the present*. 3rd ed. Toronto: Addison Wesley Longman.

Flanagan, Tom. 2008. *First Nations? Second thoughts*. 2nd ed. Montreal: McGill-Queen's University Press.

Francis, Daniel. 1997. *National dreams: Myth, memory, and Canadian history*. Vancouver: Arsenal Pulp Press.

Francis, R. Douglas, Richard Jones, and Donald B. Smith. 2004. *Destinies: Canadian history since Confederation*. 5th ed. Scarborough, ON: Thomson Nelson.

Frelinghuysen, Thomas. 1977. Speech delivered in the Senate of the United States, April 7, 1830. In Anon., *Speeches on the passage of the Bill for the*

Removal of the Indians, 6. Millwood, NY: Kraus Reprint Co.

Friesen, Jean. 1986. Magnificent gifts: The treaties of Canada with the Indians of the Northwest, 1869–76. *Transactions of the Royal Society of Canada* series 5(1):45–55.

Fumoleau, René. 1973. *As long as this land shall last: A history of Treaty 8 and Treaty 11, 1870–1939*. Toronto: McClelland and Stewart.

General Assembly of the Chilcotin Nation. 1983. *A declaration of sovereignty*. http://www.tsilhqotin.ca/pdfs/Administration/83DeclarationSovereignty.pdf

Government of Canada. 2008. *Statement of apology — to former students of Indian residential schools*. 11 June.

Granatstein, J.L., Irving M. Abella, T.W. Acheson, David J. Bercuson, R. Craig Brown, and H. Blair Neatby. 1990. *Nation: Canada since Confederation*. Toronto: McGraw-Hill Ryerson.

Gwich'in First Nation. 1992. Comprehensive Land Claims Agreement between Her Majesty the Queen in Right of Canada and the Gwich'in as represented by the Gwich'in Tribal Council. Ottawa: Minister of Indian Affairs and Northern Development.

Halsbury's laws of England. Various years. 5th ed. London: LexisNexis.

Hancock, Robert L. A. 2007. Historiographical representations of materialist anthropology in the Canadian setting, 1972–1982. Ph.D. Dissertation, University of Victoria.

Hawthorn, H.B., ed. 1966–67. *A survey of the contemporary Indians of Canada: A report on economic, political, educational needs and policies, in two volumes*. Ottawa: Indian Affairs Branch.

Heartfield, James. 2011. *The Aborigines' Protection Society: Humanitarian imperialism in Australia, New Zealand, Fiji, Canada, South Africa, and the Congo, 1837–1909*. New York: Columbia University Press.

Henderson, James Youngblood. 2007. *Treaty rights in the constitution of Canada*. Toronto: Thomson Carswell.

Hill, Richard. 2010. Linking arms: The Haudenosaunee context of the Covenant Chain. *Spiritual Quadrant* http://www.ccforum.ca/wp-content/uploads/2-Spiritual-Quadrant-English.pdf

Hobbes, Thomas. 1996. *Leviathan*. Ed Richard Tuck. Cambridge: Cambridge University Press.

Hume, Susan. 1971. North oldtimer recalls New Year's Day 1889. *Edmonton Journal*, 31 December 1971.

Hunt, F.L. 1876. 'Notes of the Qu'appelle Treaty. *Canadian Monthly and National Review* 9(3): 173–81.

Imperial Archive. n.d. Key concepts in postcolonial studies. http://www.qub.ac.uk/schools/SchoolofEnglish/imperial/key-concepts/Settler-Colony.htm

Indian and Northern Affairs, Canada. 1995. The Government of Canada's approach to the implementation of the inherent right and the negotiation of Aboriginal self-government. http://www.aandc-aadc.gc.ca/eng/1100010031834/1100100031844.

Indigenous Environmental Network. n.d. Free, prior, and informed consent. http://www.ecosanity.org/files/images/blogsanity/IEN_FPIC.pdf

Innes, Robert Alexander. 2012. Multicultural bands and the notion of 'tribal' histories. In *Finding a way to the heart: Feminist writings on Aboriginal and women's history in Canada*, ed. Robin Jarvis Brownlie and Valerie J. Korniek, 122–45. Winnipeg: University of Manitoba Press.

Inuvialuit Final Agreement. 1984. The Western Arctic claim: The Inuvialuit Final Agreement. Ottawa: Minister of Indian Affairs and Northern Development.

Ipperciel, Donald, and Jennifer Woo. 2009. Between freedom and belonging: Ignatieff and Berlin on nationalism. *British Journal of Canadian Studies* 22(2): 155–75. http://dx.doi.org/10.3828/bjcs.22.2.2.

JBNQA. 1998. James Bay and Northern Québec Agreement and Complementary Agreements, 1998 ed. Ste-Foy, QC: Les Publications du Québec.

Jenness, Diamond. 1932. *Indians of Canada*. Ottawa: National Museum of Canada.

Jennings, R.Y. 1965. *The acquisition of territory in international law*. Manchester: Manchester University Press.

Johnson, Harold. 2007. *Two families: Treaties and government*. Saskatoon: Purich.

Johnston, Larry. 2001. *Politics: An introduction to the modern democratic state*. Toronto: University of Toronto Press.

Kendall, Diana. 2011. *Sociology in our times*. 9th ed. Toronto: Nelson Education.

Kroetsch, Robert. 1977. Canada is a poem. In *Divided we stand*, ed. Gary Geddes, 13–16. Toronto: Peter Martin.

Kymlicka, Will. 1995. *Multicultural citizenship: A liberal theory of minority rights*. New York: Oxford University Press.

Kymlicka, Will. 2001. *Politics in the vernacular: Nationalism, multiculturalism, and citizenship*. New York: Oxford University Press. http://dx.doi.org/10.1093/0199240981.001.0001.

Ladner, Kiera. 2001. Negotiated inferiority: The Royal Commission on Aboriginal People's vision of a renewed relationship. *American Review of Canadian Studies* 31(1–2): 241–64. http://dx.doi.org/10.1080/02722010109481593.

Laird, David. 1874. Copy of notes made by Hon David Laird upon Qu'Appelle Treaty.aItem MSS-C550–1-31–1 (Box 40), Morton Manuscripts Collection, University of Saskatchewan Special Collections. Available online at <http://scaa.usask.ca/ourlegacy>.

Lévi-Strauss, Claude. 1966. *The savage mind*. Chicago: University of Chicago Press.

Lévi-Strauss, Claude. 1969. *Elementary structures of kinship*. Oxford: Alden and Mowbray.

Long, John. 2010. *Treaty No. 9: Making the agreement to share the land in far northern Ontario in 1905*. Montreal: McGill-Queen's University Press.

Lubicon Nation. n.d. Lubicon mailouts and related materials. *The Lubicon Archive*. http://nisto.com/cree/lubicon

Lubicon Settlement Commission. 1993. Lubicon Settlement Commission of Review Final Report. http://www.lubicon.ca/pa/negp/ls930330.htm

Lux, Maureen K. 2001. *Medicine that walks: Disease, medicine, and Canadian plains Native people, 1880–1940*. Toronto: University of Toronto Press.

Malanczuk, Peter. 1997. *Akehurst's modern introduction to international law*. 7th rev. ed. New York: Routledge.

Martin-Hill, Dawn. 2008. *The Lubicon Lake Nation: Indigenous knowledge and power*. Toronto: University of Toronto Press.

Martínez, Miguel Alfonso. 1999. *Human rights of Indigenous peoples: Study on treaties, agreements, and other constructive arrangements between states and Indigenous populations*. <http://www.unhchr.ch/Huridocda/Huridoca.nsf/0/696c51cf6f20b8bc802567c4003793ec?Opendocument>

Mauss, Marcel. 1950. *Sociologie et anthropologie*. Paris: Presses Universitaires de France.

Mauss, Marcel. 1954. *The gift: Form and functions of exchange in archaic societies*. Trans. Ian Cunnison. London: Cohen and West.

Mauss, Marcel. 1990. *The gift: The form and reason for exchange in archaic societies*. Trans. W.D. Halls. New York: W.W. Norton.

McNab, David T., and Paul-Emile McNab. 2009. Historical report on Inverhuron and Inverhuron Provincial Park. http://www.inverhuronrate.com/history-inverhuron-1-main.html

McWhinney, Edward. 1979. *Quebec and the constitution, 1960–1978*. Toronto: University of Toronto Press.

McWhinney, Edward. 1982. *Canada and the constitution, 1979–1982: Patriation and the Charter of Rights*. Toronto: University of Toronto Press.

Mill, John Stuart. 1848. *Principles of political economy*. London: J. W. Parker.

Mill, John Stuart. 1947. *On liberty and considerations on representative government*. Ed. R.B. McCallum. Oxford: Basil Blackwell.

Miller, J.R. 2000. *Skyscrapers hide the heavens: A history of Indian-White relations in Canada*. 3rd ed. Toronto: University of Toronto Press.

Miller, J.R. 2009. *Compact, contract, covenant: Aboriginal treaty-making in Canada*. Toronto: University of Toronto Press.

Milloy, John S. 1988. *The Plains Cree: Trade, diplomacy, and war, 1770–1870.* Winnipeg: University of Manitoba Press.

Ministry of Indian Affairs and Northern Development, Canada. 1998. Gathering strength: Canada's Aboriginal action plan. Electronic document, http://www.austlii.edu.au/au/journals/AILR/2000/10.html#Heading3.

Ministry of Indian Affairs and Northern Development, Canada. 2000. Gathering strength: Canada's Aboriginal action plan: a progress report. Electronic document, http://publications.gc.ca/collections/Collection/R32-192-2000E.pdf.

Ministry of Indian Affairs and Northern Development Canada. 2003. Resolving Aboriginal claims: A practical guide to Canadian experiences. Ottawa

Mohawk Nation Council of Chiefs. 1996. Letter to Ovide Mercredi. Retrieved from http://sisis.nativeweb.org/mohawk/ovide.html (last accessed 21 October 2012).

Moneo, Shannon. 2011. Secrets and Lives: Fran Hunt-Jinnouchi. *Victoria Boulevard* 21(8), 98.

Montesquieu, Charles-Louis de Secondat. 1989 [1748]. *The spirit of laws.* Trans. and ed. Anne M. Cohler, Basia Carolyn Miller, and Harold Samuel Shore. Cambridge: Cambridge University Press.

Morris, Alexander. 1880. *The treaties of Canada with the Indians of Manitoba and the North-West Territories, including the negotiations on which they were based, and other information relating thereto.* Toronto: Belfords, Clarke and Co.

Mussamore, Barbara J. 2005. 'The line over which he must not pass': Defining the office of the Governor-General, 1878. *Canadian Historical Review* 86(3), 453–83.

Nagata, J. 2001. Plural Societies. In *International encyclopedia of the social and behavioral sciences*, ed. Neil J. Smelser and Paul B. Bates, 11513–16. Elsevier. http://dx.doi.org/10.1016/B0-08-043076-7/00938-4.

Newey, Glen. 2008. *Routledge philosophy guidebook to Hobbes and Leviathan.* New York: Routledge.

Nisga'a Nation. 1999. Nisga'a Final Agreement. http://www.nnkn.ca/files/u28/niseng.pdf.

Office of the Treaty Commissioner. 2007. *Treaty implementation: Fulfilling the covenant.* Saskatoon: Office of the Treaty Commissioner.

Oxford English Dictionary: s.v. 'cultural relativism,' 'de facto,' 'de jure,' 'Indigenous,' 'share,' 'kind,' 'time immemorial,' 'usufruct.'

Pallister, Anna. 1971. *Magna Carta: The heritage of liberty.* Oxford: Clarendon Press.

Panaouamskeyen. 1991 [1727]. Abenaki letter. In *Dawnland encounters: Indians and Europeans in northern New England.* Ed. Colin G. Calloway, 115–18. Lebanon, NH: University Press of New England.

Parliamentary Select Committee. 1837. *Report of the Parliamentary Select Committee on Aboriginal tribes (British settlements) reprinted, with comments, by the 'Aborigines Protection Society,'* London: William Ball.

Payment, Diane Paulette. 2001. Plains Métis. In *Handbook of North American Indians Vol. 13: The Plains, Part 1*, ed. Raymond J. DeMallie, 661–676. Washington, DC: Government Printing Office.

Phipps, William E. 2002. *William Sheppard: Congo's African American Livingstone.* Louisville, KY: Geneva.

Ray, Arthur J., Jim Miller, and Frank Tough. 2002. *Bounty and benevolence: A documentary history of Saskatchewan treaties.* Montreal: McGill-Queen's University Press.

Relland, Michael Roger. 1998. *The teachings of the Bear Clan: As told by Saulteaux elder Danny Musqua.* M.Ed. Thesis, University of Saskatchewan.

Richardson, Boyce. 1989. *Drumbeat: Anger and renewal in Indian country.* Toronto: Summerhill.

Royal Commission on Aboriginal Peoples. 1993. *Treaty making in the spirit of coexistence: An alternative to extinguishment.* Ottawa: Supply and Services Canada.

Royal Commission on Aboriginal Peoples. 1996. *Report of the Royal Commission on Aboriginal Peoples, 5 vols.* Retrieved from http://www.collectionscanada. gc.ca/webarchives/20071115053257/http://www.ainc-inac.gc.ca/ch/rcap/ sg/sgmm_e.html

Sahtu Dene and Metis. 1993. Sahtu Dene and Metis Comprehensive Land Claims Agreement. Ottawa: Minister of Public Works and Government Services Canada.

Saskatchewan Indian. 1986. Indian government and the treaties. February/ March, 9–12.

Saul, John Ralston. 2009. *A fair country: Telling truths about Canada.* Toronto: Penguin Canada.

Schmalz, Peter S. 1991. *The Ojibwa of southern Ontario.* Toronto: University of Toronto Press.

Schochet, Gordon J. 1967. Thomas Hobbes on the family and the state of nature. *Political Science Quarterly* 82(3), 427–45. http://dx.doi.org/10.2307/2146773.

Scholtz, Christa. 2008. Aboriginal communities and the Charlottetown Accord: A preliminary analysis of voting returns. Paper presented to the Canadian Political Science Association Annual Conference, Vancouver, BC.

Schweitzer, Ivy. 2006. *Perfecting friendship: Politics and affiliation in early American literature.* Chapel Hill: University of North Carolina Press.

Sharrock, Susan R. 1974. Crees, Cree-Assiniboines, and Assiniboines: Interethnic social organization on the far northern plains." *Ethnohistory (Columbus, Ohio)* 21(2), 95–122. http://dx.doi.org/10.2307/480946.

Shewell, Hugh. 2004. *'Enough to keep them alive': Indian welfare in Canada, 1873–1965.* Toronto: University of Toronto Press.

Simpson, Leanne. 2008. Looking after Gdoo-naaganinaa: Precolonial Nishnaabeg diplomatic and treaty relationships. *Wicazo Sa Review* 23(2), 29–42. http://dx.doi.org/10.1353/wic.0.0001.

Smith, Anthony D. 1986. *The Ethnic origins of nations.* Oxford: Blackwell.

Smith, Anthony D. 1991. *National identity.* Reno: University of Nevada Press.

Smith, Shirleen. 1999. Dene treaties, anthropology and colonial relationships. Ph.D. Dissertation, University of Alberta.

South Slave Divisional Education Council. 2009. *Dene Yatié K'çç Ahsíi Yats'uuzi Gha Edîhtå'éh Kåtå'odehche: South Slavey topical dictionary: Kåtå'odehche* Dialect retrieved from http://www.ssdec.nt.ca/Dictionary/dictionary.pdf

Stanford Encyclopedia of Philosophy s.v. 'colonialism,' 'consequentialism.'

Stl'atl'imx Nation of Chiefs. n.d. Introduction and application for membership into the International League of United Nations. Electronic document, http://cwis.org/fwdp/Americas/lillooet.txt.

Stonechild, A. Blair. 1986. The Indian view of the 1885 uprising. In *1885 and after: Native society in transition,* ed. F. Laurie Barron and James B. Waldram, 155–70. Regina: Canadian Plains Research Centre, University of Regina.

Talbot, Robert J. 2009. *Negotiating the numbered treaties: An intellectual and political biography of Alexander Morris.* Saskatoon: Purich.

Taylor, Charles. 1994. The politics of recognition. In *Multiculturalism: Examining the politics of recognition,* ed. Amy Gutmann, 25–74. Princeton: Princeton University Press.

Tlicho. 2003. Land claims and Self-Government Agreement among the Tlicho and the Government of the Northwest Territories and the Government of Canada.

Tobias, John. 1983. Canada's subjugation of the Plains Cree, 1879–1885. *Canadian Historical Review* 64(4), 519–48. http://dx.doi.org/10.3138/CHR-064-04-04.

Todorov, Tzvetan. 2001. *Life in common: An essay in general anthropology.* Trans. Katherine Golsan and Lucy Golsan. Lincoln, NE: University of Nebraska Press.

Treaty 11. 1957. *Treaty No. 11 (June 27, 1921) and Adhesion (July 17, 1922) with Reports, etc.* Ottawa: Queen's Printer and Controller of Stationery.

Treaty 4. 1966. *Treaty No. 4. Between Her Majesty the Queen and the Cree and Saulteaux tribes of Indians at Qu'Appelle and Fort Ellice.* Ottawa: Queen's Printer and Controller of Stationery.

Treaty 4 Chiefs Council. 1999. *Proclamation and convention of Treaty 4 First Nations.* Fort Qu'Appelle, SK: Treaty Four Governance Institute.

Treaty 4 Elders. 1983. Elder's document on Treaty #4 by the Saulteaux, Cree and Assiniboine nations. Available online at <http://hdl.handle.net/10294/1723>.

Treaty 7 Elders and Tribal Council, with Walter Hildebrandt, Sarah Carter, and Dorothy First Rider. 1996. *The true spirit and original intent of Treaty 7*. Montreal: McGill-Queen's University Press.

Tsawwassen First Nation. 2007. Final Agreement. Available at http://www.gov.bc.ca/arr/firstnation/tsawwassen/down/tsawwassen_final_agreement_engiish_mar_20_2009.pdf

Tsosie, Rebecca. 2011. Conceptualizing tribal rights: Can self-determination be actualized within the U.S. constitutional structure? *Lewis & Clark Law Review* 15(4), 923–50.

Tucker, Robert C., ed. 1978. *The Marx-Engles reader*. 2nd ed. New York: W.W. Norton.

Tully, James. 2008. *Public philosophy in a new key, Volume 1: Democracy and civic freedom*. Cambridge: Cambridge University Press.

Turner, Dale. 2006. *This is not a peace pipe: Towards a critical Indigenous philosophy*. Toronto: University of Toronto Press.

United Nations. 1960a. General Assembly Resolution 1514 (XV): Declaration on the granting of independence to colonial countries and peoples. December 14: 947th plenary meeting. http://www.un.org/ga/search/view_doc.asp?symbol=A/RES/1514%28XV%29.

United Nations. 1960b. Principles which should guide Members in determining whether or not an obligation exists to transmit the information called for under Article 73e of the Charter. General Assembly Resolution 1541 (XV), 948th plenary meeting, December 15. http://www.daccess-ods.un.org/TMP/676624238491058.html.

United Nations. 1970. Declaration on principles of international law concerning friendly relations and cooperation among states in accordance with the Charter of the United Nations (2625 XXV). http://www.un-documents.net/a25r2625.html.

United Nations. 2007a. United Nations Declaration on the rights of Indigenous peoples. General Assembly Resolution 61/295, September 13. http://www.un.org/esa/socdev/Unpfii/DRIPS_en.pdf.

United Nations. 2007b. General Assembly adopts declaration on rights of Indigenous peoples; 'Major step forward' toward human rights for all, says president. General Assembly press release. 13 September. Electronic document, http://www.un.org/News/Press/docs/2007/ga10612.doc.htm.

Venne, Sharon. 2002. Treaty-making with the crown. In *Nation to nation: Aboriginal sovereignty and the future of Canada*, eds. John Bird, Lorraine Land, and Macadam, 44–52. Toronto: Irwin Publishing.

Walker, R.B.J. 1991. State sovereignty and the articulation of political space/time. *Millennium* 20(3), 445–61. http://dx.doi.org/10.1177/03058298910200030201.

Walker, R.B.J. 1993. *Inside/outside: International relations as political theory*. Cambridge: Cambridge University Press.

Ward, Tara. 2011. The right to free, prior, and informed consent: Indigenous peoples' participation rights within international law. *Northwestern Journal of International Human Rights* 10 2), 54–84.

West, Allyshia. 2010. Indigenous and Settler understandings of the Manitoulin Islands Treaties of 1836 (Treaty 45) and 1862. MA thesis, University of Victoria.

Wicken, William C. 1994. *Encounters with tall sails and tall tales: Mi'kmaq society, 1500–1760*. Ph.D. Dissertation, McGill University.

Wiebe, Rudy. 1982. 'Mistahimaskwa (Big Bear, known in French as Gros Ours).' *Dictionary of Canadian Biography*. Vol. 11. http://www.biographi.ca/en/bio/mistahimaskwa_11E.html.

Williams, Robert A., Jr. 1997. *Linking arms together: American Indian treaty visions of law and peace, 1600–1800*. New York: Oxford University Press.

Witgen, Michael. 2011. *An infinity of nations: How the Native New World shaped early North America*. Philadelphia: University of Pennsylvania Press.

Cases Cited

Calder v. Attorney-General of British Columbia (1969), 8 D.L.R. (3d) 59.

Calder v. Attorney-General of British Columbia (1970) 74 W.W.R. 481 (B.C.C.A.)

Calder v. Attorney-General of British Columbia [1973] S.C.R. 313.

Delgamuukw v. British Columbia [1997] 3 S.C.R. 1010.

Gros-Louis et al. v. la Société de développement de la Baie James et al. (1974) Que. P. R. 38.

Haida Nation v. British Columbia (Minister of Forests), [2004] 3 S.C.R. 5111, 2004 SCC 73.

La Société de développement de la Baie James et al. v. Kanatewat et al. [1975] Que C.A. 166.

Mitchell v. M.N.R. [2001] 1 S.C.R. 911.

R. v. Badger [1996] 1 S.C.R. 771

R. v. Marshall [1999] 3 S.C.R. 456

R. v. Pamajewon [1996] 2 SCR 821

R. v. Sparrow [1990] 1 S.C.R. 1075

R. v. Van der Peet [1996] 2 S.C.R. 507

Reference re Secession of Quebec [1998] 2 S.C.R. 217

Re Paulette (1973) 6 W.W.R. 97 (N.W.T.S.C.)

Taku River Tlingit First Nation v. British Columbia (Project Assessment Director) 2004 SCC 74.

Windsor and Annapolis Railway Company v. The Queen and the Western Counties Railway (1882), 7 App. Cas. 178.

Index